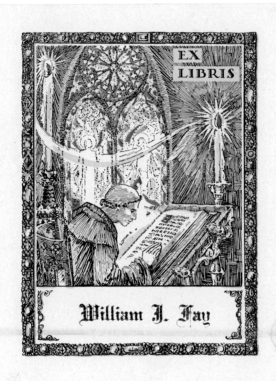

EX
LIBRIS

William J. Fay

THEOLOGICAL DIMENSIONS
OF THE LITURGY

THEOLOGICAL DIMENSIONS
OF THE LITURGY

By Cyprian Vagaggini, O.S.B.
Translated by Leonard J. Doyle

VOLUME I

THE LITURGICAL PRESS
COLLEGEVILLE, MINNESOTA

This book is translated from the second Italian edition of *Il Senso Teologico della Liturgia* and abridged after the model of the French adaptation, *Initiation Théologique à la Liturgie*, which was made under the author's direction.

FOREWORD

Not very long ago, the liturgy was seen as nothing more than a ceremonial, governed by precise rules; and a textbook devoted entirely to the study of the rubrics could be called *Course in Sacred Liturgy*. It is hardly more than thirty years since an understanding has come about in most countries, thanks to the persevering efforts of a few pioneers, that such a notion is superficial, to say the least.

It has come to be recognized that the object of the liturgy is not only the ceremonies of worship and their regulation, but also and primarily worship itself, in its essential elements as well as in its annual progression or in its material and literary framework. At the same time, with the increasing realization that it would be hard to grasp the exact meaning of the present-day liturgy as long as its history was not known, there has been an increase of research into the origin and the development of rites, texts and institutions.

These studies, which had actually commenced at the beginning of the century, have not been confined to the Roman rite, but have tried to shed light on it by comparison with other liturgies, ancient or present-day. They have made use of the remarkable works of the great seventeenth-century liturgists, and have shown extraordinary progress in a short time. The results of these inquiries have been collected and summed up in certain manuals. The best are undoubtedly Ludwig Eisenhofer's *Handbuch der katholischen Liturgik* in Germany and Msgr. Mario Righetti's monumental *Storia liturgica* in Italy.

Such a development of the historical study of the liturgy is highly gratifying. The historical study is indispensable for an exact and profound understanding of the mysteries. This end, moreover, is attained so much the more surely when the historian is not satisfied with enumerating facts and showing the modifications undergone by a book or a rite in the course of time, but strives in addition to bring to light the external and internal forces — cultural,

v

psychological, spiritual — which have intervened in this evolution. It is to be hoped, therefore, that these historical studies will be further pursued and perfected, and that they will continue to be fundamental to any attempt at explaining the liturgy.

Still, however useful it may be, the knowledge of history is only a step. The present-day liturgical movement, which stimulates historical research and is stimulated by it at the same time, tends to surpass this stage in three directions: first, in a spiritual direction, to seek in the liturgy a food for the spirit and a ferment of interior life; then in a pastoral direction, to find the means best suited for bringing the Christian people back to a liturgy which will be intelligible to them; finally in a direction more properly theological, to understand the liturgy in depth by replacing it in the framework of a theological synthesis.

During the last fifteen years it has been the pastoral renewal which exerted the greatest force in the liturgical movement. It has already obtained a certain number of reforms, and can hope for others still more important. This is cause for rejoicing. Yet we must not forget that these reforms are not an end in themselves. They are only a means of helping the liturgical pastoral art to attain its end. They are a means, a useful means, but a means which cannot suffice.

As a French priest said, "Whether the liturgy is done in Latin or in French, for my people it will always be in Hebrew!" If the liturgy is to become intelligible for the people, its meaning must be explained to them. Above all, they must be made to understand what the liturgy is, and what place belongs to it in the life of the Church and of every Christian. Only thus will the liturgical pastoral art attain its goal, which is to bring the people back to the mysteries and to Christ present and acting in these mysteries.

In order to bear real and lasting fruit, therefore, liturgical spirituality and liturgical pastoral must be based on a theological study which re-situates the liturgy in that vast divine economy made known to us by revelation and explained in a scientific manner by theology. There is perhaps nothing more necessary today for the liturgical movement than this theological study. And this study will be profitable not only to the liturgy, but also, as experience shows, to theology itself.

To be sure, much work has already been done in this field by various scholars, and the encyclical *Mediator Dei* has summed up the most noteworthy and most secure results. But much remains to be done in order to give the liturgical movement the broad, solid foundation it needs. One of the most important tasks is to make sure that the introductory studies for young clerics will make them enter really and deeply into the world of the liturgy, something which is possible only in a properly theological perspective.

The teaching of the liturgy should be a theological instruction, then, solidly grounded on the data of history and involving spiritual and pastoral consequences. It will comprise: a general liturgy, which will study the elements common to the various parts of the liturgy, always from the theological point of view; and a special liturgy, which will study from the same point of view the Mass, the sacraments and the sacramentals, the liturgical year, etc.

Such are the reasons which have prompted me to present this modest essay, in which I shall seek to shed light on the nature of the liturgy, its place in the economy of salvation, and its relations with the Bible, with faith, with theology, with the spiritual life and with the pastoral art.

I shall be happy if with this essay I can help some readers to quench their thirst more readily at the fountain of the liturgy. It is a fountain of living water which flows on into life everlasting. And the fountain is Christ.

ABBREVIATIONS

Dz: *Enchiridion symbolorum* of Henricus Denzinger and Clemens Bannwart.

MD: Encyclical *Mediator Dei*. Quotations and numbering of paragraphs are according to the Vatican Library translation (Washington: National Catholic Welfare Conference). The numbering marked "Lat." is according to the Latin text in *Documenta pontificia ad instaurationem liturgicam spectantia (1903–1953),* edited by Annibale Bugnini, C.M. (Rome: Edizioni Liturgiche, 1953), pp. 95 ff.

PG: Migne, *Patrologia graeca.*

PL: Migne, *Patrologia latina.*

Righetti: Mario Righetti, *Storia liturgica,* 4 volumes (Milan: Ancora, 1945 ff.). The first three volumes are cited in the second edition.

CONTENTS

CHAPTER 7

THE LITURGY AND THE CHRISTOLOGICAL AND TRINITARIAN DIALECTIC OF SALVATION: FROM THE FATHER, THROUGH CHRIST, IN THE HOLY SPIRIT, TO THE FATHER

CHAPTER 8

THE ONE LITURGIST AND THE ONE LITURGY

CHAPTER 9

THE LITURGY AND THE LAW OF SALVATION IN COMMUNITY

CHAPTER 10

THE LITURGY AND THE LAW OF INCARNATION

CHAPTER 11

THE LITURGY AND THE LAW OF THE COSMIC UNIVERSALITY OF THE KINGDOM OF GOD: 1. MAN AND THE INFRAHUMAN WORLD

CHAPTER 12

THE LITURGY AND THE LAW OF THE COSMIC UNIVERSALITY OF THE KINGDOM OF GOD: 2. THE SAINTS AND THE ANGELS

CHAPTER 13

THE TWO CITIES: THE STRUGGLE AGAINST SATAN IN THE LITURGY

PART 1 THE NATURE
OF THE LITURGY

1 THE GENERAL BACKGROUND OF THE LITURGY: REVELATION AS HISTORY OF SALVATION

IN ORDER TO ENTER into the world of the liturgy, we must first of all enter into the world of the Bible and place ourselves in the perspective which is that of the Bible. That is to say, we must see all things in the framework of the history of salvation. For the liturgy is a phase of that history; it is the means of our insertion into that history.

1. Revelation Takes the Form Primarily of a History of Salvation

Christian revelation, especially in the Bible, is not presented to us primarily as a speculative system, a revealed metaphysics. To be sure, revelation includes a certain number of statements of a metaphysical order which are of capital importance for revelation itself. But these statements are relatively rare and sporadic. They are not proposed as a system of metaphysical explanation of the universe, but rather as basic truths which can serve, if further developed, for the construction of such a system. And above all, however important they may be, they are not in the foreground; it is not on them that the Bible puts its emphasis. They are there like postulates: the Scripture sometimes alludes to them, but without dwelling on them.

Nor does revelation take the form primarily of a morality, a rule of life, a

3

collection of precepts. There is, of course, a moral teaching in the Scripture; but it almost always takes second place, being proposed as a consequence, a normal corollary of another element which itself occupies the foreground.

That which occupies the foreground in revelation, and especially in the Bible, is a history, a sacred history. It is the story of God's intervention in the world, to draw men to Him, to communicate His divine life to them, and thus to bring about His universal reign.

Such is the distinctive note which gives Judeo-Christian revelation its own physiognomy and differentiates it from any merely philosophical or ethical system. For example, the systems of Plato, Aristotle, Kant, are essentially philosophical systems from which a morality is derived. On the other hand, Confucianism, and also, it seems, the original Buddhism, are primarily a rule of life, a morality.

Revelation, then, is presented first of all as a unified group of historical events; as the history, always in the making, of God's interventions to make men share freely in His plan of universal dominion; and as the history of man's responses to God's appeals. If this history involves a metaphysical background, that is simply because no story can be without one.

When Caesar narrates the *Gallic War*, his story implies also a metaphysics: it implies that the notions of man, freedom, responsibility, war have an objective value; otherwise his story would make no sense. Caesar did not intend to occupy himself with metaphysics; nevertheless he could not help presupposing a certain number of concepts of a metaphysical order, and sometimes stating them explicitly. But it is clear that in a narrative of this kind metaphysics enters only as a foundation, always in the service of the story, to whatever extent is necessary to safeguard the import of the story.

The same holds for Christian revelation. The metaphysical data remain in the background and become an object of affirmation only to whatever extent is necessary to safeguard and make understandable the import of the history of salvation.

The fact that in Christian revelation the moral aspect is brought out strongly, comes from the nature of the story which revelation tells. It is a sacred story, a religious story, which, by the nature of Him who is its principal actor, God, and by the purposes which He is pursuing, encounters and involves deeply the life and the activity of man, his rights and his duties.

In Christian revelation, therefore, the moral teaching does not flow directly from a metaphysics, but first of all from a history. By looking at things as the Bible looks at them, man will see that his action is to be determined not simply by philosophical reasons or abstract considerations but, in practice, by the fact that God has intervened and is intervening, in such and such a way, in the history of the world and in our personal history: because God has acted thus and so with us, we should act thus and so toward Him.

The Ten Commandments, for example, are presented as the consequence of an alliance between God and the people whom He has chosen, formed, saved (Ex. 20:1–17). Israel's love for God will be the response to the special love which God has had for Israel (Deut. 10:12–16). The same manner of stating the foundation for moral teaching is found in St. John (e.g., 1 John 3:16; 4:7–11) and in St. Paul (Rom. 8:3–18; 1 Cor. 6:15–20; 8:11–13).

It is to be noted, moreover, that the Fathers and the ordinary teaching authority of the Church also present revelation first of all as a sacred history. It is the Bible which they propose chiefly to the faithful; it is the biblical message which is at the center of their own message. And the Credo, which is considered as a summary of revelation not only by the tradition of the Fathers[1] and of the liturgy,[2] but also by the scholastic tradition,[3] takes the form of a résumé of the history of God's interventions in the world. This is especially clear in the Apostles' Creed, which is the most ancient form of the *Credo*. We know that the later modifications tending to bring out the entitative aspect of certain points of doctrine were the work of the extraordinary *magisterium* in opposition to the errors of the heretics.[4]

In short, the whole Judeo-Christian revelation is presented first of all as a history, a history always in the making, which already has a long past and will be completed only in the future, the story of God's interventions in the world and of the response of creatures.

2. The Great Phases of the History of Salvation

It may be useful to recall in quick outline form the major facts of this history. It starts out in heaven and outside of time, develops on earth and in time, and finds its definitive fulfilment in heaven and outside of time.

1. IN HEAVEN

God — God the Father by appropriation — decides in an absolutely free manner to have creatures participate in His inmost life. There will be a Kingdom of God, (of which Christ will be the head, and) which will find its definitive fulfilment only in the heavenly Jerusalem. God predestines the elect

[1] Cf. D. van den Eynde, *Les normes de l'enseignement chrétien dans le littérature patristique des trois premiers siècles* (Gembloux, 1933). See, e.g., Irenaeus, *Adv. Haer.*, I, 10, 1–2 (PG 7, 549–553); Tertullian, *De Praescript.*, 13 (PL 2, 26–27).

[2] This was strikingly brought out in the ancient liturgy by the rite of the *Traditio symboli*, the handing-on of the creed; cf. *The Gelasian Sacramentary*, ed. Wilson (Oxford: Clarendon Press, 1894), pp. 53, 55 f. Moreover, even in most ancient times, the profession of faith in the principal articles of the *Credo* was an essential element of the Christian initiation.

[3] It is a common doctrine of scholasticism that all the data of faith are contained in the Apostles' Creed, in as much as those points which are not found explicit therein can be reduced to one of the explicit statements, whether as presupposition or as consequence. See, e.g., Alexander of Hales, *Summa*, III, q. 69, ed. Quaracchi, IV, nn. 898 ff.; St. Bonaventure, *In III librum Sententiarum*, d. 25, a. 1, q. 1.

[4] A typical case was the modifications which the Council of Nicaea introduced into the Symbol to defend the orthodox teaching against the Arians. The so-called Athanasian Creed also, with its strong insistence on the entitative aspect of the Trinity and of the Incarnation, is intended to combat heresies.

(in Christ and under His primacy). He creates the angels. But there is a drama in the angelic world: some remain faithful while others rebel and become enemies of God.

2. ON EARTH: A. First phase in Adam

God begins to carry out His plan by creating Adam as spiritual head of the human race (with subordination to Christ at least since the fall). He creates Adam, raises him to supernatural life, places him in paradise. There is unity of the universe which is subordinated to man. But God imposes a test, and man lets himself be led by the rebellious angel into revolt against God. The result is a rupture of the unity of the universe and the rise of the two cities. The first phase ends in apparent failure, but there is the promise of a Savior.

B. Second phase in Christ the second Adam: God resumes the execution of His plan in Christ the Savior

1st step: the preparation

Noe survives the deluge, and God makes a pact with him. Abraham is called by God, who binds Himself by a promise to him. With Moses there is the establishment of a "people of God," who are freed from Egypt by crossing the Red Sea in a miraculous way. Then there is the covenant on Sinai, the wandering in the desert and the entrance into the promised land. With the kings comes the building of the temple and the organization of worship. The age of the prophets and the exile make the people aware of their sinful condition and heighten their desire and expectation of a Messias to save them. The final preparation comes with John the Baptist and the Virgin Mary.

2nd step: the realization in Christ

God manifests and communicates Himself fully and definitively in the person of Christ the Savior: Incarnation, Nativity, Epiphany. It is essentially in the mystery of the Pasch that Christ fulfils His mission as Savior. After the sacramental anticipation in the institution of the Eucharist and of the priesthood, Christ traverses the two slopes of the one mystery: on the one side the Passion, death, burial and descent into hell; on the other side the Resurrection, the exaltation and the sitting at the Father's right hand. The glorified Christ sends His Spirit from His place at the Father's side.

3rd step: the extension in the Church

Under the action of the Spirit the Church, body of Christ, was born and has grown. This growth is to continue until the parousia, and it takes place essentially by means of the liturgy, that is to say, by the Mass, the sacraments, the sacramentals, liturgical prayer. The Church's other activities — teaching, governing, apostolate — are a preparation for this liturgical activity or a prolongation of it. And the individual activities of Christians have the aim of achieving in each one a correspondence with that which is lived in the liturgy.

4th step: the eschatological fulfilment

The history of salvation, in so far as it is history, that is, linked to time, comes to an end on the individual level with death, which opens heaven to the saints and purgatory to the faithful who are still imperfect; on the universal and cosmic level it comes to an end with the parousia, the general judgment and the resurrection.

3. IN HEAVEN

The Kingdom of God — of God the Father by appropriation — is established definitively, in Christ, in the one city of the faithful angels and of the men who have been saved, which addresses to God a universal liturgy of praise and thanksgiving.

Such, in brief summary, are the major facts of the history of salvation. Such is the specific world of the liturgy as well as of the Bible. This is by right, and should be also in fact, the specific world of theology, the role of theology being to explain certain aspects of this history, those which a scientific study can help to clarify. Theology must fulfill this task without ever losing sight of the fact, either in the general plan or in the details, that the concern is first of all with a history, even if that history, as we have said, involves a metaphysical basis and is itself the basis of a morality.

3. The Essential Traits of the History of Salvation

In order to situate the liturgy accurately in the framework of the history of salvation, outside of which it is incomprehensible, we must now specify the essential characteristics of that history. We shall come back to certain points in more detail in the chapters that follow.

It is a biblical history

Any fairly attentive reader of the Bible, especially of St. Paul's letters and of the Apocalypse, will recognize readily in the summary given above a simple schematization of the essential ideas underlying the whole Scripture, ideas which St. Paul has made explicit and has developed in various passages of his letters, and which the Apocalypse has brought out with much force.[5]

For the proof of this statement, recourse to the following texts will suffice. For the general picture: Eph. 1–3; Col. 1:9–23; 1 Tim. 3:15–17. For the general meaning of the relations between the old economy and the Christian economy: 1 Cor. 10:1–5; Rom. 9–11; Heb. 7:1–10, 18; see also Mark 1:15; Gal. 4:4. For the role of baptism in the Christian life and in the development of the Church, Christ's body: Rom. 6:1–12. For the role of the Eucharist: 1 Cor. 10:14–21; 11:23–30; John 6:32–59. For the heavenly Jerusalem and the cosmic liturgy: Heb. 12:21–24; Apoc. 5:8–14; 21:1–22:5.

---

[5] Cf. L. Tondelli, *Il disegno di Dio nella storia* (Turin, 1947); Ceslaus Spicq, *L'épitre aux hébreux*, I (Paris: Gabalda, 1952), 25–33.

It is a theology of history

Sacred history presents itself as a theology of history, because it reveals the ultimate meaning of history, the meaning which time and history have in the eyes of God. For, although God is immanent and involved, as it were, in this history, still He transcends it infinitely, and therefore sets it in motion, directs it, gives it a meaning.

This history is linear. It has its point of departure in God's eternal design, and it proceeds successively and irreversibly towards a point of arrival which has been fixed for it in advance and toward which it has been aimed from the beginning.

This history is one, coherent. Because it is directed by God, unique and all-powerful stage manager, with a view to the attainment of a preestablished end, there is a connection among the successive phases. The preceding ones prepare for those that follow, and the whole constitutes a realization by successive stages, perfection being attained only in the final phase.

This history is marked by a profound eschatological dynamism. The antecedent phases all tend to the subsequent ones, and all together tend to the ultimate. All the times tend to the ultimate times (*ta eschata*), which seem to exercise a force of attraction on the antecedent phases and give them an intelligible meaning.

This history does not go forward according to a mechanical and necessary process, but rather as a drama. For the angels and men are free and fallible creatures, whose freedom God wishes to respect, and who can use their freedom to go against the designs of God or to conform to them. Some of the angels and some of the men have freely accepted and seconded those designs: these are the elect. But the rest of the angels and, at their instigation, some of the men have rejected and impeded those designs. This division makes all history a dramatic struggle between two cities: on the one hand the rebellious angels and the men who have lined up with them; on the other hand the faithful angels with the elect of mankind. God dominates this drama, of which He is absolutely master, even while respecting the freedom of the protagonists. Its theater is the universe, earth and heaven.

It is the "mystery," the mystery of Christ

This whole history is called by St. Paul the "mystery" (Rom. 16:25; 1 Cor. 2:7; Eph. 5:32; Col. 1:26-27), the "mystery of the will of God" (Eph. 1:9), the "mystery which has been hidden from eternity in God" (Eph. 3:9). There is now general agreement in recognizing, contrary to what Dom Casel had thought, that this Pauline notion of the mystery owes nothing to the idea of the pagan mysteries and is simply the development and the result of an idea already expressed in the Old Testament, for example in Dan. 2:20-30: The profound meaning of the progress of history, which is obviously a religious meaning, can be known of itself only by God; it is a secret and a mystery hidden in God, and if men succeed in knowing it, this can be only because God reveals it.

In itself, and still more in the thinking of St. Paul, this mystery is wholly centered on Christ. This fact stands out still more strikingly if we accept a theory held by certain theologians. According to this theory, God from eternity, independently of Adam's sin, willed Christ and constituted Him the head of all creation; and thus the Word would have become incarnate in any hypothesis, that is to say, even if Adam had not sinned.[6]

At any rate, the history of salvation is divided clearly into two parts: before Christ and after Christ. Before Christ, at least beginning with Adam's sin, everything tends to Him, and after Christ everything derives from Him. Hence this story can be called, in the Pauline perspective, the "mystery of Christ."

It is true that in St. Paul this expression (Col. 4:3; Eph. 3:4), strictly speaking, means only the calling of the gentiles, together with the Jews, to be saved by Christ in the Church. Yet the context of the passages referred to above, where sacred history is spoken of as mystery, shows well enough that St. Paul's whole attention is concentrated on Christ as center and focal point of God's counsels and plans, center and focal point of history and of the mystery. And it is of this that he is thinking when he speaks of the mystery which "refers to Christ and to the Church" (Eph. 5:32), of "the mystery of the gospel" (Eph. 6:19), of "the mystery of faith" (1 Tim. 3:9), of "the mystery of piety" (1 Tim. 3:16). In this last passage, moreover, as also in Col. 2:2, if the variant reading τοῦ μυστηρίου τοῦ θεοῦ, Χριστοῦ, is adopted, the word "mystery" designates Christ Himself and everything that He represents for the world.

We are therefore remaining faithful to the thinking of St. Paul if we use the expression "mystery of Christ" to refer to everything that the incarnate Word, Savior and High Priest of the human race, is and does in the divine plan and in its realization. We can equivalate "history of salvation," "mystery," "mystery of Christ": the concern is always with a single reality, in as much as the center of this sacred history, this mystery, is Christ.[7]

If Christ holds this central place in history, it is because the end which God has proposed to Himself — to communicate His own life to creatures — is

---

[6] This point is disputed between Scotistic and Thomistic theologians. In the Scotist theory, now accepted by many, even in case Adam had not sinned the Word would have become incarnate; but even then Adam would have been spiritual head of the human race, though under the supreme head, Christ, who would thus have been supreme Head and Mediator, but not Redeemer. The question is extended also to the angels. The data of Scripture and of tradition do not suffice to solve it. It seems undeniable, however, that the thinking of St. Paul tends in this direction (Col. 1:15-20); but it is not explicit. This way of looking at things gives the divine plan and all of sacred history a much greater unity.

[7] For the concept of mystery in St. Paul cf. D. Deden, "Le 'mystère' paulinien," *Eph. theol. lov.*, 1936, pp. 405 ff.; G. Soehngen, *Der Wesensaufbau des Mysteriums* (Bonn, 1938); J. T. Trinidad, "The Mystery Hidden in God," *Biblica*, 31 (1950), 1 ff.

realized in the person of Christ in a full and final way. In Him this communication reaches its culmination and its highest manifestation. After Him
nothing substantially new is to be expected which is not already present in
His person. The only thing to be expected is the extension of this life to men
of good will and their admittance to this glorious condition which Christ
already enjoys.

The appearance of Christ on earth marks the beginning of the last times,
for in Christ the meaning of time and of history is realized fully. These last
times will come to an end with the glorious return of the Lord and the passage from time to eternity.

To enter into the world of the liturgy, it is most important to understand
that the whole of sacred history is the mystery of Christ, that everything before Him tends to Him and everything after Him derives from Him, that
after His coming there is nothing further to be done but to reproduce His
mystery in creatures until the end of time.

For the liturgy, as we shall see, is nothing but a certain way in which Christ,
in the present intermediate time which extends from the Ascension to the
parousia, communicates the fulness of His divine life to individual souls,
reproducing His mystery in them, drawing them into His mystery.

It is the mystery of the Church

This time in which everything is already substantially and radically realized
and in which we are only waiting until the number of the brethren is complete (cf. Apoc. 6:11), is properly the time of the Church. In the Church
Christ visibly gives His mandate to the Apostles and their successors in the
hierarchy, fortifying them with specific powers to sanctify, to teach and to
govern. At the same time, invisibly, He sends the Holy Spirit, who inwardly gives life to their work. Thus He brings the reality of His mystery
into souls and so fulfils the meaning of history.

The Church is the human and divine, hierarchical and spiritual framework
willed and established by Christ to be the necessary means by which, until
the end of time, He would communicate to men the divine life of which He
Himself is full.

The Church, again, is the messianic community of the last times, composed
of a great number of gentiles and a little remnant of faithful Jews, called
together by God around Jesus the Messias. In it the whole divine life issuing
from Christ is diffused; it prepares the final assembly in the glory of the
heavenly Jerusalem (cf. Heb. 12:22-24). The Church is that holy people,
chosen and loved by God, whom God had the aim of purchasing for Himself
when He set history into motion and guided it (cf. 1 Pet. 2:9-10).

We can make the following comparison. Christ realizes and expresses in
His own person the meaning of history because He is the incarnate expression
of God, His full and exhaustive image, since in Christ "dwells bodily all the

fulness of the Divinity" (Col. 2:9; cf. John 14:9-11; 2 Cor. 4:4-6; Col. 1:15; Heb. 1:3). So also the Church expresses and realizes in herself the meaning of history because she is the complete human-divine expression on earth of the existence and activity of Christ. By the Spirit which He communicates to her, Christ gives life inwardly to the Church, so that she can be compared in this respect to a body; for the body is the visible expression of the invisible soul, the sphere in which the soul exercises its action (cf. Eph. 1:23).

Finally, another parallel may be drawn. Whatever there is of divine life in the world is found in Christ, and no one is saved unless he is really and currently united to Christ through grace, participating thus in the fulness of the divine life which is in Him. So also, since the Ascension, whatever there is of divine life and Christian life in the world is found in the Church, and no one is saved except in real and current union, at least invisible,[8] with this Church.

For the Holy Spirit is present in the Church "as in a good vessel containing a precious treasure which is perennially young and communicates its perennial youth to the vessel in which it is contained. . . . God has placed in the Church Apostles, prophets, teachers (cf. 1 Cor. 12:28) and all the other working of the Spirit. Anyone who does not belong to the Church does not share in that Spirit, but deprives himself of life by erroneous doctrine and bad conduct. For where the Church is, there is the Spirit of God, and where the Spirit of God is, there is the Church and every grace; and the Spirit is truth. Therefore those who do not share in the Spirit are not nursed by the maternal breasts and do not drink of the limpid spring which flows from the body of Christ."[9]

Thus, in the time that extends from the Ascension to the parousia, the Church is the mother of all those who live with the divine life; she is the new Eve at the new Adam's side, immaculate spouse (cf. Eph. 5:24-27) who bears children to Christ. Only she "assigns to the Kingdom the children whom she has borne. Whoever is separated from the Church . . . is a stranger, is profane, is an enemy. He who has not the Church for a mother cannot have God for a Father."[10]

It is all this that constitutes the mystery of the Church, that "cosmic mystery of the Church" of which the *Didache* speaks,[11] the "wonderful mystery of Your whole Church" of the liturgy.[12]

---

[8] Every man of good faith who lives according to his conscience, adheres by that very fact, at least implicitly, to whatever the divine will expects of him. Thus he has at least the implicit desire to adhere visibly to the Church, such being now the will of God for every man. For this desire the man of good faith receives the grace of God, and this grace makes him a member really and currently, though still invisibly, of the one Church, the visible Church. And this much suffices for salvation.

[9] Irenaeus, *Haer.*, III, 24, 1 (PG 7, 966).

[10] Cyprian, *De cath. eccl. unitate*, 6 (PL 4, 503).

[11] 11, 11.

[12] Roman Missal, Holy Saturday, collect after the second prophecy when there were still twelve.

We see that the history of salvation, the mystery of Christ and the mystery of the Church are inseparable realities, or rather a single reality of which these different names simply designate different aspects.

This whole explanation should by no means be taken for lyrical flights of fancy, but as a perfectly sober expression of the plain reality. We shall return in another chapter to some aspects of this question. Its complete and detailed study belongs to the "theology of the Church."

Here we have offered a broad vista to show that the liturgy is incomprehensible if it is not related to the Church, just as the Church is incomprehensible if it is not related to Christ, and Christ is incomprehensible if He is not related to the general plan of God in the history of salvation.

In other words, the liturgy cannot be understood unless it is seen in the framework of the history of salvation, mystery of Christ and mystery of the Church.

2 THE LITURGY AS A COMPLEXUS OF SIGNS

What is the liturgy? The things designated by the word are first of all the Mass and the sacraments, but also the sacramentals, the Divine Office and all the ceremonies with which the Church surrounds and clothes these essential acts. Does all this constitute a homogeneous whole? What is the common denominator which allows us to bring all this under the concept of liturgy? How is the liturgy to be defined?

1. Definition of the Liturgy

The method to be followed

Concerning the question of the true definition[1] of the liturgy there is anything but unanimity among the scholars even after the encyclical *Mediator*

[1] The use of the word "liturgy" in its present sense goes back to the humanists and the liturgists of the seventeenth century. The ancients spoke of *ministerium divinum, ministerium ecclesiasticum, officia divina.*

The term λειτουργία originally designated a public service, a function exercised in the interests of all the people: first of all a work of a political or technical nature, but also a religious service.

It is in this last sense that the word is used in the Septuagint to indicate the religious service of the priests in the temple (cf. Ex. 28:35 and 43; Num. 4:33; 1 Par. 23:28). This sense is known in the New Testament (e.g., Luke 1:23; Heb. 9:21; 10:11), which applies the term also to Christ's heavenly ministry (Heb. 8:2 and 6), to St. Paul's apostolic ministry which permits him to offer as a sacrifice to God the faithful (Rom: 15:16) and their faith

Dei.[2] The question is not simply one of terminology, but of the precise determination of that one among all the necessary properties of the liturgy which is at the basis of all the others. In every science the whole orientation of the inquiry and of the exposition depends on this determination; for this fundamental characteristic is the principle of intelligibility on which every further affirmation will depend. Thus it is the whole study of the liturgy which will depend on the accuracy of the definition to be proposed.

To arrive at a valid solution, it seems to me, we must first consider, as parts of a whole, all the elements which concretely make up the liturgy; then look for the essential characteristic notes which are found in all these elements; and finally, among these essential notes, look for that which is at the basis of the rest and explains them. This is the classical way of seeking the definition of the subject in any science.

The sacrifice, the sacraments, the sacramentals, the Divine Office, the ceremonies all have in common the fact that they are *signs*. They are the sensible signs of realities which are sacred, spiritual, inaccessible to the senses.

The Mass, a visible sacrifice, has the formal value of sacrifice only as sign of an interior sacrifice, that of Christ offering Himself, that of the faithful

---

(Phil. 2:17), to the offering which the faithful make to God in helping the poor communities (Rom. 15:27; 2 Cor. 9:12; cf. Phil. 4:18; Heb. 13:16), probably also to the cultual celebrations (Acts 13:2).

Very soon, in the East, λειτουργία serves to designate the Eucharistic sacrifice (perhaps this is true as early as the *Didache*, 15, 1, and 1 *Clem.*, 41, 1–3; starting with the fourth century it is common). This is only to be expected, since the Mass is truly the summing up and the center of the whole of Christian worship. On all this cf. E. Raitz von Frentz, "Der Weg des Wortes 'Liturgie' in der Geschichte," *Eph. lit.*, 55 (1941), 74 ff.; Antonino Romeo, "Il termine λειτουργία nella grecità biblica," *Miscellanea liturgica in honorem L. Cuniberti Mohlberg*, II (Rome: Ed. Liturgiche, 1949), 467 ff.

[2] It is not necessary to recall the various definitions that have been proposed. Many liturgists have adopted that of Lambert Beauduin, who defined the liturgy simply as "the Church's worship" ("Essai de manuel fondamental de liturgie," *Les quest. lit. et parois.*, 3 [1913], 56–66). See also Emmanuel Caronti, "Per una definizione della liturgia," *Riv. lit.*, 8 (1921), 4 ff.; A. Stenzel, *Cultus publicus. Ein Beitrag zum Begriff und ekklesiologischen Ort der Liturgie* (Innsbruck, 1953).

The encyclical *Mediator Dei*, at the end of a passage showing that in the Church and especially in the liturgy it is Christ Himself who honors the Father, and that the Church does so only with and through Christ, says, "The sacred liturgy is consequently the public worship which our Redeemer as Head of the Church renders to the Father as well as the worship which the community of the faithful renders to its Founder, and through Him to the heavenly Father. It is, in short, the worship rendered by the mystical body of Christ in the entirety of its Head and members" (n. 20). The encyclical certainly does not intend to bring to an end the discussion among theologians on the technical and perfect definition of the liturgy; it intends only to make the point that the liturgy, *in as much as it is worship rendered to God*, is the worship of the whole mystical Body, Head and members.

The same encyclical, moreover, presents other definitions or rough drafts of definitions; e.g., n. 22: " . . . since the liturgy is nothing more nor less than the exercise of this priestly function of Jesus Christ"; or n. 171 (Lat. 169): "Such is the nature and the object of the sacred liturgy: it treats of the Mass, the sacraments, the Divine Office; it aims at uniting our souls with Christ and sanctifying them through the divine Redeemer in order that Christ be honored and, through Him and in Him, the most holy Trinity." Here in a special way the aspect of sanctification is more strongly emphasized.

uniting themselves to the offering of Christ. As early a writer as St. Augustine observed, "The visible sacrifice, therefore, is *sacramentum,* that is, sacred sign, of the invisible sacrifice." [3]

For the seven sacraments, it is enough to recall the teaching of St. Thomas: "That is properly called a sacrament which is a sign of some sacred thing pertaining to men; so that 'sacrament' is properly used, in the sense in which we are now speaking of sacraments, when it is predicated of 'a sign of a sacred thing, in as much as it sanctifies men.' " [4]

The sacramentals too are signs of spiritual realities; in this they do not differ from the sacraments. The same must be said of the rites and ceremonies of all kinds which the Council of Trent calls precisely "visible signs of religion and of piety." [5]

Finally, since liturgical prayer is by its nature vocal, it too falls under the concept of sign: speech is by definition a conventional sign of what we think and feel within.

In the first place, then, all the elements which make up the liturgy have this in common, that they are sensible signs of sacred, spiritual, invisible realities. All these signs have the further point in common of having been instituted either by Christ (substance of the Mass and of the sacraments) or by the Church (sacramentals, prayers, ceremonies).

In the second place, the liturgical signs, because they have been instituted by Christ or by the Church and are employed by them to signify realities dependent on them, are always *efficacious* with respect to that which they signify. This efficacy, however, is of different kinds, according to whether there is question of the sacrifice and the sacraments instituted by Christ — which operate primarily *ex opere operato* (literally "from the work wrought") — or of the signs instituted by the Church — which operate primarily *ex opere operantis Ecclesiae* (literally "from the work of the Church working").

In the third place, the sacred realities which are signified and accomplished by the liturgical signs concern *the sanctification and the worship* of the Church; by means of these signs God sanctifies the Church and the Church renders its public worship to God. These two aspects are inseparable.

But it is always through Christ that God sanctifies. At least since Adam's sin, there is no grace and sanctification which is not *in Christo,* that is to say, merited by Christ, effecting real union with Christ, and, since the Incarnation, effected, caused by Christ's humanity itself as conjoint instrument with His divinity.

In the same way, any worship rendered by the Church to God is *in Christo,* that is to say, in union with Christ and through His mediation. More properly, the Church's worship is nothing but the participation of the Church in the worship which Christ her Head renders to God. It is the worship and

---

[3] *De civ. Dei,* X, 5 (PL 41, 282).   [5] *Sess.* XXII, chap. 5.

[4] *Summa,* III, q. 60, a. 2.

the priesthood of Christ the Head continued in the Church, by the Church, with the Church, which is His body.[6]

In the liturgy, therefore, sanctification and worship are accomplished only *in Christo*.

If they are accomplished *in Christo*, they are accomplished also *in Spiritu*. As the New Testament teaches, the action of Christ and the action of the Spirit are inseparable, and no one can be united to Christ unless he finds himself in the presence and in the power of His Spirit. Not only is baptism in the Spirit[7] and not only is the Spirit received in confirmation, in penance, in the Eucharist and in holy orders,[8] but every Christian sacrifice and every Christian prayer is sacrifice and prayer in the Spirit.[9]

In this precise sense Christian worship is "spiritual,"[10] and it can be said of the Christians, using a formula of St. Paul which expresses very precisely the nature of the worship they practice, that "through Him (Christ) they have access in the one Spirit to the Father."[11]

Definition of the liturgy

By putting together all these data, we arrive at the following definition: *The liturgy is the complexus of the signs of things sacred, spiritual, invisible; signs instituted by Christ or by the Church, efficacious, each in its own way, of that which they signify; by which signs God (the Father by appropriation), through Christ the Head, and in the presence of the Holy Spirit, sanctifies the Church, and the Church as a body, in the presence of the Holy Spirit, uniting herself to Christ her Head and Priest, through Him renders her worship to God (the Father by appropriation).*

To bring out more clearly what constitutes the essence of the liturgy and to formulate a definition by proximate genus and specific difference, following the classical rules, we must now eliminate from the above description those expressions which only follow from and explain the other expressions contained therein without really adding anything new for anyone who grasps the full force of these other expressions in the light of general theology.

In the first part, we can suppress the words "of things sacred, spiritual, invisible." Actually these realities signified by the liturgy are concretely: sanctifying grace; the Author of this grace, Christ; its end, the glory to come; and the interior worship which the Church renders to God. It suffices to say,

---

[6] See MD, nn. 2, 3, 20, 22.

[7] Cf. 1 Cor. 12:13.

[8] Cf. Acts 8:15 ff.; John 20:22–23; 1 Tim. 4:14; Acts 20:28.

[9] Cf. Rom. 8:26–27; 15:15–16; Gal. 4:6; Eph. 6:18; Heb. 9:14; Jude 20.

[10] Cf. Phil. 3:3: the affirmation is direct if we read θεῷ, indirect if we read θεοῦ. Christian

worship is called spiritual not to deny its visible and sensible aspect, but to affirm that, even if it is visible and sensible, it is rendered in the Spirit.

[11] Cf. Eph. 2:18. The expression "to have access" (ἔχειν τὴν προσαγωγὴν) to God" refers to worship; cf. 1 Pet. 3:18.

therefore, that the liturgy is a complexus of signs of the sanctification of the Church by God and of the worship of God by the Church.

There is no need to specify that those signs have been instituted by Christ or by the Church : signs efficacious of the Church's sanctification and worship have necessarily been instituted by Christ or by the Church, who alone are capable of giving these signs the power to effect what they signify.

After "efficacious" it is not necessary to add "each in its own way of that which they signify"; for the efficacy of the sign, as sign, is obviously related to its signification; and, moreover, since the concern is with a complexus of signs, it goes without saying that each kind of sign will have the efficacy that is proper to it.

In a definition of the liturgy by proximate genus and specific difference it is not necessary, either, to mention explicitly that all sanctification comes from the Father (by appropriation) through Christ the Head, in the presence of the Holy Spirit, and that all worship of the Church is directed to the Father (by appropriation) by the same way. It is not necessary because this is simply the general theological doctrine of the way in which every good comes to us from God and of the way in which every return of ours to God is made (though I would not presume to say that this doctrine is much heeded or much understood, still less that it is effectively lived).

This movement "from God to God" always follows the scheme "from the Father, through Christ, in the Holy Spirit, to the Father." [12]

It is not necessary to say, either, that the Church's worship is rendered to God. This is already included in the very idea of the Church's worship. Nor is it necessary to say that the sanctification of the Church comes from God, because this is already included in the idea of sanctification.

Finally, in a definition it is not necessary to say explicitly that the Church's worship of God in the liturgy is done as a body, officially, publicly. Actually "Church," understood formally as Church, necessarily implies all this.

Thus, among the different characteristics of the liturgy, we arrive at that which is fundamental and explains the others, we arrive at that which constitutes the very essence of the liturgy, which we may now define as *the complexus of the efficacious signs of the Church's sanctification and of her worship.*

This definition applies to all the elements of the liturgy and to them only. It holds not only for that which is action of the Church — worship — but also for that which is action of God — the sanctification of the Church. It corrects the inadequacies of some notions of the liturgy which are still too widespread. For the liturgy is sometimes defined as the Church's worship, with no mention of its whole aspect of sanctification. Again the liturgy's domain is still more restricted, being limited more or less consciously to what is of ecclesiastical institution in worship. What is divine in the Mass and the sacraments is

---

[12] Cf. chapter 7 below: "The Liturgy and the Christological and Trinitarian Dialectic of Salvation."

excluded, leaving only the prayers and ceremonies with which the Church clothes, so to speak, the celebration of the Mass and the administration of the sacraments.[13]

These concepts just mentioned offend against one of the essential rules of every good definition, that it be co-extensive with the object defined. They try to restrict the concrete liturgical reality, to cut off a part of it arbitrarily. For the liturgy includes not only an attitude and an activity of the Church towards God, but also an attitude and an activity of God towards the Church. The liturgy is not a monolog of the Church thinking of God and honoring Him; it is a dialog between God and the Church, a point of contact and a place of meeting.

In the liturgy there is both the sanctification of the Church by God and the worship rendered to God by the Church. And since this double action is realized only through Christ and in Him, one may say that the liturgy is the point of encounter, in Christ, of God who sanctifies the Church and the Church who renders her worship to God.[14]

Liturgy and *sacramentum*

It will be noticed that the proposed definition of the liturgy is basically no more than a broadening of the classical definition of the sacraments: "sensible signs effecting (*ex opere operato*) the grace which they signify."

The extension occurs in two essential points: first of all, by efficacious signs are understood not only those which are efficacious *ex opere operato*, but also those which are efficacious *ex opere operantis Ecclesiae*; in the second place, some of these signs, such as the sacraments, signify grace directly, but others signify first of all the worship rendered to God, and only indirectly the grace which sanctifies men. Moreover, our definition of the liturgy states explicitly that it is the Church as such which is the direct subject of sanctification and of worship.

A thing no less notable is that this broadening which the concept of sacrament is made to undergo in order to include the whole of the liturgy simply brings us back to the ancient concept of *mysterium* or *sacramentum* which the patristic and liturgical tradition employed to designate everything that we today call liturgy. And this coincidence should not surprise us if we remember that the scholastic theologians and St. Thomas in particular worked out the notion of sacrament in the strict sense by purifying the ancient concept of *mysterium* or of *sacramentum* so as to make it signify only the essential

---

[13] Cf., e.g., Camillus Callewaert, *Liturgicae institutiones — De S. Liturgia universim* (4th ed.; Brussels: Beyaert, 1944), p. 6: the liturgy is defined as "the ecclesiastical arrangement of public worship," "public worship in so far as it is arranged by ecclesiastical authority."

[14] The encyclical *Mediator Dei* also comprises under the notion of liturgy not only that which is of ecclesiastical institution in the liturgical action, but also that which is of divine institution. See nn. 3, 171 (Lat. 169), 205 (Lat. 203).

characteristics of the seven major rites to which they reserved the name of sacraments.

We shall attempt later on to analyze the patristic notion of *sacramentum*.[15] Here it is enough to recall that for the ancients it was capable of encompassing the whole liturgical reality. For example, St. Augustine used the term *sacramentum, sacramenta* not only for the hidden teachings and for the figures of the Old Testament, as well as for the Bible itself, but also for baptism, confirmation, the Eucharist, the Apostles' Creed, the Lord's Prayer, exorcisms, fasting, all the ceremonies and prayers of the Mass, the liturgical feast of Easter, etc.[16]

And this is possible for him because he takes *sacramentum* in a very broad sense: it is a sign which has reference to the sacred realities of God's economy in the world and which manifests them to those who understand the sign and hides them from the rest. Moreover, for the ancients, the liturgical *sacramenta* really contain in some way the realities which they signify.

If we want to remain faithful to this terminology, we can say that the liturgy is the carrying out *in sacramento* or *in mysterio* of the history of salvation in the time that extends from Pentecost to the parousia. Actually, as we have explained above, the liturgy is nothing but the realization of this history under the veil of signs, and the ancient concept of *mysterium* or *sacramentum* expresses accurately the original and specific character of this realization.[17]

2. Sign

If the liturgy is a complexus of signs, the first thing to be done in order to have an accurate idea of it is obviously to explain the notion of sign and its application in the liturgy.[18]

Structure of sign

St. Augustine has defined sign as "a thing which, besides the species it impresses on the senses, leads to the knowledge of something other than itself." [19]

[15] Cf. vol. 2, chapter 19 below: "Theology and Liturgy in the Fathers."

[16] All these meanings are met with, e.g., in *Sermo* 227 (PL 38, 1099–1101); 228, 3 (PL 38, 1102); *Ep.* 98, nn. 9–10 (PL 33, 363–364).

[17] This notion of *sacramentum* or of *mysterium* is definitely traditional and is independent of Dom Casel's theory. It would be ridiculous to hold suspect the doctrine expressed by the words *sacramentum* and *mysterium*, so well founded in patristic and liturgical tradition, for the simple reason that one does not agree with the personal theory which Casel tried to attach to these words. It would be no less unjust to deny that the credit for having rediscovered a very rich vein of authentic tradi-

tional theology belongs to the monk of Maria Laach, aside from his own specific theory.

[18] For a metaphysical analysis of the concept of sign see: John of St. Thomas, *Logica*, II, qq. 21 and 22, ed. Reiser, I (Turin: Marietti, 1930), 646–722; A. M. Roguet, "Les sacraments," *S. Thomas d'Aquin, La somme théologique*, ed. de la revue des jeunes (Paris: Desclée, 1945), pp. 269 ff.; Eugène Masure, *Le signe* (Paris: Bloud et Gay, 1953).

[19] *De doctr. christiana*, II, 1, 1 (PL 34, 35). I see no solid basis for the criticism by Masure, *Le signe*, pp. 15, 188, who considers this definition too narrow, applying only to the notional sign.

The sign is therefore a sensible reality which makes known another more hidden reality. For one thing to be a sign of another, three conditions are required. It must be distinct from the thing signified, have a relation to it and be more easily known than it. In brief, what is required of a sign is the qualities of an intermediary, a substitute. If the sign did not have these three qualities, it could not play its part.

From this premise two observations can be drawn. In the first place, the sign reveals the thing signified but at the same time hides it. It reveals it in as much as it has something in common with it; but it hides it in as much as it is distinct and different from it, and expresses it only imperfectly. The sign makes the thing known, but at the same time it offers an obstacle to this knowledge because it is not perfectly transparent. For the person who does not know how to interpret the sign, it is a screen, a barrier. To get past it, one must understand the sign in so far as it is a sign, and not stop at what it is in itself. Then the sign is no longer a veil but a bridge connecting the thing with the mind.

The second observation is that the sign has no reason for being unless the reality to be known is absent or hidden. As soon as it is present to the mind without intermediary, without a veil, the sign loses its value. A system of signs makes sense only as a bridge between two beings or two worlds hidden from each other. The sign is the means which permits the human spirit to communicate with the invisible world and to express itself in the visible world.

Signs may be divided into two great categories, according to the relation which they have to the thing signified. Thus there are real signs and signs of pure reason, and among the real signs we must distinguish natural signs and free signs.

In the case of real signs the relation between the sign and the thing signified is real: it is a relation of effect to cause. Smoke is a real sign of fire because it is the effect of fire; the fact of bowing down before someone is a real sign of the respect one wants to show him. Real signs contain the thing signified in some way and make it known, as the effect contains and makes known its cause.

In the case of real signs which are natural, the relation between sign and thing signified does not depend on a free decision of man, but comes from the very nature of things. Smoke is a natural sign of fire, the track of an animal is a natural sign of its passage; a photograph is a natural sign of the one whom it represents. Such signs are understandable to all men; all that is needed is to know the reality which they express.

As to the real signs which are free, they are objects, actions or gestures freely chosen by man to express realities with which they have no natural connection, no necessary connection. It is thus that the flag has been chosen to signify the country, or the bow to signify respect.

It should be noted that, even in this case, the relation between sign and thing signified is real, and that even here the sign contains in some way the thing signified. The difference between natural signs and free signs does not proceed from the fact that they contain or do not contain the reality signified, but from the manner in which they contain it.

In natural signs the reality is contained directly, in virtue of the very nature of things. In free signs it is contained only by reason of a free choice, a free initiative of man. That is why natural signs have a universal value, while for understanding free signs it is necessary to know the intention of the one who has chosen them.

Real signs that are free are therefore, in so far as they are signs, real and sensible effects which depend on man's free choice as their efficient cause, and it is the will from which this choice proceeds that they contain and signify directly. It is only in a mediate way that they contain and signify the idea or the sentiment which a person understands them to express.

Finally, signs of pure reason are free signs which are not produced by man and therefore cannot be real effects of his will. They are sensible realities, existing independently of man, which he has chosen in a conventional way to signify other realities. Thus, for example, two men might wish to take, not just an emblem of the rainbow, but the rainbow itself in the sky, as a sign of their reconciliation.

Sign, image and symbol

Among the notions close to that of sign, those of image and symbol are rather important in the liturgy. The three terms are often used today as synonymous; but, strictly speaking, image and symbol are particular species of signs.

We speak of image when there is a relation of likeness between the sign and the thing signified. This likeness proceeds either from the nature itself or from a natural characteristic, such as the "figure."[20] Smoke is not the image of fire, but the sketch is the image of the building, or the son the image of the father.

The modern notion of symbol is much harder to determine.[21] Every symbol is a sign, but not all signs are symbols. Smoke is not a symbol of fire, but its sign; a statue is not the symbol of a person, but his image. Symbol is not identified, therefore, either with sign in general or with image.

A symbol is a free sign, whether real or of pure reason, as distinguished from a natural sign. But, although it has been chosen freely, it most often presents, in its very being or in its properties, a certain analogy with the thing symbolized, so that one might call the symbol a sort of concrete metaphor.

[20] Cf. St. Thomas, *Summa*, I q. 93, aa. 1 and 2. The notion of image or εἰκών among the Greeks was broader: everything which led to the knowledge of another was called εἰκών.

[21] Originally the σύμβολον (συν-βάλλω) was a sign of recognition, an object cut in two, of which two partners each kept a piece: the two parts brought together served to identify the bearers.

Thus the scale is the symbol of justice, incense the symbol of prayer, the sun the symbol of Christ.

In other cases the symbol has been chosen because it had a relation of belonging, of origin, of name with the thing symbolized, or some historical tie. Thus the wolf symbolizes Rome; the fish symbolizes Christ because of the word ἰχθύς; the iconographic symbols of the saints often belong to this category, as the keys of St. Peter or the sword of St. Paul.

The ancients' way of thinking about sign, image, symbol

What we call sign, image or symbol is what the Greeks called εἰκών, σύμβολον, μυστήριον, τύπος, and the Latins *imago, species, figura, sacramentum, mysterium*. Each of these terms has its history and its shades of meaning, but all agree in the general idea of sign; all designate a visible reality related to a hidden reality.

Between that visible reality and that hidden reality, between the sign and the thing signified, there is at the same time a certain identity and a certain diversity.

There is a certain identity, by virtue of which the invisible is present in the visible. This presence, however, must not be conceived as that of something contained within a container, but rather as a manifestation, a sensible way of being of a reality essentially spiritual. This holds when there is a relation of cause to effect between the thing signified and the sign, for the effect always contains its cause in some way; it has something of its cause in it, at least that sort of imprint that the cause leaves in it. This identity is real also in the case of conventional signs chosen by reason of some analogy with the thing to be signified; for analogy, even metaphorical analogy, supposes a certain identity between the objects compared.

There is a certain identity, then, between the sign and the thing signified. There is also a certain diversity. The sign is always distinct from that which it signifies. This point is so evident that there is no need to dwell on it.

While the moderns generally insist on the distinction and the difference between the sign and the thing signified, the ancients paid attention primarily to their unity and their identity. As early as the beginning of this century Harnack made this observation, *à propos* of the doctrine of the Eucharist in antiquity. Are the body and blood of Christ in the Eucharist real or symbolic? "As far as we can judge, no one saw a problem here. The symbol was a mystery, and mystery was not conceived of without symbol. What we understand by 'symbol' today is a thing which is not what it signifies; at that time 'symbol' denoted a thing which, in some real way, was what it signified. Besides, for the ancient way of thinking, the heavenly reality was always present in the form or under the form in which it was manifested, without, however, being identified completely with it on this earth. For this reason we must reject completely the distinction between a symbolic concept and a realistic concept of the Eucharist" [22] in order to understand the thinking of the ancients.

In other words, we are posing a false problem if we ask whether, for the Fathers, Christ's body is present really or only symbolically in the Eucharist. It is a false problem because it starts out from the modern idea that what is symbolic is not real. Recent research on the history of the terms εἰκών, σύμβολον, μυστήριον, τύπος, *signum, imago, figura, species, sacramentum, mysterium* [23] has confirmed fully the justice of Harnack's observation.

These remarks are of great importance for theology as well as for liturgy.

In theology they allow us in particular to interpret accurately the scriptural and patristic theme of Christ the image of the invisible God; to give its full value to the biblical and patristic typology which relates the realities of the Old Testament to those of the New, and those of the New Testament to those of the last times; to understand the whole sacramental theology of the Fathers, and especially their theology of the Eucharist; finally, to appreciate the doctrinal foundations of the struggle of the Greek Fathers in the seventh and eighth centuries against iconoclasm.

In the field of liturgy, the knowledge of this ancient way of thinking enables us to avoid misunderstandings in the interpretation of the numerous texts where the Fathers employ the terms *mysterium, sacramentum, imago, species* etc. in connection with the liturgical rites. Likewise, it enables us to interpret accurately a good number of ancient liturgical texts, many of which are still in use. Here are three of these texts, very characteristic:

Aeternae pignus vitae capientes humiliter imploramus ut apostolicis fulti patrociniis quod in imagine gerimus sacramenti manifesta perceptione sumamus.[24]	Receiving the pledge of eternal life, we humbly implore that under the patronage of the Apostles we may consume with full knowledge what we consecrate in a sacramental image.
Perficiant in nobis, Domine, quaesumus, tua sacramenta quod continent, ut quae nunc specie gerimus, rerum veritate capiamus.[25]	May Your Sacraments, O Lord, we pray, effect in us what they contain, that what we now do in appearance, we may obtain in reality.
Quorum oblationem benedictam ratam acceptabilemque facere di-	And may You see fit to make the oblation of these things blessed, rati-

[22] *Dogmengeschichte*, I (4th ed., 1909), 476.
[23] For a first orientation, see Thomas Camelot, "Simbolo e simbolismo," *Enciclopedia cattolica*, 11 (1953), 611–616, with a bibliography to which may be added: H. Willms, *Eikon. Eine begriffgeschichtliche Untersuchung zum Platonismus* (Münster, 1935); the article "Bild" in the *Reallexikon für Antike und Christentum*, written by H. E. Killy and M. Höpfner for the Greek and Roman idea, and by J. Kollwitz for the Christian; W.

Dürig, *Imago. Eine Beitrag zur Terminologie und Theologie der römischen Liturgie* (Munich, 1952); Hermann Kleinknecht, "Der griechische Sprachgebrauch von 'eikon,'" *Theol. Wört. zum NT*, II, 386 f.
[24] *Sacramentarium Leonianum*, n. 335; ed. Mohlberg, II, p. 45.
[25] *The Gelasian Sacramentary*, II, 60; ed. Wilson, p. 202 (see also the Roman Missal, postcommunion of Ember Saturday of September).

generis, quae est imago et similitudo corporis et sanguinis Iesu Christi filii tui ac redemptoris nostri.[26]

fied and acceptable — this oblation, the image and likeness of the body and blood of Jesus Christ, Your Son and our Redeemer.

But we must insist especially on the fact that the ancients' way of thinking prepares us much better than the modern way for understanding the liturgy as a whole and for understanding what may be called the style of the liturgy. If the liturgy is a complexus of signs, in which and thanks to which the mystery of Christ is fulfilled in us, it stands to reason that the more we believe in the value of the signs, the better will we penetrate the liturgy and live by it.

To enter fully into the world of the liturgy, we must be convinced that under the veil of the signs, of every sign, we really reach the thing signified, and that, conversely, the reality comes to us through this sensible veil. We must admit that the sign is the means which permits the invisible reality to be present for us and permits us to enter into contact with it.

If, on the contrary, we insist on the difference between the sign and the thing signified, to the point of considering them as belonging to two worlds foreign to each other, we shall obviously be tempted to regard the liturgy as a pointless, sterile game, in which the players are simply shaking rattles, to no effect. We shall find it hard to believe that God can, or at any rate will, fulfill the mystery of Christ in us through signs, and that through these same signs man can render an authentic worship to God.

We must recognize, of course, that the Platonic and Neoplatonic mentality had prepared the ancients to accept this economy of signs and symbols.

In the Platonic system, the world accessible to the senses is but an image and a shadow of the world of ideas. It is an expression and a participation of this supersensible world, and it is to serve as a ladder for man to return by way of the sensible to the spiritual and the eternal.

The Neoplatonists, going further, hold that Being emanates in a continuous series of forms, each less perfect than the preceding; every form impresses its own likeness on the beings which flow from it, and is in contact with the higher degree by that which is highest in itself and with the lower degree by that which is lowest in itself. By emphasizing the profound unity of the cosmos, this doctrine accustomed the minds of the ancients to reading in each individual being the bonds which attach it to the universe, and especially to recognizing the bonds of the sensible world with the spiritual world.[27]

Despite its grandeur, this representation of the world, as found in the pagan thinkers, suffered from several defects. The pagan thinkers had only a very inadequate idea of God; they conceived analogy almost entirely as a quantita-

---

[26] Mozarabic liturgy, *Liber ordinum,* ed. Férotin, col. 322.

[27] Cf. Plotinus, *Enneads,* III, 6, 11–14.

tive descent, which did not safeguard the specific distinction of beings; finally and above all, they were ignorant of the concept of creation, and thus were led to represent participation as a mere emanation of being. The result was a marked tendency to monism, heightened further by religious and mystical factors both in Neoplatonism and in the gnostic sects.

Such Christian thinkers as Clement of Alexandria, Origen, Gregory of Nyssa, the Pseudo-Dionysius, Ambrose and Augustine were imbued with this Neoplatonic mentality, and their philosophical formation helped them understand the realism of the signs, images and symbols in which the Christian economy was proposed to them. Their attitude is not dependent, however, on that which may have been transient and erroneous in this system. It rests on other grounds, much more solid.

The first of these grounds is the metaphysical truth of the existence of degrees of being, of the analogical unity of all these degrees, and of participation. This truth, the vital core of the Platonic and Neoplatonic intuition, St. Thomas was later to vindicate, having purified it of the dross with which it was covered in the pagan Greek thought.[28] The metaphysics of participation, sign and image, everything that is true in the Platonic intuition, is in fact perfectly capable of preservation in the Christian system, even in the metaphysics which Aristotle inspired in St. Thomas. This metaphysics denies every kind of monism and emanationism, affirming instead the doctrine of creation, the specific distinction in beings, analogy, production by efficient causality.

Whatever is produced by efficient causality, then, participates in the form of the agent, and first of all in the "form" of God, who is first cause. That is why all creatures are really signs, vestiges, images of God, who is present in them as efficient and exemplary cause. Moreover, in as much as they act upon one another, and especially in as much as they all belong to one and the same universe, they have a certain resemblance among themselves, they are signs of one another, and a person can pass from the knowledge of one to the knowledge of another. Such is the nucleus of truth contained in the great stoic and gnostic theme of universal harmony and "sympathy."

The second basis on which ancient Christian exemplarism rests is revelation itself. Revelation develops a certain number of themes which can be understood only in the perspectives of exemplarism: the theme of the unity of the whole history of salvation, every phase of which is at the same time the realization of the preceding phase and the rough draft and preparation for the following one; the theme of the unity of the whole cosmos, infrahuman, human, angelic and divine; the theme of the ability to know God by means of creatures, even of material creatures; the theme of the Incarnation and of Christ the perfect image of the Father. In the second part of this book we

---

[28] E.g., *Summa*, III, q. 60, aa. 2 and 3. Cf. C. Fabro, *La nozione metafisica della parteci-* *pazione secondo San Tommaso d'A.* (2nd ed.; Milan, 1950).

shall come back to these different themes and try to show how they clarify
the liturgy.

Our purpose in enumerating them here has been to convince the reader
that, when he is invited to recognize the full value of signs, images and symbols, or when the hope is expressed that he will reacquire some of the realism
of the ancients in this field, he should not immediately be alarmed and worry
about mysticism, but rather make a sincere effort to examine the question
with the maximum of objectivity.

3. Sign in the Liturgy

The use of signs in the Catholic liturgy constitutes a part of the general
phenomenon of recourse to symbolism in religions.[29] These signs always have
a religious value: they are sacred signs; they concern the relations between
God and man, and more precisely the relations between God and man in the
Christian and Catholic regime.

It must be observed also that everything in the liturgy involves recourse
to signs: the whole liturgy and each of its parts has the value of sign; of every
rite we may say, "One thing is seen and another understood." [30] Further, we
must know how to interpret these signs, and not fall back into the arbitrary
and naive explanations of an Amalarius or a Durandus.

How to interpret the liturgical signs

The first observation to be made is that the liturgical signs are never purely
and simply natural signs. They are always, at least to some extent, free signs,
whose meaning has been determined by the free will of Christ or of the
Church. In fact, the liturgical signs signify supernatural realities which surpass
absolutely the order of nature; no sensible thing can be the natural sign of
such realities.

The immersion in water and the emersion from water may well signify
naturally a disappearance and a reappearance, but they are not the *natural*
sign of participation in the death and Resurrection of Christ. A kiss is not
the natural sign of fraternal love in Christ. A bow is not the natural sign of
worship rendered to God in Christ.

If the liturgical signs, then, are not natural but free signs, their meaning
depends on the will of the one who has instituted them. To interpret them
correctly, we must know what was the intention of Christ or of the Church.
There is no other way.

One man or a group of men as private persons have not the power to create
liturgical signs or to establish their meaning. And this holds not only when

[29] For this religious phenomenon see, e.g.,
Nicola Turchi, "Simbolo e simbolismo nelle
religioni non cristiane," *Enciclopedia cattolica*,
11, 609 f., with bibliography; C. A. Bernoulli,

"Symbole," *Die Religion in Geschichte und
Gegenwart*, 5 (1935), 935–939.
[30] St. Augustine (*Sermo* 272 [PL 38, 1247])
says this of the consecrated bread and wine.

there is question of the Mass and the sacraments in their substance, but also when there is question of the secondary rites of the sacraments, when there is question of the sacramentals and of all the rest. In the former case, the only competent one is Christ, for the sacraments were instituted by Him. In the latter case the only competent one is the Church, for the liturgy as worship is an action of the Church, and therefore the signs in which worship is expressed depend on the Church and not on individuals.

But the fact remains that Christ and the Church have taken account of natural connections in the choice of the liturgical signs, and that often they have simply taken up pre-existing symbols, to give them a larger and more elevated signification.

If Christ chose water to signify the purification from sin and the birth to a new life, this was obviously because of its natural symbolism and because of the use which had been made of it in Judaism, for example by St. John the Baptist. Similarly, if Christ chose bread and wine to signify His body and blood given as food, this was because of their natural signification and at the same time because of the use which had been made of them by the Jews in feastday meals, especially in the Paschal supper. As for the laying-on of hands and the anointings, they were known and practiced in Judaism.

If we pass on to the liturgical signs adopted by the ancient Church, we find that almost all of them were already used, whether in religious or in profane context, by Semitic and Greco-Roman society. In the same way, the liturgical signs instituted by the Church in the Middle Ages are inspired by the customs of the court of Byzantium or of the Germanic courts.[31]

These observations lead us to posit as a principle that the meaning of the liturgical signs depends essentially on the free will of Christ or of the Church.

The intention of Christ relative to the liturgical signs He instituted is known to us by revelation, interpreted according to the general laws of exegesis and of theology.

As to the intention of the Church, it is most often made known to us by the texts which accompany the rites and reveal their meaning.

Thus, the symbolism (*mysterium*) of mixing water with the wine in the chalice at the offertory is established by the accompanying prayer: "Grant that through the mystery (*mysterium*) of this water and this wine we may become sharers of His divinity who was pleased to become a partaker of our humanity." The significance of the incensation of the altar is explained by the prayer which accompanies it: "May my prayer, O Lord, arise as incense in Your sight."

The meaning of the Palm Sunday procession used to be clearly explained by the fifth prayer of the blessing: ". . . that the devoted hearts of Your

---

[31] Cf. the bibliography in Josef Löw's "Simbolo e simbolismo liturgico," *Enciclopedia cattolica*, 11, 621, as also the individual words in the *Dict. d'archéologie chrétienne et de lit.* and in the *Reallexikon für Antike und Christentum*, where the different liturgical signs and rites are explained.

faithful may understand to their benefit the mystery alluded to in the act of the multitude (*quid mystice designet in facto*) who today, inspired by a heavenly illumination, went out to meet the Savior and strewed His path with branches of palm and olive. The palm branches signify His triumph over the prince of death, while the sprigs of olive proclaim in a way the coming of Him in whom there is spiritual unction. . . . And we, in fervent faith retaining both the ceremony and its signification (*factum et significatum retinentes*) . . ."

But in many cases it is hard for us today to see the exact meaning of the rites. This happens sometimes because they are not accompanied by an explanatory text; for example, the drawing with ashes of a great cross on the floor of the nave in the rite of consecration of a church. In other cases it happens because they are so reduced or effaced that a person can scarcely see them as symbols; for example, the gesture of the priest in raising his hand slightly when he gives absolution is much less expressive than the ancient laying-on of hands.

This leads us to enunciate a second principle of the interpretation of liturgical signs: in order to know the exact meaning which the Church has chosen to give them, it is indispensable to study the origin and the development of the rites.

This study is long and difficult, to be sure; but only by devoting ourselves to it, less for itself, however, than for its results, will we attain to a real understanding of the liturgy. It is the only means of avoiding the fanciful interpretations indulged in by too many medieval liturgists, beginning with Amalarius of Metz.[32] Their fault lay in proposing personal opinions instead of reporting the mind of the Church. By the reaction they aroused, their exaggerations were the principal cause of the disrepute into which even the authentic liturgical symbolism fell, beginning with the Renaissance. We cannot truthfully say that this medieval allegorism has left no traces in certain books of devotion.

Classification of liturgical signs

To go over the individual signs used in the liturgy, explaining their meaning and efficacy, would be the task of a complete and detailed study. Here we must confine ourselves to the general outlook and attempt a classification of the signs. It seems that we may divide them into four principal groups.

Speech as sign

Speech is the most important of the signs employed by the liturgy, both in the elements originating with Christ and in those which come from the Church.

[32] Died in 850. On the principal medieval allegorists and their works see Righetti, I, 45–48 and 65–68.

In the essential parts of the Mass and the sacraments, speech is the "form" which determines the meaning of the "matter": it is the words of baptism which give to the fact of being immersed in water and of coming out of the water the meaning of a participation in Christ's death and Resurrection. In every sacrament it is by speech that the material element becomes the sign of the supernatural reality in which the sacrament consists; and both together constitute, inseparably, the one sacramental sign.[33] As early a writer as St. Augustine set down, à propos of baptism, a formula which has become famous: "Take away the words and what is the water but just water? Add the words to the element and you have a sacrament (accedit verbum ad elementum et fit sacramentum), which itself is like a visible word." [34]

We need only think of the place held by the sacramental economy in the present phase of the history of salvation to grasp the importance of the role played by speech as sign in the fulfilment of this history. St. Thomas was not going too far when he compared the dignity of the word in the sacraments to the dignity of the Word in the Incarnation, and considered the sacrament as a sort of word made flesh: "It is common to all the sacraments to consist in words and corporeal things, just as in Christ, the Author of the sacraments, the Word is made flesh. And just as the flesh of Christ is sanctified and has the power of sanctifying by the Word which is united to it, so also the sacramental elements are sanctified and have the power of sanctifying by the words which are pronounced over them." [35]

Just as the incarnate Word is the substantial and personal manifestation in the world of God's intentions with regard to men, so in the sacraments, through which Christ's action is prolonged, the word is the sensible manifestation of God's intentions. In both cases God communicates through signs, He has recourse to the economy of the sacramentum. The sign which is speech is therefore extremely important in the liturgy as sanctification of the Church. And since they are the instrument of Christ's action, the words of the sacraments, in that which is essential in them, have necessarily been instituted by Him.

Speech also takes first place among the signs in the liturgy instituted by the Church. Better than any other sign it incarnates and expresses the Church's reply to the divine work of sanctification. It incarnates and expresses the spiritual and interior worship of the Church, whether in prayer under all its forms or, more remotely, in preaching, which is a sign and an instrument used by the Church to prepare the faithful for receiving grace and participating in worship. Speech as sign also has a leading part to play in the sacramentals. These are constructed in the likeness of the sacraments, and it is

[33] Cf. St. Thomas, Summa, III, q. 60, a. 6 ad 2: "In the sacraments a single thing is somehow made out of words and things, as out of form and matter, that is, in as much as the signification of the things is completed by the words."

[34] In Ioannem tract. 80, 3 (PL 35, 1840).

[35] De articulis fidei et ecclesiae sacramentis, n. 614; Opuscula theologica, ed. Verardo (Turin: Marietti, 1954), I, 148.

thanks to the words that the material elements in the sacramentals become the sign of the invisible realities which God at the Church's behest grants to those who use these sacramentals with the right dispositions.

Thus we see that among the sacred signs of the liturgy (*signa rei sacrae, sacramenta*) speech occupies first place, though in intimate union with the signs which are gestures and elements. God has willed that speech be the means of exchange between Himself and men in the Christian economy. This is the proof of the social and communitarian character of that economy, and at the same time of its agreement with the deepest tendencies of man, for whom speech is the most natural way of expressing his thoughts and feelings.[36]

Let us add that when the liturgy makes use of metaphor and extensive imagery in its language, as it very frequently does, speech becomes a sort of sign in the second degree: a sign as vehicle of other signs.

Gesture as sign

If gesture plays a relatively small part in the liturgy of praise, it does play a larger part in the sacrificial and sacramental liturgy. Gesture involves the body. Sometimes the body expresses the disposition of the soul, as in bowing, extending the hands, striking the breast. Sometimes it permits action on an external thing, as in blessings, anointings, insufflations. And sometimes the body itself is to be sanctified, or else it is to be touched as a means of reaching the soul, as in the baptismal immersion or the laying-on of hands. Almost always, in the last two cases, the gesture is accompanied by words. The words specify the meaning of the gesture, but the gesture gives weight to the words. A rite in which gestures are absent or reduced to a minimum seems tenuous and unsubstantial to us. Compare, for example, matrimony and holy orders, from this point of view, or penance and extreme unction.

Things as signs

Things, like gestures, play a greater part in the sacrificial and sacramental liturgy than in the liturgy of praise. Things were created by God for the service of man, and it is normal that man use them for his worship. He thereby makes them attain their last end, for they have been ordained to man only in as much as he is ordained to God. That is why, in using these subjects, the liturgy often recalls that they are the creatures of God: *hanc creaturam aquae* . . . .

The things used as signs by the liturgy fall into two groups: the natural elements, such as bread and wine, water, oil, chrism, salt, ashes, incense, light, palms; and objects which result from man's work, such as the altar, the cross, the sacred vestments; to this second group belong the signs which depend on sacred art.

[36] On this point see a beautiful text of St. Augustine, *De doctr. christ.*, II, 4 (PL 34, 37-38).

Person as sign

The simple fact of the faithful being gathered in a church for a liturgical celebration has the value of sign. It is the visible expression of the invisible relations between God and mankind called together and assembled by Christ. It is not just any meeting, but the *ecclesia* of God in Christ,[37] fulfilment of the "Qahal Yahweh" of the Old Testament and at the same time a sign and sketch of the gathering of the elect for the heavenly liturgy.

With still more reason, the ministers of the liturgy have the value of sign. Under various titles, they are the delegates and the representatives of Christ. This is what St. Ignatius of Antioch recalled in his letter to the Magnesians: ". . . Be zealous to do all things in the peace of God, the bishop presiding in the place of God and the priests in the place of the Apostolic college, and my beloved deacons being entrusted with the ministry of Jesus Christ . . . who came forth from one Father, existed in the unity of one Father and returned to Him." [38]

Such are the signs employed by the liturgy.[39] It must be remarked that in most cases these signs are not employed in isolation, independently of one another. The liturgy is not a collection of signs in juxtaposition, but a complexus of celebrations, functions or rites. In each of these functions the liturgy has recourse to many signs, to signs of several categories and often of all categories. For a valid exegesis, therefore, it will not be enough to look for what such and such a sign signifies in itself. We must look for what it signifies in the general context of the function in which it is used. And above all we must find out what this function signifies when taken as a whole.

The role of art in the liturgy

The question of the use of signs in the liturgy is the proper heading under which to study the principles that explain and determine the Church's recourse to art in her worship.[40]

Art is a sensible quality, which of itself has the value of sign, and which can embellish the other liturgical signs, speech as well as gestures or things. By giving an artistic character to the signs it uses, the liturgy reinforces them, since it confers on them that power of expression or of impression which art alone possesses.

[37] Cf. 1 Thes. 1:1; 2 Thes. 1:1; Matt. 18:20.

[38] *Magnes.*, 6:1–7:2 (PG 5, 668).

[39] Perhaps we should add that the liturgy sometimes employs numbers with the value of sign. This appears especially in the biblical texts which it uses, such as the text about the 144,000 *signati* of the Apocalypse on the feast of All Saints. But it occurs also in rites: the twelve crosses in the consecration of a church, or the fact of repeating certain words or gestures a certain number of times.

[40] General views on this question will be found in the encyclicals *Mediator Dei*, nn. 195 f. (Lat. 193 f.) and *Musicae sacrae disciplina*, especially nn. II and III. See further Pie-Raymond Régamey, *Art sacré au XX siècle?* (2nd ed.; Paris: Ed. du Cerf, 1957); Msgr. Johannes Wagner, "Liturgical Art and the Care of Souls," *The Assisi Papers* (Collegeville, Minn.: Liturgical Press, 1957), pp. 57–73.

All the arts are drawn upon for their contribution to the liturgy, but the first place goes to those that reinforce the sign which is speech: rhetoric, poetry and especially song. Song, the ideal means of forming or expressing a communitarian spirit, is the art form best suited to the liturgy. As for instrumental music, it may be considered here as a development of song, which has, however, more or less freed itself from song.

Signs have the right of admission into the liturgy only in so far as they are signs, that is to say, in as much as they represent the invisible realities which the Church wants to express through them. In the same way, it is not because of any value of its own that art is entitled to admission into the liturgy, but in so far as it can serve the liturgy's particular end, in so far as it can help the Church express her worship or sanctify the faithful.

In order to determine precisely the conditions under which this collaboration of art and liturgy can take place, it would be necessary to analyze the nature of art in general (and also of each one of the arts, in particular of song, architecture and painting), then find out in what religious or sacred art consists essentially, and finally show the possible relations between the proper end of art and the proper end of the liturgy, thus being enabled to give a definition of liturgical art. But such an inquiry would lead us far afield, so controversial are the notions of art and sacred art.[41] We shall limit ourselves to a few remarks.

Art and esthetic pleasure

Art must be defined in relation to the beautiful.[42] And the beautiful can be defined only in relation to that enjoyment which it causes in us, called esthetic pleasure. Hence art can be defined as the aptitude for perceiving and expressing sensibly in things the quality which makes them a source of esthetic pleasure.

It remains to define esthetic pleasure, which is something easier to experience than to translate into concepts. In terms of Aristotelian-Thomistic psychology, it is the enjoyment of the faculties of knowledge — especially of sight, hearing and imagination — conformably to their natural inclination and to the acquired dispositions of the subject.

This enjoyment has the particular characteristic of being disinterested. That is to say, its cause — and its goal — is not the physical possession of its object, but only its contemplative possession. And it is a source of peace because it gratifies fully the faculties of knowledge.

[41] See, e.g., Adriano Prandi, "Arte," *Enciclopedia cattolica*, 2 (1949), 33–44, with bibliography of previous writings, *ibid.*, 43 f. To be noted among other authors are: Jacques Maritain, *Art and Scholasticism* (New York: Scribner, 1946); A. Carlini, *La religiosità dell'arte e della filosofia* (Florence, 1934); P.-M. Léonard, "Art et spiritualité," *Dictionnaire de spiritualité*, I (1932), 899–934; G. van der Leeuw, *Vom Heiligen in der Kunst* (Gütersloh, 1957).

[42] It is not enough to say that art consists in creating; technology and science are also creative activities. Similarly, the notions of expression, of incarnation of the spirit in matter, do not sufficiently distinguish art from technology.

Beauty is not in things considered in themselves, but in things considered in relation to the faculties of knowledge. Thus art involves an objective aspect and a subjective aspect. For if the faculties are the same, essentially, in all men, the innate or acquired dispositions which help determine them vary considerably from one epoch to another, from one society to another, from one individual to another; and in one individual they are easily modified by various influences. That is why taste, which is the aptitude to experience an esthetic pleasure in the presence of certain things, may vary and hence may be formed by an appropriate education.

The esthetic perception, involving a certain accord between the object and the dispositions of the subject, is an instinctive or intuitive type of perception. It is not analytic but synthetic. It cannot be communicated directly, therefore, like a science, but only indirectly. One must seek to induce in the listener or the spectator the dispositions which were those of the artist, in such a way that the same object will awaken in him the same esthetic perception.

The intrinsic end of art (the end of the work, as the scholastics say) is therefore simply to actuate the cognitive faculties in such a way as to bring about esthetic enjoyment in the subject, and nothing else. And this enjoyment is morally indifferent, as is scientific knowledge or technical knowledge. It becomes good or bad action according to whether the further end for which it is sought (the end of the agent) is good or bad.

Thus an object or an action morally bad can be truly artistic, if it is presented in such a way as to stimulate esthetic pleasure. By the same token, it is not enough that an object or an action be morally good, or that the artist have a morally right intention, in order that the result be esthetic!

Still, because he who makes a work of art and he who admires it are men and not only artists, it is their duty to consider their act not in itself but in terms of man's last end. Art is indeed a good for man, but a particular good and not the total good. To act in an ordered way, therefore, man must subordinate his esthetic pleasure to his total good, that is, to the moral good. As far as the end of the agent is concerned, art can and must be qualified in moral terms.

Art and religion

It is here that the possibility of a religious art comes in, a sacred art; that is to say, an art which, while remaining faithful to its own requirements, subordinates itself to a specifically religious end.[43]

[43] There are degrees to this subordination. There is a submission wholly material, which consists only in taking a religious subject. But one may deal with a religious subject — compose a melody for singing, paint a Madonna, build a church — in a manner that has nothing religious about it. Many painted or sculptured Madonnas are real works of art, but works whose artistic quality bears much more on the human theme of motherhood than on the religious theme of the divine motherhood. There is not really any sacred art unless the artistic form bears on the properly religious aspect of the subject, as is the case, for example, in the paintings of Fra Angelico. When we speak of the subordination of art to a religious end, we mean this formal subordination.

The end of religion is to produce in man that substantially interior attitude which is made up of admiration, submission, faith, hope and love towards God. Art subordinates itself to this end when the esthetic enjoyment which is its own end is not only juxtaposed but really ordained to the religious end.

No one would think of denying the possibility of the harmonious collaboration between art and religion. It is sufficiently proved by achievements such as Gregorian chant, the painting of Fra Angelico, the sculptures of the portals of the cathedral of Chartres, the ancient Christian basilical architecture. But how is this collaboration to be explained?

Most of the schools of spirituality have exercises of psychological preparation for meditation and prayer. Some of these devices are of a simply physical or psychic nature, and have the aim of creating a state of recollection by acting on the senses and through them on the whole person.

St. Ignatius, for example, advises one to close the window and to stand in the dark or with a dim light for meditating; to say certain prayers by pronouncing the words slowly to the rhythm of inhalation and exhalation; to take certain bodily attitudes, for example placing the hand to the breast, keeping the eyes fixed in one position or on some object.[44]

This physical and psychic recollection is not yet prayer, but it is an effective preparation for prayer, it creates a climate in which prayer flows out more readily.

The esthetic experience can, in a certain measure and under certain conditions, play an analogous role.[45] The reason for this is that esthetic pleasure, resulting from an accord between subject and object, involves an activity of the senses and of the intellect which is intuitive, synthetic, without effort and without investigation, quite different from their ordinary activity. The subject has the impression of going beyond the usual process of knowledge and of entering into immediate and profound contact with the real. He seems to be seeing things no longer from the outside but from the inside.

If this esthetic experience is accompanied by the required moral dispositions, it easily becomes a fertile ground for prayer. For prayer also, especially if it is contemplative, implies a certain surpassing of the usual activity of the senses and of the analytical and discursive activity of the intellect. Prayer also wants to be a direct contact with the object; it also wants to be an experience.

But, just as the spiritual authors recommend that the psychological means of preparation for prayer be used only with discretion, so also prudence must be advised in the recourse to the esthetic experience. This prudence is needed because of the danger of stopping at the esthetic pleasure instead of using it to rise up to God. The danger will be greater or lesser according to the subject's dispositions and his ability to control his senses. It will vary also according to

---

[44] Cf. *Exercises*, fourth week, second and third methods of prayer.

[45] Cf. P.-M. Léonard, "Art et spiritualité,"

Dict. de spir., I, 925 ff.; Henri Bremond, *Prayer and Poetry* (London: Burns Oates & Washbourne, 1927).

the means employed by the artist: if they are not adequately spiritualized, they run the risk of riveting the attention on the sensible, that is, on the sign.[46]

Art and liturgy

Religious art is not yet liturgical art. Liturgical art requires not only that the work be beautiful and the enjoyment which it arouses be directed to the religious attitude in general, but also that it serve to promote that particular type of religious attitude which is the liturgical attitude.

As will be seen in the following chapters, it is characteristic of the liturgy to be an action, a communitarian action of an assembly in which the members all have a role to play, an action centered on the Mass and the sacraments, finally an action whose whole meaning is to have the mystery of Christ relived by those who take part in it.

It is this particular form of religion which liturgical art must express and help establish. To produce an authentic work of liturgical art, therefore, the artist must not only be truly religious, but he must really have penetrated into the world of the liturgy.

Numerous practical consequences flow from these principles for all the arts which find a place in the liturgy, especially for the arts of singing and of instrumental music, for architecture and for painting.[47]

On condition that these rules be observed, the liturgy opens the door wide to art. It has done so from the very beginning: at first to the arts of speech and of song; then, beginning with the third-fourth century, to architecture, to mosaics, to painting, to the arts of movement and to the lesser arts; finally, in more recent times, to sculpture and to polyphonic and instrumental music.

And because art and taste, involving a noteworthy subjective aspect, vary with times, places and people, the liturgy has admitted works of the most varied taste and style. And today it remains open to new quests.[48] This is so

---

[46] This danger has often provoked the reactions of the spiritual-minded against the invasion of the sanctuary by art under its different forms. St. Augustine, speaking from experience, has admirably shown the usefulness but at the same time the danger of art, especially of the chant, in raising one to God (*Confessions*, X, 33). For the attitude of the Fathers toward the chant of the Church, cf. Th. Gerold, *Les Pères de l'Eglise et la musique* (Paris, 1931); A. Dohmes, "Der pneumatische Charakter des Kultgesanges nach frühchristlichen Zeugnissen," *Vom christlichen Mysterium* (Düsseldorf: Patmos-Verlag, 1951), pp. 35-53.

[47] And it is these principles which inspire the rules established by ecclesiastical authority; cf. the encyclicals *Mediator Dei*, nn. 195 f. (Lat. 193 f.) and *Musicae sacrae*; the *Instruction on Sacred Music and the Sacred Liturgy*

according to these two encyclical letters, English translation in *Worship*, 32 (1958), 590 ff.; the instruction *De arte sacra* (*Acta Apostolicae Sedis*, 1952, pp. 542-546). For the liturgical requirements of sacred architecture see Theodor Klauser, "Directives for the Building of a Church," and His Eminence Giacomo Cardinal Lercaro, "The Christian Church," *Documents for Sacred Architecture* (Collegeville, Minn.: Liturgical Press, 1957); Pie-Raymond Régamey, "Architecture de l'autel et exigences liturgiques," *La maison Dieu*, 29 (1952), 71-87.

[48] Cf. *Mediator Dei*, n. 195 (Lat. 193): "What we have said about music, applies to the other fine arts, especially to architecture, sculpture and painting. Recent works of art which lend themselves to the materials of modern composition, should not be universally

much the more proper because there is evolution not only in the artistic sensibility but also in the religious sensibility, that is, the way in which man reacts, on the sensible level, in the presence of the religious phenomenon.

Let us note that here again there are dangers to be feared. Like sacred art in general, liturgical art runs the risk of forgetting its properly religious end and seeking "art for art's sake." Moreover, it is in danger of forgetting the requirements proper to the liturgy, especially its communitarian requirements.

Song, music and architecture have too often failed on this score.

Is it not a mistake to have given the liturgical chants a development and a perfection which have undoubtedly made them superlative works from the artistic point of view, but which have necessitated their being withdrawn from the people and entrusted to a schola?

Is it not a mistake to have built churches which are perhaps admirable and which give witness to a profound religious sense, but in which the people are so far removed from the altar that they can no longer see what is being done there?

Is it not a mistake to have raised up altars which do certainly constitute magnificent settings for the exposition of the Blessed Sacrament, but in which it is hard to recognize the Eucharistic table which the communicants should be surrounding?

It would be only too easy to multiply similar examples. All these deviations come from forgetfulness of the proper requirements of liturgical art. The liturgy makes use of art as a sign; and every sign is at the service of that which it is supposed to express and, in a certain measure, to make real. It is therefore a duty for the artist who wants to work in the liturgical field to become permeated with the realities which his art presumes to express, and to submit himself to their requirements.

Why this regime of signs?

Before inquiring what the liturgical signs signify, we must ask ourselves why the encounter between God and man takes place in a regime of signs, by means of signs. The modern man often fears that this introduction of signs between himself and God will impede the spontaneity and the sincerity of his religious life. God has asked us to adore Him in spirit and in truth, and to pray to Him in secret. Then why all these intermediaries and all this stage setting?

There is no doubt that God could have adopted a system in which religion

despised and rejected through prejudice. Modern art should be given free scope in the due and reverent service of the Church and the sacred rites, provided that they preserve a correct balance between styles tending neither to extreme realism nor to excessive 'symbolism,' and that the needs of the Christian community are taken into consideration rather than the particular taste or talent of the individual artist. Thus modern art will be able to join its voice to that wonderful choir of praise to which have contributed, in honor of the Catholic faith, the greatest artists throughout the centuries."

would have been a purely interior and individual affair, without the mediation of things or of persons. Actually, God has chosen and imposed on those who want to come to Him another way, which is the way of the Incarnation: it is through men and sensible things that God communicates Himself to us and that we go to Him.

God communicates Himself to us and we go to Him by the Word made flesh, by the Church, spiritual and visible at the same time, which prolongs Him, by the liturgy whose visible signs signify, contain and give the invisible realities. We may apply to the present phase of the history of salvation what Origen said of the story of Abraham: "Everything that is done, is done *in sacramentis.*" [49]

Such is the regime God has established; and His decisions, in the last analysis, have no other reason than His free will; man can do nothing but ascertain them and conform to them.

In submitting the whole of His relations with man to the law of incarnation, God, moreover, is merely adapting Himself to the nature of His partner. For man is made of spirit and matter, and his spirit acquires knowledge only by means of the sensible, and expresses itself only by means of the sensible. To this incarnated spirit the way of incarnation and the regime of signs are perfectly suited.

The Fathers have often observed this in connection with the *sacramenta* in general and the sacraments in particular. Thus St. John Chrysostom remarks, "Since the Word says, 'This is My body,' let us assent and believe and consider Him in this sacrament with spiritual eyes. Actually what Christ has given us is not anything sensible. Rather, the realities given are wholly spiritual, though clothed in sensible things. The same holds for baptism: the gift is given through a sensible thing, water; the spiritual reality accomplished is birth and renewal. If you had been incorporeal, He would have given you bare, incorporeal gifts; but since the soul is united to the body, He offers you spiritual realities in sensible things." [50]

This idea of the harmony of the sign with the nature of man can readily be particularized and probed if a person examines in what manner and with what effect the mind is instructed and expresses itself by means of the different liturgical signs and the different rites.

In ancient times, St. Augustine had already been struck by this power of sign and symbol over the human spirit: "All these things brought home to us in figures have the aim of feeding and somehow fanning the flame of love which, like a sort of specific gravity, carries us above or within ourselves until we come to rest. Thus proposed, these realities move and enkindle love more than if they were set forth in a starkly intellectual way and not as *sacramenta.*

---

[49] *In Gen. Hom.* 9, 1 (PG 12, 211).
[50] *In Matthaeum hom.* 82, 4 (PG 58, 743); this passage is read at the second nocturn on the second Sunday after Pentecost. Cf. St. Thomas Aquinas, *Summa*, III, q. 60, a. 4; q. 61, a. 1; *Contra Gentiles*, III, 119.

It is hard to say why this should be so. But it is certain that anything expressed by way of allegory is more moving, more pleasing and better heeded than if it were said outright in the most appropriate words. I think the soul is slower to catch fire as long as it is involved in mere earthly things; while if it is directed to bodily symbols (*similitudines*) and from the symbols to the spiritual realities expressed by them in figure, this very process enlivens it, enkindles it like a waving torch and draws it with more ardent love to its resting-place." [51]

What Augustine had surmised with his usual perspicacity, the moderns have striven to describe in detail by means of psychological analysis, and this in the religious sphere as well as the profane. Among the Catholics, Romano Guardini has shown particular interest in this aspect of the liturgy.[52] Among the Protestants a noteworthy work is that of Robert Will, *Le culte*, in three volumes,[53] the second of which is devoted entirely to the phenomenology of worship. Through very attentive observation, Will seeks to understand the source of the psychological effectiveness of the signs and rites of worship.

Apart, of course, from certain defects congenital to the mentality of a Protestant when he speaks of Catholic worship, many of Will's observations on the psychological necessity and efficacy of the liturgy in its structure as a complexus of signs are quite justified; and some of his effective passages on this subject can, with a few changes, be fully approved by a Catholic.

Thus, for example, on the psychological necessity of a worship embodied in signs: "All worship demands expressive forms: images, sounds, words, gestures, rites, persons. These forms, interposed between God and the faithful, serve as commutators for the currents of life which connect the subjective pole to the objective pole or vice versa. They give concrete expression to the soul's aspirations and raise them up. In the other direction, they make concrete the graces descending from on high and channel them into souls. Thus phenomena in the sphere of worship, placing themselves at the service both of the religious subject and of the divine object, respond to a twofold necessity, the one being of the psychological order, the other of the metaphysical order. In other words, the nature of man demands phenomena and the essence of revelation also requires them."[54]

Again: "The rites of worship appear, therefore, as means designed to preserve the objective values of religion, because they are considered as translating into phenomena the supersensible data of divine revelation. Without this translation into figures, religion, purely subjective, would run the risk

---

[51] *Ep.* 55, n. 21 (PL 33, 214).
[52] Especially in *The Spirit of the Liturgy* (Eng. ed.; New York: Benziger, 1931); *Sacred Signs* (Eng. ed.; St. Louis: Pio Decimo Press, 1956); *Liturgische Bildung* (Mainz, 1923); *Die Sinne und die religiöse Erkenntnis* (Würzburg, 1950).

[53] Paris: Alcan. The second volume was published in 1929.
[54] Robert Will, *Le culte*, II, 13. This "requires" means: requires them in order to be communicated to man in accordance with his nature.

of deteriorating into mystical states, cold ideologies or moralizations. . . . The religion which has no interest in worship wastes away in the rarefied atmosphere of an excessive spiritualism.[55] . . . In short, there is no more justification for denying to transcendental inspiration a representation by figures perceptible to the senses than there is for denying such representation to the soul's aspirations. The translation of the transcendental realities into the sensible world is a postulate of the divine essence in communication with the world,[56] as the concrete figuration of the data of religious consciousness is a postulate of human nature." [57]

Or again this observation on private religious life and worship: "The worship-experience will be an empirical prolongation and a concrete enlargement of the religious experience. The encounter with God in worship will be the end result and the combination of all the experiences provided us by our previous contact with God, by our faith and by our prayer." [58] "In short, worship, prolongation of the mediating action of Christ, is the religious symbol *par excellence*. Forming the bridge which leads from transcendence to immanence, it has the mission of helping the whole world to be penetrated with the divine presence." [59]

Any Catholic will surely welcome these observations by a Protestant; for they prove how natural, effective and morally necessary it is, from the psychological viewpoint alone, that the encounter between God and man take place in a regime of signs. They show the irreplaceable role played by visible worship in assuring a just balance in the life of religion and in preventing religion from being transformed into a mere psychological experience, into a philosophy cut off from life or into an ethics without foundation.

If Protestantism has not been able to avoid these dangers, this is due in large part to its almost complete rejection of the incarnated forms of the Catholic liturgy.[60] "It is a fact," writes Will, "that the Protestant churches, and especially reformed Puritanism, have tipped the balance of the two hemispheres — the external and the internal — in favor of the internal. The spiritual impoverishment resulting from this imbalance does not respond to the demands of our dualist nature or to the needs of popular piety or to the trends of our generation so eager for reality, objectivity and intense life." [61]

Such observations, already recognized as accurate from the psychological viewpoint, acquire still more force if we add that this imbalance is contrary to the will of God manifested in Christ, and that it ignores not only the laws of psychology but also and above all the laws to which God has chosen to

---

[55] Or, as the author said above, of a cold ideologism or an exaggerated moralism.

[56] More precisely: it is the act of a positive free will of God in His communicating Himself to the world, which, though it is a free act, corresponds wonderfully to the very nature of man.

[57] Robert Will, *Le culte*, II, 26 f.

[58] *Ibid.*, 38.

[59] *Ibid.*, 25.

[60] Only Anglicanism, with its eclectic character, forms an exception to a certain extent.

[61] Robert Will, *Le culte*, II, 9.

submit His relations with men: law of objectivity, law of incarnation, law of salvation in community.

Thus it is understandable that the discovery of the liturgy, even by men sensible especially to its psychological utility, as is the case today with many Protestants, carries with it in germ the recognition of values which, logically developed, might lead to the discovery of Catholicism.[62]

If the regime of signs is in harmony with man's condition, material and spiritual at the same time, it is equally in harmony with his social character. Man is a social being, and the Christian is a member of that body which is the Church. The homage he must render God cannot be the homage of an isolated individual. The people of God must render God a collective worship, a liturgical worship, in the etymological sense of the term.

Now the sign is the means *par excellence* for communication among men, the instrument which assures the unity of the group as well as its distinction from other groups. At the same time it is the necessary point of departure for common action. No one could conceive of a community offering God an exclusively spiritual worship. In order to be common to all, worship must have recourse to the indispensable means of human communication, that is, to signs. It is only around signs that the gathering of the community will take place, and by means of signs that its worship will be expressed.[63] Thus the fact that God has willed that men go to Him by using signs is explained by the prior fact that He has desired them to go to Him in a group, in community.

This communitarian and social character of the liturgy is rich in consequences, to which we shall have occasion to return. Let us point out at least, right now, that if the sign is made for the community, it must be within reach of their understanding, under pain of losing its psychological effectiveness. This simple observation, as we shall see later, is very helpful in solving the problems of the liturgical pastoral art.

4. The Things Signified by Signs in the Liturgy

Having explained the concept of sign in general and having observed the universal dominion of signs in the liturgy, we must determine more particularly what are the invisible sacred realities signified by the liturgical signs — realities which concern the relations between God and man.

The four dimensions of the liturgical sign in general

If the liturgy is a complexus of efficacious signs of the Church's sanctifica-

---

[62] For some twenty-five years there has been a notable movement among Protestants for the restoration of the liturgy. See, e.g., a brief review with a bibliography as far as Lutheranism is concerned, in R. Staehlin's "Der Widergewinnung der Liturgie in der evangel-

ischen Kirche," *Leiturgia* (*Handbuch der evangelischen Gottesdienstes*), I (Kassel, 1954), 74 ff.

[63] Cf. Jean C.-M. Travers, *Valeur sociale de la liturgie d'après S. Thomas d'Aquin* (Paris: Ed. du Cerf, 1946), in particular pp. 313–317.

tion and worship, it is clear that the realities signified by the liturgical signs will be that sanctification and that worship. Chapter 4 will show that these two realities are inseparable, in themselves as well as in the liturgy. They are both present, therefore, in every sign and in every rite, though most often they do not hold equal rank: in certain cases it is sanctification that is brought to the foreground, while in other cases it is worship.

Let us try to specify further in what these realities consist. We can get some idea by inquiring what are the various causes of sanctification and of worship.

The *intrinsic formal cause* of sanctification is sanctifying grace with all the infused virtues that accompany it.

The intrinsic formal cause of worship is the interior attitude of reverence towards God based on the recognition of His pre-eminence. This attitude is made up of admiration, esteem, honor, entreaty, as well as humility and avowal of submission, which includes repentance and the will to make satisfaction in case of sin. The whole is an expression of the virtue of religion, which makes us render to God whatever is due Him as first Principle, Creator and Governor of all things.

That which plays the role of *material cause* of sanctification and of worship is, first of all, the soul as subject of sanctification, and not simply the human soul, but the Christian soul, the soul that belongs to the Church; for it is the Church that is sanctified in the liturgy, and souls are sanctified only in and through the Church.

The role of material cause is played also by the moral dispositions necessary to the soul to make it a fit subject to receive sanctification and to render Christian worship to God. And on this point we must dwell.

In the adult, sanctification and worship are acts fully human, and hence free. They are never mechanical actions, comparable to physiological functions. When we say of the sacraments that they give grace *ex opere operato,* we mean always that they give it in this way to one who interposes no obstacle; and that obstacle would be the absence of the requisite moral, therefore human and free, dispositions. Without these dispositions, grace does not take effect.

To all the Protestant and rationalist criticisms, Catholic theology keeps replying that the sacraments operate according to a process which infinitely surpasses the possibilities of man left to himself, but which has nothing to do with magic. Magic is a process by which man supposes that he can force a divine power to put itself at his disposal, by physical means, without being bound to any moral effort. In having recourse to the sacraments, on the contrary, man submits himself inwardly to God, who has decided to communicate His life in this way; and, if he is an adult, he receives grace only if he has the right moral dispositions, and he remains liable to lose grace by changing his dispositions.

Among these dispositions required for sanctification we must include the obligation to live for the future in a way that corresponds to the requirements of the new mode of being, received in the sanctifying act. This obligation is always more or less explicit in the adult who receives sanctification, since sanctification involves a personal moral effort, a free cooperation. In this precise sense every sacrament is for the adult recipient a real oath.[64]

This holds equally for worship. The disposition of soul in which interior worship consists is not conceivable without the obligation, at least implicit, of living in the future as we are required to by that excellence and sovereignty of God which we affirm by our worship.

Faith also must be noted among the dispositions required by sanctification and worship. Every liturgical action presupposes and expresses the faith of those who take part in it. If it is true to say that the sacraments are *sacramenta fiaei*, sacraments of faith, we should add that the whole liturgy is in an eminent degree a *protestatio fidei*, a profession of faith.

The principal *efficient cause* of sanctification is God. Christ in His humanity is the instrumental cause, since the divinity uses His humanity as a conjoint instrument for our sanctification. The meritorious cause is the redemptive actions of Christ in His earthly life, especially His Passion and death.

The principal efficient cause of the Church's worship is Christ Himself; for the Church's worship is, after all, the worship which Christ renders to God through the Church by making the Church participate in it. The Church's interior dispositions are like an instrument in His hands.

The proper *final cause* of sanctification (the final cause common to all things is always God's glory) is the future glory of the beatific vision to which grace is intrinsically ordained as the acorn is to the oak.

The proper final cause of worship here on earth is the eternal, universal worship of the heavenly Jerusalem.

Under one aspect, the *exemplary cause* of our sanctification and our worship is Christ Himself, for it is His sanctity and His worship that the liturgy makes us continue and imitate.

But, under another aspect, the exemplary cause is all the acts of sanctification and of worship which took place before the coming of Christ, and especially those of the chosen people; for all these acts were sketches of the sanctification and the worship which would be realized in the person of Christ and then in the life of the Church.

Under a third aspect, this exemplary cause is to be sought in the sanctification and the worship of the heavenly Jerusalem, of which our liturgy is but a rough draft, still imperfect, which tends toward this model as the perfect realization in which it will find its fulfilment.

[64] We know that the first meaning of *sacramentum* is precisely: engagement, oath.

Such, therefore, are the spiritual realities which sanctification and worship presuppose and which the liturgical signs signify. That is what is "understood" in these signs in which "one thing is seen and another understood."

Not all these realities are signified by the same right in the liturgy. There is an order among them, based on their relation to the essential and formal element of sanctification and of worship, which is sanctifying grace and interior devotion. It is this principal element that the liturgical signs signify immediately and primarily. The other elements are signified only in a mediate way, in so far as they have an intrinsic and necessary connection with the primary element.

Thus the liturgical signs signify the moral dispositions of the subject such as faith and the obligation to a certain kind of life in the future, because these dispositions are implied in sanctification and in worship.

Similarly, as sanctifying grace comes to us from God, and this through the mediation of Christ, who merited it for us in His Passion and communicates it to us by having us share in His fulness of life and of holiness, the liturgical signs must signify this action of God in us, as well as Christ's Passion and His holiness. They must also signify His worship, of which our own is but a participation.

Again, the liturgical signs signify the glory to come and the eternal liturgy, to which our sanctification and our worship on earth are directed.

Finally, they signify those acts of sanctification and of worship which took place before the coming of Christ, because they were sketches of ours.

Among these realities some belong to the past, others to the present, others to the future. It may be said, therefore, that every liturgical sign has a three-fold dimension, and that it points at the same time toward the past, present and future phases of the history of salvation.

But it must be added at once that as sign of the present it really has two distinct functions. Most of the realities of the present it manifests simply as present; such is the case, for example, with sanctifying grace and with the interior attitude of veneration, or with Christ's action as cause of sanctification and of worship. But there is one reality which, though signified as present, actually concerns future actions: the obligation of the subject to live in a manner conformable to the graces received or the devotion manifested. In as much as it signifies this obligation, therefore, the liturgical sign is at one and the same time a sign of the present and of the future.

We arrive at the conclusion, then, that the liturgical sign has four dimensions. It is a *sign demonstrative* of the invisible realities belonging to the present: first of all, sanctifying grace and interior worship; then God in as much as He effects the sanctification and is object of the worship, and Christ as instrumental and exemplary cause of the sanctification and as principal and exemplary cause of the worship. It is a *sign obligating* even now the life which the subject of sanctification and worship will lead. It is a *sign com-*

memorative of Christ's saving actions, especially of His Passion and death, as well as of the acts of sanctification and of worship which took place before the Incarnation. Finally, it is a *sign portending or prophetic* of eternal glory and of the worship in the heavenly Jerusalem.

It should be observed that the realities of the past and those of the future are not signified as purely past or future, but also in some way as present.

The question of the presentness in the liturgical celebration of the redemptive actions performed at one time by Christ will be examined in the following chapter.

As far as the acts of sanctification and of worship prior to the coming of Christ are concerned, it is easy to see that they are signified as present in as much as they are fulfilled and "represented" by the Christian liturgy.

As to the glory and the worship in heaven, they are signified as present in as much as they are contained in seed and in rough draft in the grace and the worship of the earthly Church.

Thus the past and the future are signified in the liturgy as in a supratemporal present, since the realities belonging to the past or to the future and signified as such, are signified, from another point of view, as contained and concentrated in the present reality. One might say that the liturgical signs concentrate in the realities which they signify the whole history of salvation, past, present and future.

This conception of the liturgy does nothing but extend and adapt what St. Thomas said of the threefold signification of the sacraments: "That is properly called a sacrament which is ordained to signify our sanctification.[65] In this sanctification three things can be considered: the cause itself of our sanctification, which is the Passion of Christ; the form of our sanctification, which consists in grace and the virtues; and the ultimate end of our sanctification, which is eternal life. And all these are signified by the sacraments. Hence a sacrament is a sign commemorative of that which preceded, namely Christ's Passion; a sign demonstrative of that which is effected in us by Christ's Passion, namely grace; and a sign prophetic, that is, foretelling future glory." [66]

Such an extension of the Thomistic theory to the whole complexus of liturgical signs is legitimate and necessary. For the basis on which St. Thomas' statement about the sacraments is grounded, holds for all the liturgical signs, as has been seen above; and the reality of the obligating sign in the order of dispositive causality is no less evident than that of the demonstrative, commemorative and prophetic sign in the order of efficient, formal and final

---

[65] St. Thomas means: ordained *immediately* to signify our sanctification as something which takes place *hic et nunc*, here and now. Thus he excludes from the notion of *sacramentum* what we now call the sacramentals, because they signify immediately a disposition to sanctity, and not sanctity itself; thus also he excludes all that which is immediately ordained to signify the worship rendered to God, such as the Divine Office, and the Mass in so far as it is a sacrifice.

[66] *Summa*, III, q. 60, a. 3.

causality. Thus we find again the ancient patristic concept of *sacramentum* or *mysterium*. More particularly we find again the whole force of its meaning, which Origen, for example, knew so well how to exploit.[67]

For a somewhat more detailed study of this fourfold dimension of each of the liturgical signs, we must consider separately those instituted by God and those instituted by the Church. Although this study belongs more properly to special liturgy, we shall touch upon it here, so important is it to see clearly this fourfold dimension of the signs and the rites if we are to penetrate effectively into the world of the liturgy.

The four dimensions of the liturgical signs instituted by God

The concern here is with the Mass and the sacraments in that which pertains to their substance and is therefore of divine institution. This study will show that, for the two fundamental sacraments of baptism and the Eucharist, their fourfold signification is already indicated in the Scripture.

Baptism

When he says that by baptism we die to sin, St. Paul affirms that the baptismal rite is a sign demonstrative of Christ's grace which He communicates: "We died to sin . . . when we were baptized into Christ Jesus . . . our old humanity was crucified with Him in order that the body of sin might be destroyed, that we might no longer be slaves to sin" (Rom. 6:2 ff.); or when he says that baptism is "a bath of regeneration and renewal by the Holy Spirit" (Tit. 3:5; cf. Eph. 5:26; John 3:5).

That baptism is a sign obligating to a new life is the whole theme of chapter 6 of the letter to the Romans: "How shall we who are dead to sin still live in it? . . . We were buried together with Him (Christ) by baptism into death, that, as Christ has risen by the glory of the Father, so we also may walk in newness of life. . . . See to it, therefore, that sin no longer reigns in your mortal body so that you obey its lusts. And do not offer your members to sin as weapons of iniquity, but present yourselves to God as men who have come to life from the dead . . . But now, set free from sin and become slaves of God, you have your reward in sanctification" (Rom. 6:2 ff.; see also Col. 3:1–4:5):

This explains how Tertullian [68] and several Latin ecclesiastical writers after him [69] were expressing a profoundly scriptural thought when they likened baptism to the *sacramentum militiae*, which in ancient times was simultaneously a military oath and a rite of religious initiation and consecration.[70]

---

[67] Cf. Hans von Balthasar, "Le mysterion d'Origène," *Rech. de sc. rel.*, 26 (1936), 513 ff.; 27 (1937), 38 ff.

[68] J. de Ghellinck's *Pour l'histoire du mot sacramentum*, I (Louvain, 1924), 66–113.

[69] See A. Blaise's *Dictionnaire latin français des auteurs chrétiens* (Strasbourg, 1954) at the word "Sacramentum," where he quotes St. Cyprian, Arnobius, Optatus of Milevis, St. Hilary, etc.

[70] Cf. Franz Dölger, *Antike und Christentum* (1930), p. 280.

Moreover, in the pagan mysteries, the rite of initiation was often considered as an oath and an enrollment into a militia.[71] And the ancient baptismal rite itself already included the explicit renunciation of Satan and all his pomps and his angels,[72] which constituted a real oath.

Thus Tertullian could say, "We have been called to the militia of God . . . when we reply in the words of the *sacramentum*." [73] In the same sense, St. Cyprian has the confessor of the faith say, "I did want to fight bravely; mindful of my *sacramentum*, I took up the arms of *devotio* and of the faith." [74] And every grave sin committed by a Christian was considered as an attempt to "obtain a discharge from the *sacramenta benedictionis*," that is, from the obligations contracted by the baptismal oath.[75]

Baptism is a sign commemorative of Christ's redemptive actions and especially of His death. This is what St. Paul tells us in the passage of the letter to the Romans already cited: "Or do you not know that all of us who have been baptized into Christ Jesus have been baptized into His death? For we were buried with Him by means of baptism into death" (Rom. 6:3-4). Baptism is also a sign commemorative of facts in the history of salvation prior to the coming of Christ, for example of the crossing of the Red Sea (cf. 1 Cor. 10:1-11) or of the salvation of Noe in the ark (cf. 1 Pet. 3:20-21).

Finally, St. Paul teaches how baptism is a prophetic sign of future glory in the same text to the Romans: "If we have indeed grown to be one (with Christ) in the likeness of His death, we shall be so in the likeness of His resurrection also. . . . If we have died with Christ, we believe that we shall also live with Him" (Rom. 6:5-8).[76]

The Eucharist

The essential texts here are the narrative of the institution in the synoptics: Matt. 26:17-29; Mark 14:12-25; Luke 22:7-20; the reflections of St. Paul in 1 Cor. 10:16-21 and 11:23-30; finally, the Eucharistic discourse in the sixth chapter of St. John.

The Eucharist is a sign demonstrative first of all of Christ's body and blood here present: "This is My body . . . this is My blood"; but also of the divine life they communicate to us and of our union with Christ and among ourselves: "He who eats My flesh and drinks My blood abides in Me and I in him" (John 6:56); "Because the bread is one, we who are many are but one body, for we all partake of the one bread" (1 Cor. 10:17).

The Eucharist is an obligating sign. St. Paul explains this to the Corinthians to make them understand that they must break completely with idolatry:

---

[71] Cf. Tertullian, *De corona*, 15 (PL 2, 102) *à propos* of the Mithraic initiation.

[72] Cf. Tertullian, *De spectac.*, 4 (PL 1, 635).

[73] *Ad martyr.*, 3 (PL 1, 624).

[74] *De lapsis*, 13 (PL 4, 476).

[75] Tertullian, *De pudic.*, 14 (PL 2, 1007).

[76] Cf. Tit. 3:5-7. It must be recognized that this fourfold signification of baptism was much more evident in antiquity, when baptism was conferred by immersion. Cf. Righetti, IV, 65, 68 f.

"You cannot drink the cup of the Lord and the cup of demons; you cannot partake of the table of the Lord and the table of demons" (1 Cor. 10:21). The idea of obligation is included, moreover, in the theme of the Eucharist as a new alliance (Matt. 26:28; Mark 14:24; Luke 22:20; 1 Cor. 11:25). This new alliance recalls the old one with its strong emphasis on the obligations flowing from the pact concluded with God (Ex. 24:1–8; Deut. 29 and 30).

The Eucharist is a sign commemorative of the Last Supper and of the Passion. Christ had said to His Apostles, "Do this in memory of Me," and St. Paul comments, "Every time you eat this bread and drink the chalice, you keep proclaiming the death of the Lord" (1 Cor. 11:26). The Eucharist also commemorates events in the history of Israel, such as the alliance concluded in the blood of the lamb at the foot of Sinai or the gift of manna to the Hebrews wandering in the desert (cf. John 6:31–33 and 49–51; 1 Cor. 10:1–4).

Finally, the Eucharist is a pledge of the glory to come. This eschatological dimension of the Eucharist is often indicated in the New Testament: "Every time you eat this bread and drink the chalice, you keep proclaiming the death of the Lord, until He comes" (1 Cor. 11:26). "It has been My heart's desire to eat this paschal supper with you before I suffer; for I tell you that I shall not eat it again until it is celebrated in the kingdom of God . . . I shall not drink again of the fruit of the vine until the kingdom of God has come" (Luke 22:15 ff.). One may see another indication of the eschatological dimension of the Eucharist in the fact that it was instituted in the setting of the Jewish paschal supper, the eschatological sense of which is beyond question. The value of the Eucharist as pledge of resurrection and of immortality is attested also by St. John: "He who eats My flesh and drinks My blood has life everlasting, and I will raise him up on the last day" (John 6:55).

Confirmation

While the fourfold signification is clearly affirmed by the Scripture for baptism and for the Eucharist, it must be deduced by theological reasoning for the other sacraments.

Confirmation is a sign demonstrative of grace, in as much as it signifies the coming of the Holy Spirit into the soul.

It is an obligating sign, in as much as it is a seal, a mark of belonging and of consecration to Christ, and of enrollment in His army.

It is a sign commemorative of the Passion, because the merits acquired by Christ on the cross make it possible for the Spirit to be communicated to us. Confirmation recalls also the communications of the Spirit in the Old Testament, which prefigured and announced those of the New.

Finally, confirmation is the sign prophetic of the full gift of the Spirit which we still await, and which will revive the bodies of the elect and transform them to the likeness of Christ's glorified body.[77]

[77] Cf. Rom. 8:11 ff. In the ancient and present-day rites of confirmation it is easy to find

Penance

Penance is a sign demonstrative of reconciliation with God and with the Church and of the return to supernatural life, to that life of grace which is a participation in the fulness of Christ's life.

The character of obligation in penance is strongly marked in the firm resolution to sin no more.

Its character of memorial of Christ's Passion is based on the fact that it is Christ's merits which make possible the reconciliation with God and the Church, empower the Church to remit sins, and make the penitent's dispositions useful in the supernatural order. In fact, these dispositions — regret, confession, firm resolution — have no supernatural value except in so far as they are a participation in the dispositions with which Christ, especially in His Passion, was animated toward the sins of men.

Finally, penance is a sign prophetic of eternal life because the grace reacquired in penance is the seed of which glory is the normal fruit.[78]

Extreme unction

Extreme unction, says St. Thomas, "is the sacrament which in some way brings to a conclusion the whole process of spiritual healing, and through which man is prepared, as it were" (he means: immediately) "to participate in glory."[79]

It manifests grace, in as much as grace is a tonic against the moral weakness which results from sins even though the sins be already forgiven.[80]

It obliges with regard to the acts still to be performed before death, for every forgiveness of sins implies such an obligation.

It commemorates Christ's Passion, meritorious cause of this spiritual recovery.

And it announces the future glory which is the normal consequence of this recovery and for which this sacrament is an immediate preparation.[81]

this fourfold signification of the sacrament. The laying-on of hands and the epicletic invocation which accompanies it manifest the gift of the Spirit. The *consignatio*, that is, the tracing of the sign of the cross on the forehead, and the formula "I sign you with the sign of the cross" commemorate the Passion of Christ and make it understood that henceforth the subject is consecrated to Christ, whose mark he bears. As to the eschatological dimension, it appeared explicitly, for example, in a formula of the Gelasian sacramentary: "The sign of Christ unto life everlasting" (I, 44; ed. Wilson, p. 87).

[78] These various senses have always been brought to light by the liturgy of penance. In the present Roman rite the following prayer in particular will be noticed: "May the Passion of our Lord Jesus Christ . . . profit you for the remission of sins, increase of grace and the reward of eternal life." In the ritual of public penance the fourfold signification is still more evident. See, e.g., in the Roman Pontifical the preface for the reconciliation of penitents on Holy Thursday; for the history of this formula see Righetti, IV, 195 f. See also the formula of absolution "May the Lord Jesus Christ . . . " at the end of the same rite.

[79] *C. Gent.*, IV, 73.

[80] Cf. *Summa*, III, suppl., q. 30, a. 1.

[81] In the present ritual it is the first signification that appears most clearly: the anointing is intended to heal and fortify the sick person's body and soul (cf. the three final prayers).

Holy orders

Holy orders is a sign demonstrative of grace and of the priestly character as a very special participation in the priesthood of Christ.

It is a sign obligating the life of the priest vowed to the service of Christ and to the priestly ministry.

It is a sign commemorative of the saving acts of Christ and especially of His Passion, because it is in these acts that Christ exercised His priesthood and merited the priestly grace which is now communicated to the priests. It recalls likewise the priesthood of the Old Testament, which was but a rough cast of the priesthood of Christ and that of the Christian priests.

Finally, it is a sign prophetic of the glory to come, in as much as this will be the fruit of the priesthood of Christ and of His priests.[82]

Matrimony

Matrimony manifests grace, which is here a grace of union between the two partners with a view to the procreation and education of children who will become members of the Church and citizens of heaven; this grace being, moreover, a participation in the grace of Christ, which in the Church and through the Church begets children to God.

It obliges or engages the life of the partners, who must submit to the requirements of Christian marriage.

It recalls the Passion of Christ, who by delivering Himself up for the Church acquired her as spouse (cf. Eph. 5:25 ff.), that is, acquired the right and the means of sanctifying men and making them, by various titles, His collaborators in begetting others to the divine life. It recalls at the same time the holy marriages of the Old Testament, which prefigured the true Christian nuptials.

Finally, it is a pledge of future glory, which the Apocalypse (19:7; 21:2 and 9) calls the nuptials of the Lamb.[83]

The four dimensions of the liturgical signs instituted by the Church

The liturgical signs instituted by the Church may be divided into three groups: the ceremonies, that is to say, the gestures, attitudes, movements with which the Church accompanies and, so to speak, clothes that which is of divine institution in the celebration of the Mass and the administration of the sacraments, and with which also she accompanies the recitation of the Divine Office; the prayers which the Church has inserted into the celebration of the Mass and the administration of the sacraments, and especially the prayers which make up the Divine Office; finally, the sacramentals.

[82] The various prefaces of ordination show clearly that the priesthood gives grace and the Holy Spirit, is connected with the Jewish priesthood and obligates with regard to the life of the one ordained.

[83] It must be recognized that the present ceremonies of the Roman Ritual for the blessing of matrimony are very sober, not to say impoverished. The Byzantine ritual, for example, is much more developed.

Although worship and sanctification are two inseparable elements everywhere in the liturgy, it must be recognized that in the rites instituted by the Church, including the sacramentals, the aspect of worship is clearly more important than the aspect of sanctification. It is therefore worship that these signs will signify above all, and they will signify worship according to the four dimensions with which we are acquainted: they will be manifestation of the present, obligation for the rest of one's life, memorial of the past and pledge of the future.

The present reality which the sign manifests is first of all that interior attitude of the Church in which liturgical worship formally consists; it is also the interior attitude of Christ, His worship of God, of which the Church's worship is but a participation and an instrument.

The reality both present and future to which the sign obligates is obviously the moral life of the subject.

As to the past commemorated by the sign, it is first of all the worship which Christ rendered to God on earth, chiefly in His Passion, which is at the point of departure of the Church's worship; but it is likewise the whole worship of the patriarchs and of the chosen people, prefiguring that of Christ and of the Church.

Finally, the future reality of which the sign is the prophecy and the pledge is the perfect worship of the heavenly Jerusalem.

To understand with what proper shadings these four significations are found in every liturgical sign instituted by the Church, we must examine separately the three groups of signs distinguished above. Then we shall say a word on the feasts and the liturgical cycles.

Ceremonies

The gestures, movements and attitudes which the liturgy prescribes for its participants have the purpose of expressing, and at the same time of reinforcing, in the one who performs them and in those who see them, the interior dispositions which are basic to worship. They signify the Church's interior worship according to its four dimensions.

For example, a genuflection made before the Blessed Sacrament manifests the sentiments of reverence and adoration which the Church has for Christ, obligates the future behavior of the subject,[84] commemorates all the past events implied by the Eucharist, from the Incarnation to the Ascension, and proclaims the perfect reverence and adoration of the elect in heaven.

---

[84] No doubt the Christian who makes a genuflection thinks only vaguely of this obligation which his gesture implies. But if he did not have some intention of living conformably to his faith, of showing forth in his life the belief which his gesture presupposes, the genuflection would not be truly an act of worship. The ancients, who supposed that *religio* was derived from *re-ligare*, had understood at least that every act of worship binds man to God. "Worship," writes St. Thomas, "is called religion because through these acts man in some way binds himself to God so as not to stray away from Him and also because, by a certain natural instinct, he feels himself obligated toward God" (*C. Gent.*, III, 119).

One might give an analogous explanation of all the gestures and all the attitudes prescribed by the liturgy, taking into account, of course, the nature and the proper object of each one. Whether the concern is with a bow made before the cross or the altar, with marks of respect toward the bishop, the priest or the faithful themselves, one must always apply the saying "One thing is seen and another understood."

Prayers

Liturgical prayer under all its forms holds first place among the signs instituted by the Church to render her worship to God. And the reason for this is that speech predominates over all other signs in the relations between man and God. This prayer of the Church has also a fourfold dimension.

It manifests primarily and immediately the Church's sentiments of adoration, thanksgiving, petition and repentance. At the same time it manifests Christ's interior prayer, since the Church's prayer is but a participation in that of her Lord.

It obligates the one who is praying, who makes the Church's prayer his own personal prayer; for every act of worship implies a moral obligation.

It recalls Christ's prayer on earth, especially in His Passion, and also all the prayers of the Old Testament.

Finally, it is a sign prophetic of the perfect prayer of adoration, praise and thanksgiving in which the angels and the elect will join forever (cf. Apoc. 5:8-14).

Sacramentals

We may define the sacramentals, in the present sense of the term, as rites of a structure analogous to that of the sacraments, instituted by the Church and used by her for obtaining with her impetration effects that are principally spiritual.[85]

There are two aspects to every sacramental. It is primarily a prayer, a petition addressed to God by the Church; but it is also, thanks to this prayer of the Church, a means which God uses to sanctify men or things.

The idea of sanctification obviously does not have the same meaning when applied to persons and when applied to things. Only persons, and formally speaking only souls, are capable of sanctity. Then how are things sanctified by the prayer said over them?

---

[85] Cf. *Codex Iuris Canonici*, canon 1144. The extension, and hence the definition, of the concept of sacramental has varied in the course of history. In the thirteenth century the old notion of *sacramentum* was abandoned, with the aim of pointing up that which distinguished the sacraments properly so called from the other rites which were more or less analogous. Then the latter began to be called *sacramentalia* or lesser sacraments. The term was applied at that time not only to the secondary rites of the sacraments but also to the ceremonies, to prayers like the *Pater*, to the Divine Office, to good works like fasting, almsgiving, etc. It is only at a later date, starting with Bellarmine, that "sacramental" has begun to have its present meaning.

We must answer that God takes them under His protection by a special right, removes them more or less permanently from the devil's influence or even from the deleterious influence of natural causes, and above all makes them the occasion of graces for those who use them with the right dispositions.

By the same token, the object blessed or consecrated rediscovers, in a manner still imperfect yet real, its original destiny, which is to be at the service of the divine life communicated to man. There is a renewal of the harmony that reigned in paradise before the fall, and at the same time a prefiguration of the perfect order that will prevail in the new heavens and the new earth.

Both as prayer and as means of sanctification, the sacramental has a fourfold signification.

From the first point of view, it manifests the Church's interior prayer and also that of the glorified Christ; it obligates the one who says this prayer or allows it to be said in his name; it recalls Christ's earthly prayer and Passion, as well as the prayers of the old alliance; finally, it announces the prayer of the heavenly Jerusalem, where the petition, perfectly satisfied, will become thanksgiving and praise.

From the second point of view, the sacramental, if its immediate object is the sanctification of the soul, is a sign demonstrative of the habitual graces granted the Christian to dispose him for sanctifying grace or for its increase; if, on the other hand, the concern is with a sacramental which primarily asks the divine protection on a material object, it is a sign demonstrative of that protection and of what it implies. Moreover, every sacramental, be it only the blessing of an object or a simple sign of the cross, must manifest dispositions of the soul and hence obligate to future acts. This is particularly true of such rites as the consecration of virgins, monastic profession, admission to the clerical status. Finally, every sacramental recalls the Passion of Christ, meritorious cause of all sanctification, and announces the heavenly Jerusalem, where all sanctity will be complete and where the material world will be perfectly at the service of the divine life.

Feasts and liturgical cycles

The feasts, and still more the liturgical cycles, group a certain number of rites around an essential theme. For a full understanding of the meaning of a feast and of the meaning taken on by the different rites in that feast, the theme must be considered according to the usual four dimensions. Such is the true object of a theology of the liturgical year. An example will suffice here to show the fecundity of this method.

The feast of the Epiphany, or more exactly of the epiphanies, is first of all the memorial of three facts in which Christ's divinity is revealed: the adoration of Christ by the wise men, His baptism, His first miracle at Cana. Beyond these happenings from the gospel, it commemorates the expectation of the Old

Testament and the theophanies which kept it alive. The Epiphany is also the sign demonstrative of the constant illumination of men by God, of that luminous coming which is realized in every liturgical celebration. It is the sign obligating to the effort which it imposes on men to prepare themselves worthily for this feast and to live henceforth in conformity with the mystery celebrated. Finally, it is the sign prophetic of Christ's return, of the definitive illumination and revelation. To get a complete view of the feast, one must look at it under all these aspects. Recourse to the breviary and the missal will suffice to prove that the liturgical texts themselves direct us into all these avenues of consideration.

Conclusion

At the end of this chapter, the liturgy appears to us as a wonderful mirror in which is reflected and summed up the whole complexus of the relations between God and men. It is the projection in the present of the whole history of salvation, past, present and future. It is the summary of the whole mystery of Christ and of the Church, and the place where, by Christ's mediation, God keeps descending among men and men keep rising to God.

Such is the perspective in which a person must place himself if he wants to understand the liturgy, and above all if he wants to live it in reality. We shall see in the course of this work [86] that the biblical texts used by the liturgy cannot be interpreted accurately except in reference to the fourfold dimension of the liturgical signs. This principle holds also for the texts composed by the Church. To be sure, we must not expect to find the complete scheme set out explicitly in every text; but it is always implied, it is always the frame of reference in which the thought or the prayer is developed.

Here are some examples taken from the Christmas liturgy.

In the collect of the vigil, the Church makes this petition: "You gladden us, O Lord, with the annual expectation of our redemption. Joyfully do we welcome Your only-begotten Son as Redeemer. Grant that we may welcome Him also with a tranquil conscience when He comes as Judge." The vigil of Christmas is considered here as a sign demonstrative at the same time of the coming of Christ the Redeemer and of the desire which we have for that coming. Besides, in asking for security on the day of judgment, the collect makes it clear that the celebration of this feast is to be the point of departure for a moral effort: it is only if our participation in the mystery is reflected in our actions that we will be able to await the judgment without fear, and therefore we ask God to grant us the grace to perform good acts. The mention of the annual expectation of our redemption suffices to recall the historical fact of Christ's coming; and the mention of His glorious return indicates explicitly the eschatological dimension of the feast.

In the postcommunion of the midnight Mass we say this prayer: "It is our

[86] Cf. below, vol. 2, chapter 14: "The Use of Scripture in the Liturgy."

joy, O Lord our God, to celebrate in mysteries the birth of our Lord Jesus Christ. Grant, we pray You, that by living worthily we may become fit to be His companions." The liturgical celebration of the Nativity through the mysteries is a sign of our interior feast. It invites and obligates us to a holy life. It has meaning only in reference to the historical birth of Christ. It announces the perfect union in heaven, toward which it is to lead us.

It would be easy to find this fourfold signification in many other texts of the Christmas liturgy.

These examples suffice to show how the whole history of salvation, in its various phases, is signified in the rites and the feasts of the liturgy. We must add once more that it is signified not only as a reality to be recalled, contemplated, admired, but also as a living, acting, efficacious reality. If the liturgy is one of the stages of the history of salvation, it must *make* that history and not only tell it. It must apply the mystery of Christ to men.

But how do the words and the gestures which constitute the liturgical rites have such efficacy? How is it that "with a little pure water and three divine names pronounced in a human language one makes a son of God"? [87]

[87] Eugène Masure, *Le signe*, p. 215.

3 THE LITURGY AS A
COMPLEXUS OF EFFICACIOUS SIGNS

The spectator who sees one of the tragedies of Sophocles presented in our day can speak of the efficacy of the play: through this complexus of signs the Greek life of the fifth century before Christ is truly represented, made present. Similarly, the reader of a novel about the future which describes the society of tomorrow, transformed by the progress of science, can speak of the efficacy of the book: thanks to the book, the future is already present to his eyes, and perhaps to his desires.

Sophocles' tragedy and the novel about the future are signs, and they have the effect proper to signs, which is to make known an invisible or absent reality and, contingently, to bring about a psychological reaction in face of that reality. In this sense it can be said that every sign is efficacious and makes present what it signifies. But this efficacy and this presence are only on the level of knowledge and, contingently, of feeling and of will. They are purely intentional, in scholastic terminology.

The case is quite otherwise with the liturgical signs. They also are efficacious and make present what they signify, but in a real and objective manner, far transcending the level of intentionality. Before entering into detail, let us quote a passage of the encyclical *Mediator Dei*, which will dictate our plan for us:

"The worship rendered to God by the Church in union with her divine

55

Head is the most efficacious means of achieving sanctity. This efficacy, where there is question of the Eucharistic sacrifice and the sacraments, derives first of all and principally from the act itself (*ex opere operato*).

"But if one considers the part which the immaculate Spouse of Jesus Christ takes in the action, embellishing the sacrifice and sacraments with prayer and sacred ceremonies, or if one refers to the 'sacramentals' and the other rites instituted by the hierarchy of the Church, then its effectiveness is due rather to the action of the Church (*ex opere operantis Ecclesiae*), in as much as she is holy and acts always in closest union with her Head." [1]

1. The Efficacy of the Liturgical Signs Instituted by God

It is the task of a theology of the sacraments to explain the Catholic doctrine of efficacy *ex opere operato*. We shall be content with recalling here its general meaning, after which we shall seek to specify the manner in which the realities signified by the sacraments are made present in the liturgical action by virtue of this efficacy *ex opere operato*.

The *opus operatum* and three characteristics of the liturgy

The encyclical does not say that the efficacy of the liturgical signs instituted by God comes exclusively from the *opus operatum*, but does say that it is so derived "first of all and principally." It is the Church's teaching that, if the conditions of validity are fulfilled and if there is no obstacle placed by the improper dispositions of the subject, the sacraments confer grace *ex opere operato*, that is, by the mere fact that the action is placed, and not in virtue of the minister's or the subject's merits. On the part of the minister it is required only that he have the faculty and that he have the intention of doing what the Church does. On the part of the subject it is required that he be qualified to receive the sacrament and that he place no obstacle to the reception of the grace.

All these qualities or dispositions are indispensable conditions for the sacrament's giving grace, but it is not from them that the grace comes. It is the sacrament that confers grace. And by that we mean, of course, that it is God who confers grace as principal cause, but that He confers it by means of the sacrament, which is its instrumental cause. Such is the teaching of all the theologians since the Council of Trent.[2]

There is a diversity of opinion, however, on the way in which this instrumental causality is to be understood. Some interpret it as a moral causality: the sacrament exerts an influence on the will of God and prompts Him to give His grace, so that He remains the only efficient cause. Others see in it an intentional causality: the sacrament is a sign which manifests God's will to grant us His grace; this sign entitles the recipient of the sacrament to God's

---

[1] Nn. 26–27.   [2] Cf. Dz 849–851 and 799.

gift of grace. Others again understand the instrumental causality of the sacraments as a real physical causality: the sacramental rite has a real and direct influence, as an instrument, in the conferral of the grace which God grants by its mediation.

The fact that the sacraments act *ex opere operato* gives us a glimpse, already, of the objective quality of the liturgy.[3] What is first in liturgical action is the accomplishment of a divine work, the realization of a mystery whose author and principal actor is God. Man's dispositions intervene only as a condition; they are not the cause of grace. All that is required of man is not to place any obstacle to God's action in him, to welcome the divine gift just as it is and to conform himself to its exigencies.

The liturgy requires an interior life, even a deeply interior life; but the ideal to which it tends and to which it leads is an interior life so invaded and dominated by the object, which is the mystery of Christ communicated through the signs, that it becomes forgetful of itself.

Thus we see how the realism of the Catholic liturgy transcends the psychologism of Protestant worship, which recognizes in the rites only the value of an exhortation. If the faithful have the certainty that their encounter with God in the liturgy takes place on a rock more solid than the shifting sands of their subjective feelings and their puny moral forces, this is due to the efficacy *ex opere operato* of the sacraments.

From the objective character of the liturgy is derived its theocentric character. The liturgy is centered on a reality which is not constructed by man but received from God. In the sacraments it is God Himself who acts, and His whole action has the aim of making souls participate in the mystery of Christ and of communicating His own life to them. In the liturgy, and principally in the sacraments, where grace is given *ex opere operato*, man's part is above all to receive from God and to let himself be drawn by God.

Finally, the liturgy owes to the *opus operatum* its realist character. God's action in the sacraments not only reaches man on the level of knowledge and of will, but transforms him in his very being: baptism and holy orders do not bring about a mere moral renewal, they effect a change which must actually be called physical.

How the realities signified by the sacraments are made present

The realism implied by the efficacy *ex opere operato* of the sacraments allows us to understand very easily how the sacramental rites make present the realities of which they are the demonstrative, obligating and prophetic signs. It is easy to understand also how they are signs commemorative of the events of the Old Testament. On the other hand, there is a special difficulty in understanding how they make present the redemptive acts performed by Christ during His earthly life.

[3] This question will be taken up again and developed in chapter 6: "The Liturgy and the Law of Objectivity."

The sacraments first of all manifest and make present sanctifying grace, of which they are instrumental cause and of which the efficient cause is God Himself, employing Christ's humanity as conjoint instrument. They also suppose and manifest in the subject that disposition of veneration in which consists formally the worship which he renders to God through Christ. The sacraments signify also as present the moral obligation of the subject, since without this intention they would not be received fruitfully.

In so far as they are a pledge of the future, the sacraments announce the glory to come and the worship in the heavenly Jerusalem. They make them present in a certain way, for they contain them as the acorn contains the oak. By an inverse phenomenon, they make present the acts of sanctification and of worship in the Old Testament, of which they are the flowering and the fulfilment.

Thus, by reason of their efficacy *ex opere operato*, the sacramental signs have the power of making present everything that they signify. This power is not confined to sanctifying grace but extends, according to the various ways, to all the realities we have just enumerated.

It is more difficult to determine precisely how the sacramental signs make present the saving actions performed at one time by Christ, in particular His Passion and His death. How should we understand and apply to the different sacraments the words "the memory of His Passion is recalled" of the antiphon "O sacred banquet"?

Explanation of Dom Casel's theory

About thirty years ago Dom Odo Casel began to present a theory which has given rise to a whole controversy, some theologians simply rejecting the ideas of the monk of Maria Laach, others trying to distinguish between what seems well founded and what seems to them to be exaggerated. Let us attempt to give an overall view of this "doctrine of the mysteries" or *Mysterienlehre*.[4]

For Dom Casel, what is made objectively present in the sacramental action is not only the effect of Christ's Passion and of His other redemptive acts, in other words not only grace; it is the redemptive action itself, in particular the Passion, not indeed in all its least circumstances, but in what was essential in it, in its substance.

Thus the liturgical rite performed in time and space is a "memorial" of Christ's saving actions and in particular of His Passion. In the liturgy these acts are rendered objectively present, are re-presented. They are numerically the same, but present in a manner wholly original.

This way of being present transcends time and space, while the liturgical action goes forward in time and space. Dom Casel calls this way a "mysterious"

[4] See: the articles in *Jahrb. für Liturgiewis.*, 6 (1926), 113–204; 8 (1928), 145–224; *Das christliche Kultmysterium* (Regensburg: Pus- tet, 1935); Theodor Filthaut, *Die Kontroverse über die Mysterienlehre* (Warendorf: Schnell, 1947).

way, a "mystery," thus giving a new sense to this traditional term.[5] For him, the "mystery" is a rite of worship which, under the veil of signs and in a manner transcending space and time, renders objectively present the saving action performed at another time by Christ, and above all His Passion, in its numerical individuality.

What is made present in the Eucharist is not only Christ who once suffered and now reigns in heaven, but the Passion itself, the suffering itself.

Dom Casel tried to base his theory on the texts of the Fathers and of the liturgy, and he even thought that this concept of "mystery of worship" had been the Christian response, true and transcendental, to those religious aspirations of mankind which were manifested in ancient times in the aberrations of the pagan mystery cults. In these mysteries, representing under the symbol of the rites the history, and in particular the death and resurrection of a divinity from whom salvation was expected (for example Mithras, or Isis and Osiris), the initiate was persuaded that he was reliving in himself, by way of worship and through a mysterious assimilation, the history of his god, in particular his death and his resurrection, and that thus he was obtaining salvation.

Criticism of Dom Casel's theory

What are we to think of this theory? Both from the historical point of view and from the philosophical and theological point of view, it runs into numerous difficulties, of which we shall indicate the principal ones.

The historical inquiries occasioned by Dom Casel's thesis have established the following three points in a manner which may be considered as definitive.

The first point is that the *Mysterienlehre* cannot appeal directly to the concept of μυστήριον in the New Testament and especially in St. Paul. We have already ascertained that St. Paul applies this concept only to the history of salvation, and does not extend it explicitly to worship.[6]

The second point is that Dom Casel, under the influence of Reitzenstein, has exaggerated the significance of the pagan mysteries. Actually these mysteries are very largely based on nature, and symbolize mostly the cycle of vegetation, disappearing in winter to reappear in spring. This is a far cry from the idea of an historical personage saving his devotees by his death and resurrection.

Moreover Dom Casel has greatly exaggerated the connection between Christian tradition, in particular that of the second and third centuries, and the pagan mysteries. It has been established now that Christian worship was constituted in its essentials without any influence from these mysteries and that when the Fathers have recourse to the concepts of μυστήριον and *sacramentum* to explain the Christian rites, they are influenced above all by the Scrip-

---

[5] Dom Casel thought to find this meaning of "mystery" in the patristic and liturgical texts, but his exegesis forced the texts.

[6] See above, pp. 8–10.

ture, where they find the idea of the history of salvation and of the value of the Old Testament events, institutions and personages as types. If there is any indication of pagan influence, it is nothing more than an echo of the Neoplatonic mentality then in vogue, for which the realities of this world are primarily images and symbols of the realities of the heavenly world.[7]

The third point is that the idea of "mystery of worship," in the exact sense which Dom Casel gives it, is unknown either to the Fathers or to the liturgies.[8] When the Fathers speak of μυστήριον or *sacramentum* in connection with worship, they give these terms the meaning of sensible signs of a sacred reality having a relation with the communication of the divine life to the world through Christ, signs which *in some way* contain and produce that reality. But to want to specify in what way, as Dom Casel does, is to go far beyond the Fathers.

To the difficulties of an historical order are added the objections of a philosophical and theological character. Dom Casel's purpose is apparently to emphasize the realism of the bond which attaches sacramental grace not only to the person of Christ but also to His redemptive actions and especially to His Passion. This bond must be real, since it is by these acts that Christ is the cause of the grace which the sacraments confer. The aim will be, therefore, to make the faithful understand that the sacramental rites put them really in the presence of Christ's redemptive acts and in contact with them.

But there are two elements that can be distinguished in Christ's redemptive actions. One is momentary : the acts themselves in as much as they are performed at a given moment. The other is permanent : the interior disposition, the stable *habitus* from which these acts of Christ proceeded throughout His earthly life.

Since Dom Casel's thesis is that these same acts, numerically the same, are rendered present in the sacramental rite, we must analyze metaphysically the nature of action and discover the source of the individuation of actions, to see whether it is possible, even by a miracle, for a past action to be made present once more, identically the same, numerically the same.

We know that in itself action is something momentary : it comes into being at a given moment through the faculty from which it proceeds, and it ceases to exist when the efficient causality of that faculty is interrupted. This holds for every human action performed in this life, even properly spiritual

---

[7] See below, vol. 2, chapter 19: "Theology and Liturgy in the Fathers."

[8] See, e.g., the studies of G. Soehngen, *Der Wesensaufbau des Mysteriums*; H. Marsh, "The Use of μυστηριον in the Writings of Clement of Alexandria," *Journal of Theological Studies*, 1936, pp. 64 ff.; Hans von Balthasar, "Le mysterion d'Origène," *Rech. de Sc. rel.*, 26 (1936), 513 ff.; 27 (1937), 38 ff.; Gerhard Fittkau, *Der Begriff des Mysteriums bei Johan-*

nes Chrysostomus (Bonn: P. Hanstein, 1953). Johannes Betz in his *Die Eucharistie in der Zeit der griechischen Väter*, Band I/1 : *Die Aktualpräsenz der Person und des Heilswerkes Jesu im Abendmahl nach der vorephesinischen griechischen Patristik* (Freiburg: Herder, 1955), defends Casel's thesis from the historical point of view. See the review of his work by J. Barbel in *Theologische Revue*, 53 (1957), 61–71.

actions like those of understanding and volition. The exercise of these faculties is connected with bodily organs; hence their acts are involved in time like
the rest: they also are placed at a certain moment in time and cease to exist
when the action of their efficient cause is interrupted.

Since in itself an action is something momentary, the element of time
enters into its individuation in an essential way. Its localization in time distinguishes it numerically from every antecedent or subsequent act of the
same species and constitutes a determining factor in its individuation.

Thus it is metaphysically impossible — and impossible even by a miracle,
being self-contradictory — that an action which took place at a given moment of time be made present, numerically the same, at another moment
of time. It is therefore impossible that Christ's redemptive actions, in as much
as they were momentary actions, be rendered present, numerically the same,
at another moment of time. If there has been interruption in time, it is no
longer the same act, but a new act.

To this Dom Casel replies that in the sacramental rites the redemptive
act is made present in a wholly original way, which transcends space and
time. But, on the one hand, this supra-spatial and supra-temporal presence
is in contradiction with the very nature of the human act; and, on the other
hand, it would remain to be explained how an act which was individuated
by the moment of time in which it took place could be preserved, to be rendered present again in its own individuality, if that previous moment came
to an end and fell into nothingness.

Thus the answer is given also to Dom Casel's statement that Christ's redemptive actions are made present in the sacramental liturgy not in their
particular circumstances of space and time, but in their substance. The indi-
viduating elements, hence also the element of time, belong to the substance
of the individual act as such, and it is contradictory to hold that such an act
is made present in its substance without being made present in the circumstance of time.

It would be a delusion to reject the metaphysical analysis of action and take
refuge in an anti-intellectual intuitionism. Besides leaving untouched the
problems raised by this analysis, such an attitude would mean questioning
fundamental philosophical principles without which theology and faith
itself could not exist.

Among the objections urged against Dom Casel's theory, let us point out
this one also, an objection of no little weight: If the Mass made Christ's Passion present in its numerical individuality, it would be a bloody sacrifice, and
Christ would acquire new merits in it.

All these difficulties, historical, philosophical, theological, prevent us from
following Dom Casel and invite us to hold to a more traditional position.

Attempt at solution

The sacramental rites, therefore, do not make present the redemptive acts once performed by Christ, in as much as they are non-permanent acts, individuated by the circumstance of time. Yet those actions, now past and not re-presentable in their numerical individuality, continue to exercise an influence on the grace which is granted us, of which they remain efficient, instrumental, meritorious and exemplary cause.

It is the teaching of St. Thomas that everything Christ did and suffered during His earthly life continues to exercise an efficient causality on all the graces of salvation granted to men at all times. For Christ's actions were not simply human, entitled as such to an efficacy limited in time and space, but theandric, human-divine actions. Their human element was an instrument, and the divine power was at work, using that instrument. "This power," St. Thomas tells us, "by its presence is in touch with all places and times." [9] Thus Christ's actions, though limited in time and space in so far as they are human, reach to all times and all places in so far as they are theandric.[10]

Moreover, these actions continue to exercise a meritorious causality on the grace that is given us. They act, so to speak, on the will of God, who keeps these actions present to His mind and grants us grace because of them.

Finally, they are exemplary cause of our sanctification and of our worship. For our sanctification is a participation in Christ's sanctity, and our worship is the prolongation of His, which He rendered to God precisely in these actions. Thus Christ's redemptive acts are made present in the liturgy in almost the same way that the image makes present the model which it "represents."

Hence the commemoration of Christ's redemptive acts, considered even in their numerical individuality, is not reduced to a mere remembrance of past events. They are really present in the sacramental rites by their effects. Through these effects the faithful are placed in real contact not only with the person of Christ, but with that which He did and suffered in His earthly life.[11]

On the other hand, these actions of Christ involve a permanent element: the interior disposition, the stable *habitus* from which they issued and of which they were but momentary expressions. This disposition was permanent and constant in Christ, without interruption or diminution, from His Incarnation to His Ascension, and it remains in the glorified Christ. Through

---

[9] *Summa*, III, q. 56, a. 1 ad 3.

[10] The teaching of St. Thomas on this point was studied recently by J. Vilanova, "Per una teologia de l'any liturgic," *Cardinali I. A. Schuster in memoriam* (Montserrat, 1956), pp. 27–44.

[11] Perhaps the encyclical *Mediator Dei* is alluding to Dom Casel's theory when it says of the mysteries of Christ commemorated in the course of the liturgical year, "These mysteries are ever present and active not in a vague and uncertain way as some modern writers hold, but in the way that Catholic doctrine teaches us. According to the doctors of the Church, they are shining examples of Christian perfection, as well as sources of divine grace, due to the merit and prayers of Christ; they still influence us because each mystery brings its own special grace for our salvation" (n. 165 [Lat. 163]).

the liturgical action, the faithful are put in contact with that disposition, which is always in act.

In the Eucharist, where Christ is present in person and not only by His divine power, the presence of that disposition is especially vivid and real. We may call it a personal presence, since it flows from the presence of the person of Christ.

In the other sacraments, where Christ is present not in person but by His divine power, the faithful are put in contact with this disposition of Christ in a "virtual" way. This presence and this contact are not simply those of an object known, recalled, loved; they are of what the theologians call a "physical" order to indicate that they exceed the purely psychological level. The fact is that every communication of sacramental grace has for instrumental cause the humanity of the glorified Christ, including that interior disposition from which His redemptive acts proceeded in the course of His earthly life.

A last point must be made clear. The redemptive actions performed by Christ from His Incarnation to His death were innumerable, and each one of them was more than sufficient to redeem us. Nevertheless, in the order of things willed in fact by the Father and freely accepted by Christ, they all contributed as partial causes to form the total and unique cause of our salvation, which cause was fully constituted only at His death on the cross.

All of Christ's redemptive actions tended, therefore, to the cross as their fulfilment, and it is the cross which gave them their meaning. Thus the cross sums up and synthesizes Christ's whole redemptive activity, and every mystery of Christ's life involves the mystery of the cross.

As for the Resurrection, the Ascension, the sending of the Holy Spirit, they are not meritorious acts, and hence they are not, properly speaking, redemptive acts, any more than Christ's glorious return will be. Nevertheless, in the sacraments and in fact in the whole liturgy, just as the representation of the different redemptive mysteries of Christ is never separated from the representation of the mystery of the cross, so the latter is never separated from the commemorative representation of the glorious mysteries, nor from the prophetic representation of the parousia.

The reason for this is that all the phases of Christ's life, on earth and in heaven, are so closely knit together that they form only one mystery: the mystery of Christ Redeemer. Starting with the Incarnation, everything is oriented toward the death on the cross as its fulfilment. But the death itself takes on its meaning only with the Resurrection, the Ascension and the sending of the Holy Spirit, because it is only in these mysteries that Christ gathers the fruits of His death and communicates them to us. What Christ communicates to us is above all the Spirit, given in the Church through the sacraments. Finally, this communication of the Spirit has for its end the definitive and universal restoration of the kingdom of God as the parousia.

In short, every sacramental sign, as commemoration of the redemptive acts performed by Christ, makes present in the sense indicated above, not only this or that mystery, but all the mysteries of Christ's earthly life, from the Incarnation to Pentecost; and it is moreover a sign prophetic of the parousia. Thus, in virtue of its efficacy *ex opere operato*, it makes present and fulfils the mystery of Christ in its fulness, though in different ways corresponding to its different aspects.

2. The Efficacy of the Liturgical Signs Instituted by the Church

After having said that the efficacy of the sacraments derives above all and before all from the action itself (*ex opere operato*), the encyclical *Mediator Dei* goes on to say that the efficacy of the rites instituted by the Church "is due rather to the action of the Church (*ex opere operantis Ecclesiae*), in as much as she is holy and acts always in closest union with her Head."

It says "is due *rather* (*potius*) to the action of the Church" because the efficacy does not depend exclusively on that action. In the first place, God has regard, in the bestowal of His graces, to the holiness of the minister and of the subject. Besides, it is a common opinion of the theologians that certain effects of these rites are obtained infallibly from the fact that the rite is performed, and therefore in virtue of an efficacy analogous to the efficacy *ex opere operato*.

The first of these effects obtained outright at the moment the rites are performed or the prayers recited in conformity with the Church's prescriptions is the Church's prayer itself. This is just what the liturgical signs instituted by the Church have as their immediate aim to signify. Thus, the Divine Office celebrated by priests or religious delegated to this office will always be the prayer of the Church, whatever be the moral worth of the officiants.

Another infallible effect of the rites instituted by the Church is the consecration of persons or of things through the sacramentals established for this purpose. A religious profession, the consecration of a virgin, the consecration of a church or an altar obtain their effect with certainty as soon as they fulfill the conditions of validity.

As to the other effects of the rites instituted by the Church — actual graces of all kinds, protection against the devil, temporal graces ordained to the spiritual welfare — God grants them out of regard for the prayer which the Church addresses to Him in these rites, out of regard for the Church's action. It is the first time, if I am not mistaken, that an official document of the *magisterium* has recourse explicitly to this notion of the *opus operantis Ecclesiae*.[12] We must find out what is the nature of this efficacy, and then what is its basis.

---

[12] The expression is a recent one, but the idea is already encountered in St. Thomas (*Summa*, II-II, q. 83, a. 12; III, q. 82, a. 6), who distinguishes the action of the minister "in the person of Christ" and "in the person of the Church."

Nature of the efficacy *ex opere operantis Ecclesiae*

When we speak of efficacy *ex opere operantis* in general, as opposed to the efficacy *ex opere operato*, we mean that the action of God in conferring grace is not connected simply with the valid performance of the rite but also with the holiness of the minister and of the subject.

This does not mean that the effect produced is due solely to the holiness of the *operans*. As in the case of the sacraments, it is God alone who remains the principal cause of the grace. But the giving of this grace is proportioned to the holiness of the *operans*, or more exactly to the holiness of his action. His action, therefore, exercises a moral causality under the form of impetration, satisfaction or merit.

This *opus operantis* can be of different kinds. The distinction is generally made between *opus operantis* of the minister or of the subject, and *opus operantis* of the Church. It seems that we may achieve greater precision by distinguishing first of all between *opus operantis* of the minister or of the subject in the Church and *opus operantis* of the Church herself, and then distinguishing in the latter between liturgical (that is, public and official) *opus operantis* and non-liturgical (public but not official) *opus operantis*.

This more precise analysis permits us to make two statements.

The first is that every *opus operantis* of a supernatural order takes place always in the Church. It is always the Church who acts, and no action has any supernatural value without real and present union with the Church. And, in spite of this, there is a difference between the *opus operantis* of an individual or a group of individuals in the Church and the *opus operantis* of the Church herself.

The second statement is that the *opus operantis* of the Church is not always a liturgical *opus operantis*, even when its object consists in prayers or rites which are outwardly similar in all things to the liturgical prayers or rites. Thus, the solemn recitation of the rosary in a parish, under the pastor's direction, at the request of the hierarchy, seems to be really a public action of the Church and not merely the action of a group of the faithful in the Church; and the graces which it obtains from God are obtained *ex opere operantis Ecclesiae*. Yet it is not a liturgical action.

It must be admitted, then, that the nature and the efficacy of the *opus operantis Ecclesiae* are not the same within the liturgy and outside of the liturgy. When the faithful at the request of the hierarchy gather around their pastor to recite the rosary, it is certain that their prayer is already a prayer of the Church and a prayer of Christ Himself. For, if the Savior promised His disciples, "Wherever two or three are gathered in My name, I am in the midst of them," with so much the more reason is He present in an assembly called together by His representatives and presided over by them. Christ makes this public prayer of His members His own prayer, and it is understandable that, to account for its efficacy, the theologians have recourse to this notion of the *opus operantis Ecclesiae,* which is nothing but the *opus operantis* of Christ Himself, making His own this action organized and performed by His Church.

There is a difference, however, between *a* prayer of the Church and *the* prayer of the Church. There is a difference between the recitation of the rosary, even done at the request of the hierarchy, and the Church's official prayer, that liturgical prayer which she has instituted in the name of Christ and which in His name she addresses to the Father. It is in this liturgical prayer that the *opus operantis Ecclesiae* is exemplified in the highest degree.

Why do the sacraments act *ex opere operato* while the rites instituted by the Church act only *ex opere operantis Ecclesiae* ? In other words, why does God give grace infallibly in the sacraments without making it depend on the holiness of men, while in the rites instituted by the hierarchy He proportions His gifts to the holiness of the Church ? The only true answer is that God has so willed, His will being known to us by revelation, of which the Church is the depositary.

It is a fact that Christ has not given His Church the power to institute rites acting *ex opere operato* (except for certain effects which we have mentioned above). But He has given her the power to institute rites which, though performed by individuals, represent not only the prayer and the worship of those individuals but the prayer and the worship of the whole Church, body of Christ and spouse of Christ, and which derive their efficacy not only from the holiness of those individuals but from the holiness of the whole Church, body of Christ and spouse of Christ. We must now specify more exactly whence these rites derive their efficacy.

Basis of the efficacy *ex opere operantis Ecclesiae*

One might be tempted to ask whether there is really an essential difference between the efficacy of a liturgical rite performed officially by the Church and the efficacy of an exercise performed by a group of the faithful. Is it not merely a question of intensity, of quantity, the Church being the assembly of all the Christians and her sanctity the sum of all the individual sanctities ? If every prayer said by a Christian or a group of Christians is truly a prayer of the Church, what is the basis for that particular efficacy which is attributed to the Church's *official* prayer ?

That the idea of *opus operantis Ecclesiae* is correct from the theological point of view is proved by its official consecration by the *magisterium.* Besides, the same encyclical *Mediator Dei* says of the relations between liturgical prayer and private prayer, "Unquestionably liturgical prayer, being the public supplication of the illustrious spouse of Jesus Christ, is superior in excellence to private prayers." [13]

[13] N. 37. On the efficacy of the Church's prayer, surpassing that of private prayer, let us cite

If anyone does not see clearly the basis for this special dignity and efficacy of liturgical prayer, it is because he is forgetting that the Church is not like other societies, in which the power, even if it is of divine origin, belongs to the people as a whole, who delegate it to certain ones among their number.

The Church is not formed from below, but from above. It is the body of Christ before being the body of the Christians. To form it, Christ gathers men to Himself, transforming them inwardly by communicating His divine life to them. He makes some men His representatives with the rest, and He entrusts them with special powers of sanctification, of teaching and of governing, which make them indispensable mediators between their fellow men and God.

To consider the Church merely as the sum total of the Christians, therefore, would be to have a false idea of the Church. It involves a divine element which distinguishes it essentially from any other society. It has to have a hierarchy instituted from above and endowed with powers which are a participation in Christ's own powers.

The hierarchy by itself is not the Church, but no more are the faithful without the hierarchy the Church. The Church is that indissoluble whole, that body, which is made up of: Christ, who is its head; the hierarchy whom He has established and who represent Him; and the people who are united through the hierarchy to Christ the head. St. Cyprian expresses it perfectly: "They are the Church: the people united to the bishop and the flock gathered under its shepherd. Hence you should know that the bishop is in the Church and the Church in the bishop, and that if anyone is not with the bishop, he is not in the Church." [14]

Such is the idea of the Church which a person must get if he is to understand the extent to which the *opus operantis Ecclesiae* transcends the *opus operantis* of an isolated Christian or of a group of Christians.

Individual prayer is efficacious in the measure in which the one who offers it is united to the Church and to Christ; while liturgical prayer, whoever its officiants may be, is infallibly an action of the Church and thereby an action of Christ Himself. It owes its efficacy to the holiness of the Church, that holiness which the Church possesses not merely from its members but directly from its Head.

Is not this, after all, what the encyclical *Mediator Dei* gives us to understand when it says of the rites instituted by the hierarchy that their efficacy comes from the action of the Church "in as much as she is holy and acts always in closest union with her Head"?

this text of St. Ambrose: "Great is the Lord. The merit of some leads Him to forgive others; pleased with the former, He relieves the latter of their sins. Why do you deny your fellow man any influence over you, when the Lord grants a slave the right to intervene and to obtain what he asks for? . . . If you have no hope of pardon for grave sins, have recourse to those who pray, have recourse to the Church, who will plead for you. Out of regard for the Church, the Lord will grant you the forgiveness that He might have denied to you" (*In Luc.*, V, n. 11 [PL 15, 1638]).

[14] *Ep.* 66, 8 (PL 4, 406).

4

THE LITURGY AS A COMPLEXUS OF
EFFICACIOUS SIGNS OF THE CHURCH'S
SANCTIFICATION AND WORSHIP

We have defined the liturgy as the complexus of the efficacious signs of the Church's sanctification and worship. After having explained the notion of sign in the liturgy and that of efficacious sign, we have yet to explain the notion of sanctification and of worship in the liturgy. The concern here is with the proximate and specific end of the liturgy; the common and remote end being, as for everything else, the glory of God.

On God's part, this specific end is our sanctification, which, in as much as it is effected in us within the Church and as members of the Church, is the sanctification of the Church. On our part or on the part of the Church, the end is the public and official worship of God. Thus the liturgy is seen as the privileged place of encounter between God and man: under the veil of the signs, God descends toward man, and man rises to God.

1. Bond between Sanctification and Worship

In the concrete liturgical reality, the action of God in sanctifying and the response of the Church in rendering her worship are closely intertwined and cannot be completely separated, being the two correlative aspects of one and the same reality. The reason for this is the intimate compenetration of the divine action and the human response in the work of man's sanctification and of worship.

Actually the divine action in the work of sanctification can never be received by an adult in an inert and mechanical way, but only in a vital and free way. This acceptance, this consent imply the recognition of the divine excellence and of man's submission to God as something to which God has a right. Now such recognition is the very soul of worship. Hence the mere fact of receiving God's sanctifying action implies, in the adult, an act of worship.

Vice versa, any act of Christian worship, being a supernatural and meritorious work, is impossible for man without a profound sanctifying action of God in him, an action which gives, maintains or increases the state of grace and precedes, accompanies and follows the act of worship.

That is why St. Thomas, in connection with the sacraments, insists on the indivisibility of sanctification and worship. For him, the act of religion is performed "either by offering something to God or by receiving something divine," [1] and to receive the sacraments is an act of adoration.[2] In his whole treatise on the sacraments the fundamental principle of explanation is that the sacraments have been instituted for a twofold purpose : to sanctify man and to bring it about that he renders to God the worship due Him.[3] Now it is clear that this holds not only for the sacraments but for the whole of the liturgy.

Although these two aspects are inseparable, the one or the other may be brought out more clearly in one or another part of the liturgy.

Thus, it is evident that in the sacrament of penance the aspect of sanctification predominates. The same may be said of extreme unction if, as St. Thomas holds, its immediate purpose is to strengthen the sick person against that spiritual weakness which is a vestige of sin. Still, even in penance and extreme unction, the aspect of worship cannot be missed. The sinner in submitting to penance proclaims the sovereign majesty of God, His right to our subjection, and he subjects himself effectively to God; these are so many acts of worship. Moreover, it is with a view to participating in the Eucharistic sacrifice, highest expression of the Church's worship, that the sinner submits to penance.

One might make the same observation about many other elements of the liturgy — various sacramentals, exorcisms — in which the aspect of sanctification predominates.

In other parts of the liturgy, such as the Divine Office and the prayers with which the Church accompanies the administration of the sacraments and of the sacramentals, it is the aspect of worship that predominates.

The Eucharist, as sacrament and sacrifice, unites the two aspects in the highest degree. God's sanctification of men through Christ is realized in the highest degree in the Eucharist as sacrament, provided it is received with the proper dispositions. And the summit of the Church's worship of God in

[1] *Summa*, II-II, q. 81, a. 3 ad 2.   [3] III, q. 63, a. 6; cf. *ibid.*, a. 5.
[2] Cf. II-II, q. 89, prolog.

Christ is realized in the Eucharist as sacrifice. From this we can see how inadequate it would be to define the liturgy solely as worship.

This is not the place to dwell further on the aspect of sanctification in the liturgy. It is enough to recall that in Catholic doctrine the sanctification of man through the sacraments as instruments of grace is conceived as something very real, which transcends immeasurably the psychological level, the level of knowledge and of love, and goes to the very roots of man's being and activity.

Through sanctifying grace there is a true participation of the divine nature, even though this participation be accidental and mysterious. There is participation also in the Incarnation and there is configuration to Christ. And all this is procured for us by the indwelling of the divine Persons and will lead us to the glory of the beatific vision as its natural fulfilment.

As for the actual graces which it is the purpose of the rites instituted by the Church to obtain for us, in so far as they are sanctifying rites, these actual graces are directed to the recovery or the increase of sanctifying grace in us. This holds also for the graces of a temporal order which some of the rites instituted by the Church have the immediate end of obtaining for us from God, since the Church requests these temporal graces, and God grants them, only in so far as they can help us the better to achieve our salvation.

Finally, when the concern is with the sanctification of the body or of external objects, this sanctification is a protection or a divine acceptance of these things, for the spiritual good of those who possess them or use them with the proper dispositions.

2. Religion and "Devotio"

Worship is an expression of the virtue of religion. And an eminent fruit of the virtue of religion in general and of worship in particular is that disposition of soul which the ancients called *devotio*. We must clarify these two notions.

Religion

Following St. Thomas, who goes back through previous theologians to Cicero, scholastic theology relates the notion of religion to that of justice. Justice in turn is considered by the scholastics, heirs of the Greek tradition in this matter, in the scheme of the four cardinal virtues, not without hesitation, however, about the manner of defining it.[4]

Thus the virtue of religion is a form of justice: it makes us render to God what is due to Him in so far as He is the first principle, Creator, Governor and end of all things.[5] But as it is impossible for man to render to God quite

---

[4] On all this see Odon Lottin's *Psychologie et Morale aux XII° et XIII° siècles*, III (Louvain: Abbaye du Mont César, 1949), 313–326; "Vertu de religion et vertus théologales," *Dominican Studies*, 1 (1948), 212 ff.

[5] *Summa*, II-II, q. 81, a. 5.

strictly what is due Him, it is added that religion is not, properly speaking, a species of the genus justice, but only a virtue annexed to justice. This is what is meant by calling religion a "potential part" of justice.[6]

Recent theologians have questioned the incorporation of the virtue of religion into this Greek scheme of the four cardinal virtues. Both historical reasons (our better knowledge of the conditions under which this scheme originated and was accepted by the scholastic tradition) and theoretical reasons (relations of the virtue of religion with the moral and theological virtues) invite us to reconsider the question.[7]

Nevertheless, for our purpose it is not necessary to enter into the heart of the discussion, since all the authors are agreed on three fundamental points which are crucial to understanding the relation between liturgy and religion: 1) the general meaning of the virtue of religion in the Christian life as man's recognition of his deep debt to God the author of all existence; 2) the fact that the virtue of religion transcends the other moral virtues; 3) the fact that it is so closely connected to the theological virtues that these are like the matter which the virtue of religion uses — maintaining at the same time that the theological virtues are the source of the virtue of religion and that this virtue in its turn is an excellent soil for the development of the theological virtues.

Since being is one, it is a natural law that every effect returns in some way to its cause. The return to God takes place in all creatures. In man, it is achieved through the virtue of religion, in as much as man is a creature endowed with knowledge and conscience, capable of loving God, wholly dependent on Him in his existence and his activity. Man therefore knows this total dependence in which he finds himself. Faced with the majesty of God, he conceives necessarily a feeling of admiration, fear, respect and submission before this formidable Being who transcends him and overwhelms him; and this spontaneous movement is already an act of adoration.

Then, when he reflects on this sentiment which has sprung up in his soul, he consents to it with full freedom and makes it his response to that debt of dependence which he has recognized toward Him who is first principle and last end of all things. Understanding, moreover, that God is his sovereign good, he desires to possess Him, and asks Him to grant him all that is necessary in order to attain that end. He strives also to lead in his daily existence a life which will be conformed to the will of God.

All these dispositions of soul proceed from a single fundamental attitude, the total response of man to the strict debt which he feels he owes to God. This attitude is the religious attitude. We see how deeply it invades man's whole life and how it orients and accompanies all the other virtues in a given direction, that is, in the effort to satisfy, in the manner proper to man, his obligation to God.

[6] II-II, q. 80.
[7] Cf. Odon Lottin, *Morale fondamentale* (Tournai: Desclée, 1954), pp. 350–363 with bibliography.

For this reason all theologians, in comparing the virtue of religion with the other moral virtues, agree in giving it a super-eminent place.

Those who do accept the concept of religion as annexed to the cardinal virtue of justice do not fail to exalt it above the other moral virtues by saying that these other virtues regulate the acts which refer immediately to something created, while religion regulates the acts which refer directly and immediately to God in as much as we render Him that which is due Him as Creator of all things.[8]

As for the theologians who refuse to accept religion as annexed to justice, they appeal precisely to the transcendence of religion with relation to the other moral virtues, a transcendence which they hold is not sufficiently respected if religion is made a mere adjunct of justice.

Dom Lottin, who is one of their principal representatives, proposes the distribution of the moral virtues into five classes: 1) the virtues which regulate our behavior toward ourselves: temperance and fortitude; 2) those which regulate our behavior toward our equals: benevolence and justice; 3) those which regulate our behavior toward the creatures superior to us, such as parents, teachers, country: submission to authority; 4) the virtue which regulates our behavior toward God: religion; 5) the direction of the whole by right reason: prudence. Evident in this classification is the eminent place reserved to the virtue of religion: since it alone has God for its object, it is superior to all the others and thus marks the summit of the moral life.[9]

Just as all theologians agree in giving religion a preeminent place among the moral virtues, so they are equally in agreement when they affirm the close connection between religion and the theological virtues.

St. Thomas says that the theological virtues are those which have God Himself for their immediate object, and that this is the case only for faith, hope and charity, and not for religion. For, he says, religion does indeed have God as the *end* to which it refers its acts immediately and directly, and for this reason it is superior to the other moral virtues; but it does not have God for its immediate *object* as do the theological virtues.

He recognizes, however, that between the theological virtues and religion there is a very close and very special bond.

In the first place the theological virtues are the root which the supernatural virtue of religion presupposes; for we can honor God by a supernatural act of religion only if we believe that He is Creator, Governor and last end of all things, if we hope that He will accept our homage, and if by charity we conform our will to His. Thus the theological virtues and especially charity are the principle of religion: "by their command they cause the act of religion."[10]

---

[8] *Summa*, II-II, q. 81, a. 6.

[9] Odon Lottin, "La définition classique de la vertu de religion," *Eph. theol. lov.*, 24 (1948), 350.

[10] *Summa*, II-II, q. 81, a. 5 ad 1: "suo imperio causant actum religionis."

Further, St. Thomas recognizes with all the theologians that religion is also a general virtue which makes use of all the other virtues, including the theological virtues, to fulfill itself, offering the acts of these other virtues as homage to God. Thus all the other virtues are like the matter of which the virtue of religion makes use.[11]

There are even theologians who claim that religion is so close to the theological virtues that it might be counted among them, at least on the theoretical level,[12] or even be considered as the synthesis of them.[13]

It can be seen that the control exercised over the whole Christian life by the virtue of religion is quantitatively and qualitatively most profound.

Beginning with a contemplative admiration of the excellence of God as Creator, Governor and end of the universe, religion arouses in the soul the reflective and free sentiment of complaisance and of reverential submission which is translated into interior adoration.

This disposition of the will, which is the soul of all worship, finds its natural expression outwardly in attitudes, gestures and words. The will, moreover, does not confine itself to mobilizing the exterior faculties; it commands also the intellect and the imagination, and even the whole person, which it places at the Creator's disposal. This is the interior sacrifice, supreme expression of religion of which the exterior sacrifices are but visible manifestations and for which the things offered outwardly are mere substitutes. The most perfect expression of this interior sacrifice is martyrdom, for which the religious life in all its forms and virginity consecrated to God are substitutes.

Thus the virtue of religion is the bond which unifies the whole moral life and even, when the concern is with the supernatural virtue of religion, the whole supernatural life of the Christian.[14]

Devotio

Among the acts of the virtue of religion St. Thomas studies prayer and *devotio* in a special way.

The notion of *devotio,* which occupies an important place in the liturgy, corresponds to something much more profound than what is commonly called "devotion" or "a devotion" today. "*Devotio,*" says St. Thomas, "is derived from *devovere*" (to devote oneself to, to give oneself entirely to, even unto death); "therefore those are called *devoti* who in some way devote themselves to God so as to be entirely subject to Him. For this reason the pagans in ancient times called those people *devoti* who vowed to their idols to suffer

[11] *In Boeth. de Trin.,* lect 1, q. 1, a. 2; in Mandonnet edition, q. 3, a. 2, near the end.

[12] R. Hourcade, "La vertu de religion," *Bulletin de litt. eccl. de Toulouse,* 1944, pp. 181–219.

[13] A. Martinet, *Institutionum theologicarum*

quarta pars seu theologia moralis (Paris, 1867), q. 355 (quoted by Lottin, *Morale fondamentale,* p. 354).

[14] Cf. Odon Lottin, *Morale fondamentale,* p. 362.

death for the safety of their army, as Titus Livius says (VIII, 9; X, 28) of the two Decii. Hence *devotio* is seen to be just this: a certain ready will to give oneself to whatever concerns the service of God." [15] "*Devotio* is an act of the will whereby a man offers himself to God to serve Him." [16]

Thus *devotio* is an attitude of the will by which it puts itself at God's service. Man vows himself to God by directing his own desires and wishes toward the sole aim of God's service, always ready to engage himself in whatever concerns God's honor. It is a calm and virile attitude of the will, the fruit of a reflective decision.

Devotio is, as it were, the fundamental psychological attitude which results from the virtue of religion and penetrates one's whole life, giving orientation and form to all the further activities in which this service is concretized.[17] It is like the soil in which worship buds and flowers.

3. The Sacramental Characters and Christian Worship

The Latin word for worship, *cultus*, comes from *colere*, "to care for, to cultivate." Worship, in the broadest sense, is veneration for a being, based on the sentiment of its excellence and of one's own inferiority and subjection in the face of that being. It is therefore, radically, an interior attitude, made up not only of admiration, esteem and honor but also of humility and submission.[18]

This attitude can be expressed in different acts; but there is properly an act of worship toward a being only if that being is the direct object of the act. Prayer is an act of worship, for it is addressed directly to God. But almsgiving, even if done for love of God, could not be called an act of worship except in a very broad sense.[19]

In the secular sphere, one may speak of worship or cult with regard to parents, rulers, the fatherland. In the religious sphere, all worship is addressed to God, for He alone possesses excellence and authority in fulness; creatures can be the object of veneration or cult only in so far as they participate in the life of God and thereby in His excellence and His authority. Thus the cult of the angels and the saints is addressed really to them, but does not stop at

---

[15] *Summa*, II-II, q. 82, a. 1 c.

[16] *Ibid.*, ad 1.

[17] Cf. J. Chatillon, article "Devotio," *Dict. de spir.*, IV, 702–716.

[18] Translator's note: The same meaning is found in the derivation of the English word "worship" from "worth-ship." The Oxford English Dictionary, which gives this derivation, also has the following definitions under "cult":

1) worship; reverential homage rendered to a divine being or beings (obsolete except as in sense 2);

2) a particular form or system of religious worship; especially in reference to its external rites and ceremonies;

3) by transference, devotion or homage to a particular person or thing, now especially as paid by a body of professed adherents or admirers.

Since the Italian *culto* has all these meanings, I shall render it by "worship" or "veneration" or "cult" as the context demands.

[19] On the Thomistic notion of worship cf. J. Lécuyer, "Réflexions sur la théologie du culte selon S. Thomas," *Rev. thomiste*, 55 (1955), 339 ff.

them; it rises necessarily to God Himself, the source of everything in them that makes them worthy of veneration.

In Christianity, worship is addressed not only to the God whose excellence and authority shine forth in creation, but very formally to the God whose excellence and authority have been manifested in Christ. It is Christ Himself, moreover, who inaugurated this Christian worship as head and Redeemer of the human race, and He continues to render it to God the Father in and through His Church. The Church's worship is nothing but a participation in our Lord's worship.

It is by the sacraments above all that the Christian community is enabled to unite itself to Christ's worship. When we study St. Thomas' theology of the sacraments, we find one of its major characteristics to be the intimate connection he establishes between sacraments and Christian worship. For him, the end of the sacraments is twofold: to sanctify man by cleansing him of sin and to fit him for Christian worship — not for just any worship, but for specifically Christian worship, that which Christ rendered to God and which is prolonged in the Church.[20]

Not all the sacraments have the same relation to worship. Three of them imprint a character, the end of which is precisely to empower for Christian worship: baptism and confirmation enable the subject to participate actively in the other sacraments and above all in the Eucharist, while holy orders confers the power of giving the sacraments to others.

If Christian worship is simply Christ's worship continued in His mystical body, the sacramental character which enables man to participate in Christ's worship is necessarily a participation in the priesthood of Christ.[21] Through the character which He imprints in the faithful, Christ makes them participants in His priesthood, or rather He exercises His own priesthood in them, just as the principal cause exercises its action by means of the instrument and the instrumental power which it imparts to the instrument.

In all the sacraments man shares in some way in Christ's priesthood, at least in so far as he shares in its effects and, by the very reception of the sacrament, performs an act of worship. But in the three sacraments which imprint a character, this participation is much more intimate and profound, because the character deputes a person to do or to receive actively something which is proper to the priesthood of Christ.

The character may be regarded, therefore, as a consecration, which separates from profane use and reserves for the use of the divine worship. "Man is sanctified through all the sacraments," writes St. Thomas, "in as much as sanctification involves purification from sin, which is effected through grace. But in a special way some sacraments, those which imprint the character, sanctify man by a certain consecration, deputing him for the divine worship;

---

[20] *Summa*, III, q. 62, a. 5.   [21] *Summa*, III, q. 63, a. 3.

just as we say also of inanimate objects that they are sanctified by being designated for the divine worship." [22]

In connection with the sacramental character, therefore, St. Thomas presents a grand synthesizing perspective from which the whole sacramental economy appears as ordained first of all to the Christian worship of God, and as prolonging in us the worship rendered to God by Christ. The other essential end of the sacraments, which is our sanctification, is itself ordained to worship. This fact must be underlined, for it is often misunderstood: In the liturgy the sanctification of man is ordained to the adoration and the glorification of God, and not vice versa. The two inseparable ends of the liturgy are not two parallel or independent aims, but one subordinated to the other: sanctification looks to worship.

It is evident that the whole sacramental economy and the whole liturgy receive from this fact a strongly theocentric color: in the liturgy everything, including the sanctification of man, is ordained to the homage to be given to God.

There is all the more reason to consider as strictly subordinate to the end of adoration and worship everything in the liturgy that has the immediate purpose of admonishing and instructing, such as readings and preaching. The didactic and moralizing aim of the liturgy is subordinate to the aim of worship. Hence this didactic and moralizing aspect must always be regulated in such a way that the end to which it is finally ordained is never lost sight of.

If we consider further that the sacraments and, with more reason, the whole liturgy instituted by the Church, are ordained to the Eucharist, as St. Thomas teaches and as we shall explain later on, we can understand how the whole work of sanctification, and *a fortiori* the whole work of teaching and governing in the Church, is ordained to the worship of God in the Mass. Thus we get some idea, once more, of how everything in the liturgy and in the Christian life, theocentrically conceived and lived, has for its center the Eucharistic sacrifice.

Moreover, with this doctrine of the sacramental character, the whole system of sanctification and worship appears solidly founded on the priesthood of Christ and on the worship rendered to God by Christ, as well as on its present participation and extension to the whole Church, especially to the hierarchy through the character of holy orders, but also to every one of the faithful through the characters of baptism and of confirmation.

Hence comes the peculiar value of Christian worship, prolongation and participation of Christ's worship of God, without parallel in anything that man could ever think of or achieve. We can see how far are philosophy, history of religions or religious psychology, left to their own resources, from being able even to suspect such depths, and how superficial is the idea which these sciences can form of Christian worship by their own lights alone.[23]

---

[22] *Summa*, III, q. 63, a. 6 ad 2.   [23] That is why the Catholic theologian,

We can see also how only he who is signed with the baptismal character is capable of a Christian worship and can take a real part in the liturgy, especially in the sacrifice of the Mass. This explains the ancient discipline which did not admit the unbaptized even to mere attendance at Mass.

4. The Christian Priesthood and the Priesthood of All the Faithful

The doctrine of the sacramental character as "character of Christ, to whose priesthood the faithful are configured according to the sacramental characters, which are nothing but certain participations in the priesthood of Christ, derived from Christ Himself" [24] — this doctrine gives its exact meaning, neither exaggerated nor minimized, to the notion of the universal priesthood of the faithful, and thus enables us to understand in what consists their active participation in the liturgical action and especially in the Mass.

The problem

Some decades ago the question of the universal priesthood of the faithful once more claimed the attention of the theologians, who since then have studied it in the Scripture and in the patristic, liturgical and theological tradition.[25] There are two incentives for this study : the liturgical renewal, bringing about a desire to understand better the active role of the faithful in the liturgy and to give it practical value; and the efforts to state precisely the function of the laity in the Church.

All research in this matter must start out from this fact : The Scripture, the patristic and liturgical tradition, as well as the medieval and modern theologians, attribute to all the faithful the character of *priests* and employ the term *sacrifice* in connection with a certain number of actions or situations : prayer, mortification, virginity and the monastic life, martyrdom, fulfilment of the duties of one's state in life, the apostolic ministry, the teaching of doctrine, participation in the Eucharistic sacrifice, the fact that the husband and wife administer the sacrament of matrimony to themselves, the life of fathers and mothers of families, the administration of certain sacramentals, Catholic Action. Besides this, there are many general statements on the existence of a special kind of priesthood which belongs to all the faithful.

All these aspects have been made explicit in the history of theology not at one

---

though finding interesting observations of religious psychology in the studies devoted to Christian worship by non-Catholic authors such as William James, Petazzoni, Jung, Otto, cannot help noticing how superficial those studies are. The observation is still more valid for the works of modernists like Tyrell and Bonaiuti.

[24] St. Thomas, *Summa*, III, q. 63, a. 3.

[25] The most recent study and the best from the theological point of view is that of Yves Congar, *Lay People in the Church: A Study for a Theology of the Laity* (Westminster, Md.: Newman Press, 1957), pp. 112-257. Also worth consulting are: P. Dabin, *Le sacerdoce royal des fidèles dans la tradition ancienne et moderne* (Paris: Desclée, De Brouwer & Cie, 1950); Joseph Lécuyer, "Essai sur le sacerdoce des fidèles chez les Pères," *La maison Dieu, 27* (1951-53), 7-50.

time, but successively. The great stages of this development can be summed up in the following way.

Already found in the Scripture is the general and explicit affirmation of a priesthood of all the Christians: 1 Pet. 2:4–10; Apoc. 1:5–6; 5:9–10; 20:6. To these texts which use the word "priesthood" itself with reference to all the faithful must be added those in which it is said that now, in Christ, we draw near (προσέρχομαι) to God: Heb. 4:14–16; 7:19; 10:19–22; or that in Christ we have access (προσάγω) to God: Eph. 2:18–22 (cf. Eph. 3:12; Rom. 5:2; 1 Pet. 3:18). This idea of drawing near and of having access has indisputably a meaning of priestly worship: one draws near to God to perform an act of worship, and it is mostly the priests who draw near and have access to God.[26] Finally, the Scripture affirms explicitly that the faithful offer worship and sacrifice to God: Phil. 3:3 (worship in general); Phil. 4:18 (sacrifice as financial aid to the missionaries); Rom. 12:1 (sacrifice of their own bodies; cf. Phil. 2:17; 2 Tim. 4;6); Heb. 13:15–16 (sacrifice of praise and of fraternal charity); Rom. 15:16 (St Paul offering in sacrifice the gentiles as fruit of his own apostolate).

Besides the points already expressed directly in the Scripture, patristic tradition develops especially the ideas of sacrifice and priesthood in martyrdom and virginity; we find explicit also the thought that there is a sacrifice and a priesthood in preaching and in the role of fathers and mothers of families.[27]

The Middle Ages dwell on the Eucharistic priesthood and sacrifice of the layman, with reference to the sacramental characters of baptism and of confirmation. Finally, the ideas of sacrifice and priesthood in the administration of matrimony, in the use of the sacramentals and in Catholic Action have been brought out by the modern theologians.

The question posed by these data of the Scripture and of the patristic and theological tradition is: how to group them in a system of general explanation of the priesthood common to all the faithful. What will be the theological principle of explanation of all this matter?

The attempts made have been many and various. We shall pass over the clearly heretical deviations which, from Tertullian to Luther, abolish any essential distinction between the hierarchical priesthood and that of the faithful. Among the Catholics the opinion ranges from the minimist position, which understands the priesthood of the faithful in a purely metaphorical or even equivocal sense, to the positions which so exalt the reality of the priesthood common to all the faithful that they risk sometimes blurring the essential distinction between this and the hierarchical priesthood; hence the warnings of *Mediator Dei*.[28]

---

[26] Cf. in the Septuagint: Ex. 29:10; Lev. 4:14; 7:6; Num. 18:2–7; Jer. 7:16; and also 1 *Clem.*, 31, 3; *Ad Diog.*, 3, 2. The theme has been studied by Karl L. Schmidt, article προσάγω in *Theol. Wört. zum NT*, I, 131–134; and Johannes Schneider, article προσέρχομαι, *ibid.*, II, 680–682.

[27] Cf. the works of P. Dabin and Joseph Lécuyer cited above, note 25.

[28] Nn. 82–84 (Lat. 81–83).

Attempt at systematization

Taking account of the suggestions proposed recently by theologians, we have drawn up an outline in which we have tried to arrange in order the different degrees of participation in Christ's priesthood, both in the hierarchical priesthood and in that which is common to all the Christians.

PRIESTHOOD OF CHRIST

in itself;

shared with the Christians:

I. Through the character of holy orders
(hierarchical priesthood)

A. To offer in Christ's name the Eucharistic sacrifice in itself;

B. To offer it in its presuppositions and consequences:

1. *With regard to the faithful:*
   a. In the presuppositions and consequences of a liturgical nature:
      1) Administration of the other sacraments;
      2) Institution and use of the sacramentals, ceremonies and prayers.
   b. In the presuppositions and consequences of an extraliturgical nature:
      1) Governing of the Church;
      2) Teaching of doctrine.

2. *With regard to unbelievers*: missionary apostolate.

II. Through the character of baptism and confirmation
(priesthood of all the faithful)

A. To participate actively in the Eucharistic sacrifice;

B. To participate in it in its presuppositions and consequences:

1. *Of a liturgical nature:*
   a. Sacramental:
      1) To receive penance, extreme unction and holy orders;
      2) To administer to themselves and to live Christian matrimony.
   b. Non-sacramental:
      1) To receive the sacramentals and to administer some of them;
      2) To take part in liturgical prayer.

2. *Of an extraliturgical nature:*
   a. Holiness of life:
      1) Mortification;
      2) Virginity and religious life;
      3) Duties of one's state;
      4) Practice of charity toward the neighbor;
      5) Private prayer.
   b. Apostolate, especially in Catholic Action.
   c. Confession of one's faith, even unto death if the occasion arises.

A series of annotations will serve to explain the meaning of the outline.

On the notion of priesthood

The first question which gives rise to different opinions among the theologians about the priesthood of the faithful is the very notion of priesthood. Is the note of mediation essential to the concept of priesthood, so that if there is no mediation there is no priesthood either? In that case the priesthood of the faithful would be without any analogy with that of Christ or of the heirarchy, since it lacks the note of mediation.[29]

Now the Scripture, when it speaks of the priesthood of all the faithful, certainly intends to point out an analogy between this priesthood and that of the Old Testament. The analogy consists in the offering of victims and therefore of sacrifice: "You also, as living stones, are built up as a spiritual edifice in view of a holy priesthood, to offer spiritual victims,[30] acceptable to God through Jesus Christ" (1 Pet. 2 :5).

A relation is therefore established between the priesthood of the faithful and the offering of victims, and therein is found the term of comparison with the priesthood of the old alliance: the faithful of the New Testament are all priests, analogously to the priests of the Old Testament, because they also offer victims.[31] The priesthood of the faithful is therefore defined not in relation to a mediating action but in relation to the offering of victims in sacrifice.

On the idea of sacrifice

But what is the precise notion of sacrifice that must be adopted? This question too is debated among the theologians. It can be said that sacrifice, in the broadest sense, consists in placing something at the complete disposal — to the point of total destruction if necessary — of a person or of another object, in recognition of the superiority of the latter over the former. Thus, we can speak of sacrificing a sum of money to something or someone, sacrificing our career or our reputation, sacrificing a person or an animal.

The idea of sacrifice includes necessarily: 1) the idea of offering, of putting something at someone's disposal; 2) the idea of destruction, at least contingent, of the thing offered: agreed to in advance by the offerer, the destruction may not really take place after all; 3) the idea of acknowledging the superiority of the thing or person to whom sacrifice is offered.

In religious sacrifice, man sacrifices to the divinity his own person or some

---

[29] At most, one might speak of the mediation which the layman exercises by his prayer of praise and of intercession between God on the one hand, other men and infrahuman creatures on the other hand. But it does not seem that the Scripture or even tradition has any such priesthood in mind.

[30] In Greek, πνευματικὰς θυσίας. We know that θυσία is the word used by the Septuagint to designate the victim offered in sacrifice.

[31] The text of Heb. 5:1, which puts the idea of mediation in the foreground, does not purport to be a definition of the priesthood in general, but speaks of the high priesthood of the line of Aaron: "Every high priest, in fact, who is raised up from among men, is ordained for the advantage of men in their relations with God, that he may offer gifts and sacrifices for sins."

of his goods, to acknowledge the sovereign dominion of the divinity. If it is goods that are offered, they represent and include in some way the life and the very person of the offerer. Otherwise there would not be a real acknowledgment of the superiority and the dominion of the divinity, since this dominion obviously extends to the offerer's life and personality. One who would intend to exclude this acknowledgment from the sacrificial act would offer an offense to the divinity rather than a sacrifice.

Thus other things can be matter of religious sacrifice only because they have some relation to the person. Either they symbolize him, or they are an effect or manifestation of him, or they belong to him. It may happen, on the other hand, that the sacrifice remains wholly interior, involving only the act of will, the gift of self, which is its essential element.

On the priesthood of Christ

Christ is our Head and our Mediator by the free will of God, who established His solidarity with us and our solidarity with Him. His priesthood and His sacrifice are therefore a priesthood and a sacrifice of Head and of Mediator.

Christ's sacrifice is formally the act of will by which, as responsible Head and Mediator of all mankind, from the very first moment of His existence, He has placed at God's disposal His own person, to the point of total destruction of His life, such being the Father's will, to acknowledge God's sovereign and absolute dominion over Himself and over all mankind.

Christ's sacrifice, and therefore His priesthood, extends to His whole life, because He offered His sacrifice from the very first moment. All the acts of His life were sacrificial, because everything He did was offered by Him as matter of sacrifice. But these acts had sacrificial value only in reference to the sacrifice of His life itself.

This last was begun also at the Incarnation, but was completed only on the cross, in the effective destruction of the life offered in sacrifice. That is why all of Christ's sacrificial acts are connected to the death on the cross as the sacrificial and priestly act which gives them their meaning and their value.

The Last Supper was a sacrifice by its relation to the cross, of which it was a sacramental anticipation. Similarly, the Mass is a sacrifice by its relation to the cross, of which it is a sacramental reproduction. Hence in the Mass there is not only an oblation but also an effective immolation — though not a bloody one — as on Calvary. The mediation which the glorified Christ now exercises with the Father is also a priestly mediation in reference to the sacrifice of the cross. The cross therefore dominates the whole life of Christ, as it dominates the whole Church and all of history.

On the priesthood of the Christians

The priesthood and the sacrifice of the Christians, like those of the Old

Testament, are meaningful only by their reference to Christ's priesthood and sacrifice. They are a derivation and a participation of that priesthood and that sacrifice.

In other words, the concepts of Christian priesthood and sacrifice involve an analogy of attribution. They are applied first of all to the priesthood and the sacrifice of Christ Himself, and only derivatively to the priesthood and the sacrifice of the Christians; even then, they include Christ's priesthood and sacrifice.

It is in this perspective that it becomes possible to put in order the manifold forms assumed by the priesthood of the Christians, which are so many ways in which the one priesthood of Christ is exercised in them and by them.

In Christ Himself priesthood and sacrifice are realized in the first place on Calvary, and only derivatively in His whole life, at the Last Supper, at the Mass, in heaven.

Among the Christians priesthood and sacrifice mean primarily the hierarchical priesthood and the sacrifice of the Mass, and only derivatively and dependently on these, the priesthood common to all the faithful and other sacrifices outside of the Mass.

For the hierarchy priesthood and sacrifice are realized primarily in the Eucharistic celebration, and secondarily, as preparation or consequence, in the government of the Church, the teaching of doctrine, the apostolate to unbelievers, etc.

As to the laity, their priesthood and their sacrifice are realized primarily in their participation in the Eucharist, and only secondarily in their holiness of life, in martyrdom, in apostolic action, in as much as all this is presupposition or consequence of their participation in the Eucharist.

Just as it is on the cross especially that Christ is priest, so it is principally in the Mass that the hierarchical ministers and the laity exercise their priesthood.

On the nature of the hierarchical priesthood and its distinction from the priesthood common to all the faithful

Like all Christian priesthood, the hierarchical priesthood is a participation in that of Christ, but a participation which differs essentially, in nature as well as in degree, from the participation common to all the faithful. It is based on a special sacrament and a special character : holy orders.

In the exercise of his priesthood the hierarchical minister acts as representative and as direct and special instrument of Christ. This is what we mean by saying that he acts directly "in the person of Christ" and not directly "in the person of the faithful." He represents the faithful only in as much as he represents directly Christ, Head of the Church, Head of that body which is inseparable from Him.

Such is the doctrine inculcated vigorously by *Mediator Dei* against some ambiguous tendencies and expressions : "But we deem it necessary to recall that the priest acts for the people only because he represents Jesus Christ, who is Head of all His members and offers Himself in their stead. Hence he goes to the altar as the minister of Christ, inferior to Christ but superior to the people." [32] "The unbloody immolation at the words of consecration, when Christ is made present upon the altar in the state of a victim, is performed by the priest and by him alone, as the representative of Christ and not as the representative of the faithful." [33]

Among the laity there is no priesthood and sacrifice except in dependence on and union with the hierarchical priesthood, and with the hierarchical priesthood exercised in the celebration of the Eucharistic sacrifice. In fact, the priesthood of the faithful has for its center their participation in the Mass, a participation which involves dependence on and union with the priesthood which Christ exercises in the Mass by means of the hierarchical priesthood.

The faithful in the Mass, by virtue of their baptismal character, play a priestly role, in as much as they offer as their own sacrifice, including in it the gift of themselves, the sacrifice which Christ offers by the hands of the priest. Although only the priest is the instrument of Christ for the consecration of the bread and wine, still all the faithful present, with him and through him, and thus with and through Christ, offer the Victim of the Mass, and, by participating in the Mass, above all by communion, they perform an act truly sacrificial and priestly, although this act is only analogous to the specific act of the hierarchical priesthood.[34]

The believer makes the Eucharistic sacrifice his own only in so far as, together with the priest, he offers his own life; for only the offerer's life is the matter of the sacrifice offered to God. If the believer completely excluded this total offering of himself from the Mass, he would not be participating in the sacrifice in any way. The more conscious, real and perfect is this offering, the more real and perfect is his participation in the Mass.[35]

Thus the Christian priesthood and sacrifice, the various forms of which are shown by the Scripture, the Fathers and the theologians, are analogical concepts. The hierarchical priesthood, being a mere instrument of Christ's priesthood, is reduced entirely to the same genus and the same species as Christ's priesthood. Between the priesthood of the faithful and that of Christ there is an analogy of proper proportionality, and at the same time an analogy of attribution. For in both cases the priesthood means the power to offer one's own life in witness of God's sovereignty; on the other hand, the priesthood of the faithful depends on that of Christ as on a first analogate, because after Adam's sin no man has had the power to offer himself to God except in reference to the sacrifice of Christ. Finally, between the priesthood of the hierarchy and that of the faithful there is only an analogy of attribution, in as much as the latter is the effect of the former.

---

[32] N. 84 (Lat. 83).
[33] N. 92 (Lat. 91).

[34] Cf. *Mediator Dei*, n. 93 (Lat. 92).
[35] Cf. *ibid.*, nn. 98–104 (Lat. 97–103).

5 THE MASS AS CENTER AND

SYNTHESIS OF THE WHOLE LITURGY

In the preceding chapters we have tried to explain what the liturgy is, by putting it into its natural setting, which is the history of salvation. It has appeared to us then as that complexus of efficacious signs under the veil of which the mystery of Christ is realized for us from Pentecost to the parousia, with its two aspects of sanctification and worship.

At this point, in order to give a sort of confirmation of the accuracy and the fruitfulness of this notion of the liturgy, we would like to apply it to the Mass and show thereby that the Mass is the center and the synthesis of the whole liturgy.

Actually every Mass realizes in a sort of foreshortened way the whole object of the liturgy, and the other rites are only preparations for, or consequences of, this essential act; they simply bring to light one or another aspect of the unique mystery which every Mass expresses and fulfils in its entirety.

The fulness of the Mass comes from the fact that it is a sacrament and a sacrifice at the same time.

It is the sacrament which contains and communicates Christ in person, Author of all sanctification as God, and Mediator of all sanctification as Man.

As a sacrifice, the Mass is Christ's own sacrifice of Himself, source and type of all worship rendered to God by men. Christ offers this sacrifice to God through the ministry of the priest; and the Church makes it her own, as the highest expression of her worship, in as much as she offers it with the priest just as Christ does, and offers herself in sacrifice with Him.

Thus the Mass realizes to the maximum the sanctification of the Church by God in Christ and the worship rendered to God by the Church in Christ, in other words the whole aim of the liturgy. The Mass is the first and the greatest of the rites in which the encounter between man and God is effected from Pentecost until the parousia.

1. The Fourfold Dimension of the Liturgical Signs in the Mass

In the Mass better than in any other liturgical function the sign expresses and produces the realities which it signifies.

The Mass is first of all a sign demonstrative of Christ Himself, who is present in person and not only in power under the "figure" of bread and wine. It also manifests and realizes to the highest degree the union between God and man in Christ, because it establishes between Christ and the communicant a union which is not merely moral but primarily sacramental. It is also in the Mass that the union among the members of Christ reaches its highest point, because here all communicate in a single principle of spiritual life by eating the same bread and drinking of the same chalice.

At the same time the Mass signifies and realizes our worship better than any other liturgical act, since sacrifice is the highest expression of worship, and Christ's sacrifice on the cross, reproduced sacramentally in the Mass, is the source and the type of all Christian worship and sacrifice. It is especially through the communion that Christ unites all the faithful to His sacrifice. Together with the priest, in fact together with Christ Himself, the faithful offer the sacred Victim to the Father, thus making Christ's sacrifice their own, giving their whole life a sense of sacrificial worship of the Father in Christ, and exercising to the full the priestly power they have received in baptism.

The Mass is likewise the greatest obligating sign of the whole liturgy by the fact that it is the greatest and the most efficacious of the signs of the sanctification which man freely receives and of the worship which he freely renders to God. Among all Christian acts, the Mass is *par excellence* the new alliance in the blood of Christ. He who takes part in the Mass, especially by communion, accepts this pact and ratifies it. And a pact involves an obligation.

This was what made St. Paul say, "You cannot drink the cup of the Lord and the cup of demons; you cannot partake of the table of the Lord and the table of demons" (1 Cor. 10:21). And he adds, "Whoever eats this bread and drinks the blood of the Lord unworthily shall be guilty of the body and blood of the Lord. Let each one examine himself, therefore, and thus let him eat the bread and drink the cup. For whoever eats and drinks, eats and drinks to his own condemnation if he does not recognize the Body."[1]

---

[1] 1 Cor. 11:27 f. The first Christians were vividly aware of the obligation inherent in every act of worship and especially in the Eucharist. We have evidence of this, for ex-

The Mass has the same supreme value as sign commemorative of past realities, for it is nothing but the sacrifice of the cross renewed in a sacramental way. Thus there are actualized in the highest degree the priesthood of Christ and the worship rendered by Christ during His mortal life, and also all the sacrifices, all the acts of sanctification and of worship prior to the Incarnation, which were but figures of the sacrifice of Calvary, now renewed *in mysterio*.

Thus the sacred reality which is fulfilled in every Mass is really the terminus of an immense number of lines of force which were converging toward it from the beginning of creation as their realization and their reason for being. For the whole of the Old Testament was a preparation and a sketch which would find its fulfilment in Christ's earthly life; and Christ's earthly life, in its turn, would take on its whole meaning only as the source of the divine life in men. But it is chiefly in the Mass that Christ communicates His divine life to us. Therefore what is fulfilled in the Mass is the point of convergence of the whole previous history, since this, in the designs of God, was directed toward the historical Calvary, while the historical Calvary tended toward the mystical Calvary of the Mass.

As a sign portending the future, and therefore as a prophetic action, the Mass likewise holds first place in the liturgy. In the Mass, under the veil of signs, there is a new epiphany of the incarnate Word in person, of the Word made flesh, immolated, raised up, glorified. It is already the Lord's return, but in figure and not in a visible and glorious form. The Mass is already the banquet of messianic times awaited by the Old Testament, but not yet in its glorious form.

And it is for this reason that a profoundly eschatological meaning is inherent in the Mass: it announces, proclaims and calls out, with every fiber of its being, the glorious return of the Lord and the banquet in the Father's kingdom, because an action veiled under symbols tends with its whole weight toward the reality which is unveiled and without symbols. Hence "every time you eat of this bread and drink this cup, you are proclaiming the Lord's death until He comes" (1 Cor. 11:26).

The simple fact of participating in the Eucharistic body and in the Lord's blood is a way of proclaiming before the world the redemptive death of the

ample, in the famous letter in which Pliny the Younger, governor of Bithynia, informs Trajan about the liturgical gatherings — most likely Eucharistic assemblies — of the Christians: "And they asserted that this had been the whole of their guilt or error, that it was their custom to assemble before sunrise on a fixed day and in antiphonal style to sing a hymn to Christ as to a god, and *to bind themselves by a sacramentum* not to any crime, but that they would not commit any fraud, theft or adultery, that they would not deceive, that they would not deny a trust when called upon to deliver

it up" (cf. Loeb Classical Library ed., book 10, letter 96). In the same way Hippolytus in the *Apostolic Tradition*, 23, after having spoken of the participation in the Eucharist, last act of the Christian initiation, adds, "And when these things have been accomplished, let each one be zealous to perform good works and to please God, living righteously, devoting himself to the Church, performing the things which he has learnt, advancing in the service of God" (ed. Gregory Dix [New York: Macmillan, 1937], p. 42).

Lord who is now glorious but hidden. This sacramental proclamation of Christ's death is proper to this intermediate time between the Ascension and the parousia : " . . . until He comes."

At the parousia, when the Lord presents Himself to the world in all His glory, the Eucharist will come to an end. For the mystery ceases when the reality it was proclaiming under veils is fulfilled and appears in full light. Then the messianic banquet will continue without veils.

This eschatological significance of the Mass was felt strongly by the first Christians. This is the sense of the prayer of thanksgiving after the Eucharist reported by the *Didache* : "Remember, Lord, Your Church, deliver it from all evil and make it perfect in Your love, and gather it from the four winds, sanctified, for Your kingdom, which You have prepared for it. . . . Let grace come, and let this world pass away. . . . Maranatha : Come, Lord, So be it."[2]

Thus the Mass is that one out of all the liturgical functions which expresses and realizes in the highest degree the Church's sanctification and worship. At the same time it is the place in which all the phases of the history of salvation and of the mystery of Christ converge for us : the past here finds its fulfilment, the present is here realized in a plenary way, and the future is here announced and prepared for. We see the whole rich symbolism expressed in this wonderful antiphon :

> "O sacred banquet, in which Christ is consumed,
> the memory of His Passion is renewed,
> the mind is filled with grace,
> and a pledge of future glory is given us!"

2. The Fourfold Dimension of the Mass according to the Anaphoras

The idea that the Mass is for us the summing up of the whole history of salvation and of the whole mystery of Christ is always found more or less explicit in that central part of the Mass which is called anaphora or canon. The anaphoral formulas are very diverse in the different Christian liturgies. All, at any rate, take the form of a prayer of thanksgiving, a "eucharist" addressed to the Father to thank Him for the benefits He has granted us, chiefly through the mediation of Christ. The mystery of Christ, center of the history of salvation, is always recalled in the anaphora with more or less detail.

All, or almost all, of the known formulas recall explicitly the mystery of Christ in its phase of historical realization, that is, the great events of our Lord's life, at least from the Last Supper — and here the words of the institution of the Eucharist are inserted — to the Ascension.

In the mention of the other stages of the mystery of Christ there is great

---

[2] 10 :5 f. In a Coptic papyrus, probably from the fifth century, *Maranatha* is translated "The Lord came." Cf. G. Horner, "The New Papyrus Fragment of the Didache in Coptic," *Journal of Theological Studies* (1924), p. 230.

variety from one anaphora to another : sometimes a simple allusion, sometimes a long development; again, they are merely implied in a generic term expressing the whole mystery of Christ as it is realized in the Mass.

The most ancient text of an anaphora that has been preserved is that of the *Apostolic Tradition* of Hippolytus. This is perhaps rather an outline than a fully developed anaphora. At any rate, the text is conspicuous for its sobriety. Hardly an allusion can be found in it to the creation and to the old economy which prepared for the new. Yet we know, from Justin[3] among others, that these two themes were common in antiquity. Actually the Eastern anaphoras have remained more faithful to the original plan than the Western.

The Eastern anaphoras

In the East, it is especially from the fourth century on that the anaphoras become more numerous and fully developed. It must be recognized that some of them indulge in a prolixity which emphasizes still further their contrast with the Roman sobriety. But, on the whole, compared with the present Roman canon, they have two advantages : first, they are constructed according to a logical, coherent plan; second, they preserve and develop, harmoniously for the most part, all the great themes of the traditional Eucharistic prayer. Thus it is to these Eastern anaphoras that we must turn by preference to see how the liturgy itself expresses in its texts the fourfold dimension of the Mass.

We give here, with its divisions and connections marked, the central part of the Greek anaphora of St. Basil, in which the traditional plan of the Eucharistic prayer appears very clearly.[4]

" . . . Together with these blessed legions, O loving Master, we sinners too cry out and say : Truly holy and all holy are You, and there is no measure to the greatness of Your holiness. You are holy in all Your works, for whatever You do to us is done with justice under a rightful sentence.

God's plan

"Having formed man from the slime of the earth and honored him with Your likeness, You set him down in a paradise of delights, promising him immortality and the enjoyment of eternal goods if he had observed Your commandments.

Frustration of this plan

"But he disobeyed You, true God who had created him, succumbed to the serpent's guile and made himself subject to death by his own transgressions. And You, O God, by a just sentence, drove him out of paradise into this world and made him return to the earth from which he had been taken ;

---

[3] *Dialogue with Trypho*, 41 (PG 6, 564).
[4] Ἱερατικόν (Rome, 1950), pp. 191–195, 196–197, 203, 204.

Promise of a Redeemer

"But You graciously disposed that by means of a new birth he should obtain salvation again, salvation in Your Christ.

Resumption of God's plan

"For You, benign Creator, did not reject Your creature forever, You did not forget the work of Your hands, but in Your mercy You visited him in many ways.

1. *Preparation in the Old Testament.* "You sent the prophets; You worked wonders by means of the saints who were pleasing to You in every generation; You spoke to us by the mouth of Your servants the prophets, telling us of the salvation to come; You gave us the Law to help us; You assigned the angels to us as guardians.

2. *Realization in the life of Christ.* "Then, when the fulness of time had come, You spoke to us in Your own Son, by whom You created the world. He, being the brightness of Your glory and the express image of Your substance, and upholding all things by the word of His power, did not think it a thing to be held to, to be equal to You, God and Father;

— *Incarnation.* "But, while remaining eternal God, appeared on this earth and lived among men, and, having taken flesh from the Virgin, lowered Himself, taking the form of a slave, made in all things similar to the body of our lowliness, in order to conform us to the image of His glory. For since through a man sin had come into this world and, through sin, death, Your only-begotten Son, who is in the bosom of You, God the Father, being born of a woman, the holy Mother of God and ever Virgin Mary, born under the Law, saw fit to condemn sin in His own flesh, that those who had died in Adam should be brought to life in Him, Your Christ.

— *Teaching.* "Having become a citizen of this world, He gave us the precepts of salvation, set us free from the seductions of idols and brought us to know You, true God and Father, acquiring us for Himself as a chosen people, a royal priesthood, a holy nation;

— *Passion.* "and, purifying us in water and sanctifying us in the Holy Spirit, He gave Himself in our place to the death into whose power we had been sold because of sin.

— *Resurrection.* "But, having descended, through the cross, into hell, that He might fulfill all things in Himself, He undid the painful bonds of death, and arose on the third day, opening to all flesh the way of the resurrection from the dead. Since it was impossible that the Author of life should be overcome by corruption, He became the first fruit of the dead, the first-born among the dead, that He might hold the first place in all things.

— *Ascension.* "Then, ascending into heaven, He sat at the right hand of Your majesty on high.

— *Parousia.* "And He will come again to render to each one according to his works.

3. *Sacramental fulfilment in the Eucharist.* "And He left us these memorials of His redemptive Passion which we have now offered You as He commanded us.

— *Institution and renewal.* "For, on the point of going to His voluntary, glorious and life-giving death, the night when He gave Himself for the life of the world, having taken bread into His holy and immaculate hands, and lifted it up to You, God and Father, He gave thanks, blessed it, sanctified it, broke it; gave it to His holy disciples and apostles, saying: Take, eat, this is My body, broken for you for the remission of sins." *People*: "Amen."

"In the same way, taking the cup of wine, having tempered it with water, He gave thanks, blessed it, sanctified it, gave it to His holy disciples and apostles, saying: Drink of it, all of you, this is My blood, the blood of the new alliance, shed for you and for many for the remission of sins." *People*: "Amen."

— *Memorial and pledge.* "Do this in commemoration of Me. For every time that you eat this bread and drink this cup, you are announcing My death and confessing My Resurrection.[5] We too, O Lord, calling to mind, therefore, Your saving Passion, the life-giving cross, the three days in the tomb, the Resurrection from the dead, the Ascension into heaven, Your sitting at the right hand of Your God and Father and Your glorious and terrible second coming, offer You from Your gifts that which belongs to You completely."

In this admirable text the Mass appears truly as the center and the synthesis of the different phases of the mystery of Christ. Within the sacramental action it puts us in contact with the past, present and future realities.

At the same time it unites us to all the members of the Church: the saints, the departed, the living; and, through communion, it obligates us to live as men who share God's life. This is expressed in the following two prayers, which belong also to the liturgy of St. Basil:

"Unite each to the other, O Lord, in the communion of the one Holy Spirit, all of us who partake of the one Bread and the one Chalice. Do not let any of us partake for our own damnation of the holy Body and Blood of Your Christ, but rather let us find mercy and grace together with all Your saints who have pleased You from the beginning of the world; protoparents, forefathers, patriarchs, prophets, apostles, preachers, evangelists, martyrs, confessors, doctors and all the spirits of the just who passed away in the faith, especially our all-

---

[5] This sentence is a later addition; it is not found in the authentic text.

holy, immaculate, blessed above all, glorious Lady, Mother of God and ever Virgin Mary. . . .

"O our God, God of salvation, teach us to thank You worthily for the benefits You have granted us and do grant us. Do You, our God, who have received these gifts, purify us from every stain of flesh and spirit and teach us to achieve our sanctification in fear of You, that, receiving the particle of the gifts sanctified by You with the testimony of a pure conscience, we may unite ourselves to the holy Body and Blood of Your Christ and, receiving them worthily, we may have Christ dwelling in our hearts and may become temples of the Holy Spirit. Yes, O our God, do not let any of us offend against these Your tremendous and heavenly mysteries, or become sick in soul or body by partaking of them unworthily. But grant that to our very last breath we may worthily receive the particle of Your holy gifts as Viaticum for eternal life, as an acceptable defense before the dread tribunal of Your Christ, that we also, together with all the saints who have pleased You from the beginning of the world, may become partakers of Your eternal goods which You have prepared, O Lord, for those who love You."

The Roman canon

All these ideas are found again in the present Roman canon, but more dispersed and less developed, so that at first glance it is rather hard to recognize them.

Actually, in the Roman canon, many of these ideas are expressed in the first section, which is variable and which is called the preface. As the changing of the preface for every Mass was considered the ordinary rule at Rome in ancient times,[6] it can be said that the custom was to divide the various aspects of the mystery of Christ among the different prefaces, while in the anaphora of St. Basil they were all expressed together in every Mass in a more logical and more synthetic manner.

Even now, in reading the various prefaces of the present Roman canon, it is easy to see how the most important phases of the mystery of Christ which we find all together in the Greek anaphora of St. Basil are recalled separately. By comparing the prefaces of Christmas, Epiphany, the Cross, Easter, Ascension and Pentecost, we can follow the whole development of the mystery of Christ in its phase of historical realization.

In the fixed part of the Roman canon the fulfilment of the mystery of Christ is expressed in the following texts:

From the *Qui pridie* through the *Unde et memores* it is the liturgical and sacramental phase of realization, with the memorial of the institution of the Eucharist, of the Passion, the death, the Resurrection, the Ascension.

---

[6] The Leonine sacramentary had 267 prefaces in the last eight months of the year alone; the Gelasian still kept 54; the Gregorian reduced them to 14; the present Roman Missal has 15.

The *Supra quae* recalls the preparation in the Old Testament, with the sacrifices of Abel, of Abraham, of Melchisedech, which prefigured the sacrifice of the cross, now renewed in the Mass.

The *Nobis quoque peccatoribus,* asking for our admittance into the society of the saints, expresses the union of the Eucharistic sacrifice with the heavenly Jerusalem, to which the *Communicantes* had already made allusion.

The two *Memento* prayers indicate the connection of the sacrifice with all the faithful, living or dead.

Finally, the eschatological phase of the mystery of Christ is mentioned in various formulas, such as *Haec commixtio et consecratio corporis et sanguinis Domini nostri Iesu Christi fiat accipientibus nobis in vitam aeternam* or *Corpus Domini nostri Iesu Christi custodiat animam tuam in vitam aeternam.*

The version of the Roman canon known as that of Moelcaich in the Irish missal of Stowe of the eighth-ninth century demonstrates splendidly the eschatological thinking of the Mass when, immediately after the words of the consecration, at the sentence "Every time you do these things you shall do them in remembrance of Me" it adds: "you shall preach My Passion, proclaim My Resurrection, hope for My coming until I come to you again from heaven." [7]

3. In the Liturgy Everything Is Ordained to the Mass

If, as we have explained, the Mass signifies and realizes better than any other liturgical function the mystery of Christ's Redemption and its fulfilment in us, it is to be expected that the whole liturgy will be ordained to the Mass, that it will flow from the Mass as its source and lead to it as its terminus. This is a truth which theology can establish and which the rites do not fail to express.

Theological affirmation

As St. Thomas teaches, the Eucharist is the greatest of the sacraments because it contains Christ in person and not only a power coming from Him. Moreover, "all the other sacraments are ordained to this sacrament as their end. The sacrament of holy orders is obviously ordained to the consecration of the Eucharist. The sacrament of baptism is ordained to the reception of the Eucharist. Such also is the orientation of confirmation, so that a person will not abstain from the Eucharist out of fear. Again, through penance and extreme unction man is prepared to receive worthily the body of Christ. Matrimony also is referred to this sacrament, at least by its symbolism, in so far as it represents the union of Christ and the Church, of which the sacrament of the Eucharist is a figure." [8]

With regard to the relation of matrimony to the Eucharist, it can be added that the end of marriage is to bring into the world children destined to become members of the Church and children of God in Christ; and if the seed of this

---

[7] Cf. Leo Eizenhöfer, *Canon missae romanae*   [8] *Summa,* III, q. 65, a. 3.
(Rome: Orbis Catholicus, 1954), p. 33.

sonship is given in baptism, it finds its flowering only in the participation in the Eucharistic sacrifice. Hence marriage fully attains its goal here below only on the day when the children born of it are admitted to the Eucharistic banquet, which itself is a pledge of the heavenly banquet. This shows, incidentally, what significance the first communion and the later communions of their children should have for the parents.

Not only are all the other sacraments ordained to the Eucharist, but they produce their proper grace only in virtue of their relation to the Eucharist. Only the Eucharist has of itself the power to confer grace, while the other sacraments confer it only in virtue of the desire which their recipients have of receiving the Eucharist also.

This was taught by as early a writer as the Pseudo-Dionysius. His doctrine, worked out precisely by St. Thomas and taken up by numerous theologians after him, passed into the catechism of the Council of Trent. The Eucharist, says the Pseudo-Dionysius, "is the perfection of all perfections.[9] . . . The participation in the other hierarchical symbols reaches its fulfilment by means of the divine and perfective gifts of the Eucharist. For hardly any hierarchical sacrament is fufilled unless the most divine Eucharist, as crown of every rite, realizes the union of the initiate with the One and consummates his communion with God through the gift of the divine consummative mysteries. Therefore every other sacramental initiation of the hierarchy, being imperfect in itself, and not carrying to its fulfilment our union and communion with the One, is deprived, by this lack in itself, of the character of a perfect initiation. And since the end and crown of the whole initiation is the communication of the divine mysteries to the initiate, hierarchical science has rightly taken from the reality itself this proper name (of communion and synaxis) for the Eucharist."[10]

St. Thomas is acquainted with this doctrine of the Pseudo-Dionysius[11] and develops it in the *Summa* : "This sacrament (of the Eucharist) has of itself the power to confer grace. No one has grace before receiving this sacrament except by a certain desire (*votum*) to receive it, his own desire in the case of adults, or the Church's desire in the case of infants, as has been said above. The fact, therefore, that even from the mere desire to receive this sacrament there may proceed the grace which gives spiritual life, follows from the efficacy of the virtue of this sacrament. Hence when this sacrament is actually received, grace is increased and the spiritual life is perfected."[12]

This teaching is taken up by the catechism of the Council of Trent. Inviting pastors to explain to the faithful all the riches contained in the Eucharist, it advises them to "compare the Eucharist to a fountain, the other sacraments to rivulets. For the Holy Eucharist is truly and necessarily to be called the fountain of all graces, containing as it does, after an admirable manner, the

---

[9] Τελετῶν τελετὴ: perfection of perfections, or sacrament of sacraments, perfection of sacraments.

[10] *Hier. eccl.*, III, 1 (PG 3, 424–425).

[11] See *In Sent.*, 4, d. 8, q. 1, a. 1 (ed. Moos, p. 308, n. 19; 310, n. 34).

[12] *Summa*, III, q. 79, a. 1 ad 1.

fountain itself of celestial gifts and graces, and the Author of all the sacraments, Christ our Lord, from whom, as from its source, is derived whatever of
goodness and perfection the other sacraments possess."[13] Hence comes their
power of sanctification, but also their value as worship.

And that which is true of the sacraments and of the liturgy in its entirety is
true with still more reason of all the other means of sanctification and of worship employed by the Church as such or by Christians as private persons:
government, apostolate, teaching, ascetical and mystical life. All this has no
value except in so far as it is connected with the Eucharistic sacrifice, whether
as preparation or as consequence; there must be in all this a certain "desire" of
the Eucharist. We shall see later on how important this is for the problem of
the relations between liturgy and spirituality and between liturgy and pastoral.

If the other sacraments are thus ordained to the Eucharist, the reason ultimately is that all the sacraments have the end of sanctifying man and rendering worship to God in Christ. Both these activities have their source in Christ's
sacrifice on the cross, of which the Mass is the sacramental representation. It is
therefore by taking part in the Mass, by communicating, that the Christian
will be put into direct contact with that which is the source of the whole
liturgy.

Liturgical expression

The bond of the sacraments with the Eucharist was manifested in ancient
times by the practice of administering and receiving them only in immediate
connection with the Mass. Thus the faithful, by taking part in the Eucharistic
sacrifice, could bring to their highest degree the values of sanctification and of
worship included in the sacraments they had just received.

We know that baptism, confirmation and communion formerly constituted
a single, homogeneous rite, the rite of initiation, begun at the baptismal font
and completed only at the Eucharistic table. The reconciliation of the penitents
also took place normally at the Mass of Holy Thursday, "that, receiving the
nuptial garment, they may be fit to partake of the royal table from which they
had been kept away."[14] Even today the rite which prepares the sick to enter
into the glory of heaven is begun with extreme unction and ended with the
reception of the Viaticum. Holy orders are conferred during Mass, and those
who receive them are to participate in that Mass by communion. Finally, matrimony should normally be celebrated in the framework of the Mass; and the
very nature of things demands that the couple seal their union by participating
together in the Eucharistic sacrifice.

Thus, even though it is not required for the validity of the sacraments that
they be administered in close connection with the Mass, they are so intimately

---

[13] Part 2, ch. 4, n. 47; translated by John
A. McHugh and Charles J. Callan in *Catechism
of the Council of Trent for Parish Priests* (New
York: Joseph F. Wagner, 1934), pp. 241–242.
[14] *Pontificale Romanum*, last collect of the
rite of reconciliation.

linked to the Eucharist and to communion that the liturgy quite naturally tends to manifest that link in its rites. The practical lesson is that everyone, in so far as it depends on him, should conform to this natural tendency and help the faithful to understand and live its profound significance. For the thing in question here is the understanding of the mystery of Christ and its effective realization for the Christian people.

All that we have said of the sacraments as ordained to the Eucharistic sacrifice holds with still greater reason for the liturgical rites instituted by the Church : ceremonies, sacramentals, prayers, Divine Office. The fundamental reason is the same : all these rites have no other aim than the divine worship in Christ and the sanctification of man in Christ. But both of these exist only as participation in the sacrifice of the cross, a sacrifice which is renewed sacramentally in the Mass. All these rites draw their meaning, therefore, from the fact that they are more or less immediate dispositions to the communion in the Eucharistic sacrifice or derivations from that sacrifice.

And it is after all the very nature of things that has led the Church to celebrate the most important of the rites she has instituted in close connection with the Mass. The consecration of a church, the blessing of an abbot, the monastic profession, the consecration of virgins all take place during Mass. The obsequies of the dead are performed in connection with the Mass and by the same priest who has celebrated the Mass. It was an ancient custom — still practiced on certain days in some countries — to bless food (bread, wine, oil, grapes, Paschal lamb, etc.) during the Mass, most often at the end of the canon.[15] The conventual Mass is to be preceded generally by the chanting of Terce, and in a general way the Divine Office is linked to the Mass of the day by the fact that the same collect is recited in it.

4. The Sense of the Liturgical Feasts and of the Liturgical Cycles

The fact that the whole mystery of Christ, past, present and future, is condensed in the Mass under the veil of efficacious signs, and that the other parts of the liturgy are ordained to the Mass as their center, permits us to understand the meaning of the liturgical feasts and cycles. Every Mass contains Advent, Christmas, Epiphany, Holy Thursday, Good Friday, Easter, Ascension, Pentecost, Christ the King, All Saints. A liturgical feast cannot be anything that is not already really contained in every Mass.

What, then, is the precise relation between every Mass and such and such a liturgical feast ? In itself, every Mass expresses synthetically and realizes in its own way the whole mystery of Christ. But our psychological capacity is limited, and we cannot grasp all at one time the riches of grace of the mystery of Christ. Hence we must have this mystery taken apart, as it were, and analyzed successively in its various aspects, that we may concentrate our attention on one at a

[15] Cf. Joseph A. Jungmann, *The Mass of the Roman Rite* (New York: Benziger, 1950–55), II, 259 ff.

time and thus succeed gradually in becoming permeated more and more with the full meaning of every Mass.

A liturgical feast, therefore, is the pointing out by the liturgy of one or another of the various aspects of the mystery of Christ, a single mystery realized in its entirety in every Mass.[16]

These feasts are grouped liturgically into cycles. There is the cycle of the time and that of the saints.

The cycle of the time comprises the Advent-Epiphany period and the Septuagesima-Pentecost period. The first recalls the whole mystery of Christ, but does so under the aspect of the Lord's manifested coming, on the various levels and in the different phases in which the mystery of Christ unfolds: expectation and preparation in the Old Testament, historical realization in Christ's earthly life, present prolongation in the Church by the sacramental way and the extrasacramental way, and finally eschatological fulfilment. Similarly, the Easter cycle considers the whole mystery of Christ, but in the perspective of the Redemption, viewed also in the four times of the history of salvation.

In an analogous way, the feasts of the Blessed Virgin, of the angels and of the saints simply bring to light an aspect of the mystery of Christ included in every Mass.

The feasts of our Lady call attention to the place which Mary occupies in this mystery. They call to mind the marvels that God has accomplished in Mary to fit her to play the part which He had assigned to her in the realization of the mystery of Christ on its various levels. Or else they recall Mary's actions either during her earthly life or now in glory. Thus in the liturgy alongside the mystery of Christ there develops in a parallel way, but in a very broad sense and a sense wholly subordinated to the mystery of Christ of which it forms a part, the mystery of Mary, prepared for in the Old Testament, realized historically in her earthly life and now working mystically in souls by disposing them to receive and live the mystery of Christ.

The feasts of the angels have for their object the role played by the angels in this same sacred history on its various levels, from the beginning of the world to the triumph of the Apocalypse. As we shall see later on, the history of salvation, even in its liturgical expression, is a cosmic history in which the angels also participate.

As to the feasts of the saints, they point out the fruits which the Redemption has borne among men. The mystery of Christ acts in every man with special gradations. No one realizes all its aspects in himself, but each one reproduces one or another trait of it in an original fashion, and thus each one has his own physiognomy and his own place, established by God, in the realization of this mystery. The feast of All Saints brings out forcefully the eschatological aspect,

[16] Cf. Odo Casel, "Zur Idee der liturgischen Festfeier," *Mysterium. Gesamelte Arbeiten laacher Mönche* (Münster, 1926), pp. 53–61.

the triumphal aspect, of the mystery of Christ: the heavenly Jerusalem is the term of the whole history of salvation and therefore of the whole liturgy.

In this perspective it is understandable that all the feasts be celebrated with the same Mass. The different formularies which adorn and illuminate an "ordinary" which is always identical simply draw special attention to one or another of the elements which go to make up the single and integral mystery of Christ.

In concluding these chapters in which we have tried to show what the liturgy is, viewed in the framework of the history of salvation, we cannot help marveling once more at the cosmic dimensions, spatial and temporal, of that complexus of efficacious signs by which God sanctifies the Church and the Church renders her worship to God.

In the light of the mystery of Christ lived in the liturgy so understood, the world, all of history and the whole Christian life acquire a surprising unity and simplicity. It is a reflection of the unity and simplicity which all things have in the eyes of God in Christ Jesus.

God's intention, His plan in creating the world and guiding its history is extremely simple: "Christ is the same yesterday and today, and forever" (Heb. 13:8). The liturgy is nothing but the actualization of this truth under the veil of efficacious sacred signs, an actualization fully realized by the communion in the Eucharistic sacrifice, prepared for in the other sacraments and in the sacramentals, contemplated and acclaimed in the divine praise "until He comes."

PART 2 THE LITURGY AND THE GENERAL LAWS OF THE DIVINE ECONOMY IN THE WORLD

THEOLOGICAL DIMENSIONS OF THE LITURGY

6 THE LITURGY

AND THE LAW OF OBJECTIVITY

For an accurate understanding of the nature of the liturgy and of its function in the Christian economy, it is indispensable to view it in the great perspectives of revelation. That is why we have been careful in explaining the concept of liturgy always to situate it in the framework of the history of salvation.

But, up to now, we have been able to show those relations only in a very general way. We have scarcely alluded to the application to the liturgy of the great laws which govern the relations between God and creatures. These general laws of the whole Christian economy can be reduced to six :

1. The law of objectivity.
2. The Christological and Trinitarian dialectic of salvation.
3. The law of the single liturgist and of the single liturgy, which further explains the preceding one.
4. The law of salvation in community.
5. The law of incarnation.
6. The law of the cosmic universality of salvation.

We shall analyze these laws, founded on the very nature of things or established by God's free will. Thus we shall see that they apply to the liturgy as well as to all the other systems of relation between God and the world. What is more, we shall learn that it is precisely in the liturgy that they find their most concrete application for us.

1. Objectivism, Subjectivism and Liturgy

The first law is the law of objectivity. It means that the way by which God comes to us and we attain to Him is not left to our free choice but is imposed on us. It is imposed on us either by our nature, and therefore by God as Author of that nature, or by a positive decision of God. To reach salvation, there is no other way but to accept freely this route mapped out by God, to submit ourselves to this given fact.

Of course, our own self and our freedom come into play also. In fact, what God demands is the gift of this free personality. But our subjective self cannot be developed, cannot be fulfilled, cannot be saved, except by submitting freely to the objective reality which is proposed to it. The subject has value only if it is governed and measured, as it were, by the object.

This object, which God has made the means of our encounter with Him, is: Christ; the Scripture and the sacraments; the Church, people of God outside of which there is no salvation, and hierarchical society subject to the pope and the bishops; the teaching of the *magisterium*.

Now the whole liturgy, as system of relations between God and man, is ruled by this law of objectivity. The liturgy is merely one particular case of this general rule.

That is one of the reasons why the liturgy is so distasteful to a certain modern mentality. For, if the ways of God are governed by the law of objectivity, the ways of modern man obey the law of subjectivity and, outside of the Church, end up in the most absolute subjectivism.

We are used to hearing that the subject is one of the conquests of modern man. In fact, it is said to be his highest conquest, because all the others hark back to this one. Subjective experience is the goal to which the whole modern world tends, the only value which it recognizes. This experience, moreover, is considered not as a product of the subject in contact with the object, but as a thing worth while in itself and for itself, independently of the object.

Some go so far as to regard the object as a secondary, negligible element, a mere reflex of the subject, which creates it by objectivating its own ego. And they draw consequences from this: life is absolute freedom in never-ending conquest over itself; God is an objectivated creation of this freedom; religion represents a still unrefined stage and expression of creative spontaneity; all religions are equally good because they are all the fruit of a religious experience.

When the subjectivist mentality has reached this point, it is obviously at the antipodes of the liturgical mentality. For the liturgy introduces us into a real, objective world, which man must take just as it is, to which he must adapt himself.

To be sure, we recognize that the subject is present and active in the liturgical action, that there is even an accord, a correspondence of subject to object without which the liturgical action would have no effect, since everything would then be reduced, for the subject, to pure externalism and mechanics.

But, on the other hand, we assert that the subjective in the liturgical action is not a *deus ex machina* which creates the whole. This action always depends on an objective reality, is regulated and measured by an objective reality. The liturgy teaches us that for man there is no creation or conquest if there has not previously been submission not only to the laws of nature but also to the norms freely determined by God, norms which surpass the laws of nature yet never contradict them.

For an idealist following Kant or Gentile or Croce, for a vitalist and intuitionist like Bergson, for an existentialist like Jaspers, Heidegger or Sartre, what can these things mean : to unite oneself to Christ really present in the Mass under the veil of sensible signs ; to be saved by the reception of sacraments working *ex opere operato* ; to pray with the people of God ?

All this, for an idealist, is completely meaningless, or else it is only an external stimulus, still very primitive, which moves the intellect and the will, a mere stimulus to internal freedom and experience.

But in this we are far indeed from the objectivism of the liturgy, for which union with Christ is something quite different from a mere union of thought and of will. There is question here of the whole reality of grace as physical elevation to the divine order, the whole reality of the sacraments as productive of that grace.

It is impossible, therefore, to enter into the world of the liturgy without an objectivist mentality, or, if you prefer, a realist mentality, in which the values of subjectivity and of interiority are realized only by the correspondence of the subject to an object distinct from it and independent of it.

Such is the specifically Catholic balance of the pair subject-object : to affirm the reality and the distinction of the two terms without permitting that one be suppressed in favor of the other, but at the same time to proclaim that the subject is strictly subordinated to the object and completely ruled by it.

The maintenance of this equilibrium, where the liturgy is concerned, is more difficult than one might suppose. The mere fact of emphasizing one factor more or less has its repercussions on one's idea of the liturgy and of its role in the Christian life.

It would not be without danger, for example, to make too large a place for introspection, for self-analysis, for the experience of the states and reactions of the subject, with the more or less conscious tendency to stop at this experience, these reactions, this "fruition" or enjoyment, as if they were the most important things and the things to be sought primarily in our relations with God.

It would be equally dangerous, on the other hand, for the understanding of the liturgy and for its efficacy, to insist on the data, on the object, to the point of no longer caring about the correspondence it requires of the subject, the effort of interiorization it demands of the subject.

A dead extrinsicism which awakens no echo in the subject, and a subjective psychologism of egocentric tendency — these are the two great enemies of the true liturgical spirit.

2. An Objectivist Attitude Favors the Efficacy of the Liturgy

The liturgy can have its full effect, its full yield, only in a climate in which the transcendence of the object is imposed on the subject, and the subject strives to interiorize the object by corresponding to it with its whole being.

But, in this search for the necessary balance between objectivity and subjectivity, between exteriority and interiority, there can be among Catholics themselves, and within the limits of a perfect orthodoxy, a certain diversity of attitudes; and these attitudes will not all be equally favorable to the full understanding and the full efficacy of the liturgy.

Of course, there cannot be question of anything but gradations in the manner of safeguarding the intangible data. For no one can conceive of a Catholic spirituality which does not admit an objective basis, and therefore is not sacrificial, sacramental, ecclesial and liturgical. And on the other hand no one can conceive of a really Catholic liturgical spirituality which does not allow an essential place for the cooperation of the subject, his personal correspondence to the exterior data.

Pius XII in the encyclical *Mediator Dei* has called attention to this point, which should be absolutely clear to everyone.[1] There was reason to give this warning to those who were making themselves the heralds of a self-styled "objective" piety, which they identified with liturgical piety and opposed to "subjective" piety, but who were actually proposing nothing but "a caricature of piety which would transform the liturgy into a kind of magic," as Père Roguet said.[2] We shall come back to this question in the chapter devoted to liturgical spirituality.

The attitudes of Catholics in this field, then, will differ only by degrees. But these gradations will definitely influence the manner of understanding and living the liturgy.

Suppose that a Catholic in his religious behavior is solicitous above all for his own self, what he feels in himself, his awareness of his own acts or his own psychic states. Obviously he will tend to diminish, or even to reduce to the indispensable minimum, his contacts with the world of the liturgy, and to take refuge in a more individual and extraliturgical form of piety. Such a kind of piety will seem to him less hampering to his need of freedom and initiative, and more satisfying to his concern with self-analysis and self-consciousness;

[1] Nn. 26–32.   [2] In his edition of the encyclical, p. 15, note 28.

while more numerous contacts with the liturgy would seem a hindrance or at least a distraction from the aim he has in mind.

For one who wants to penetrate the world of the liturgy to the depths and draw as much profit out of it as possible, these dispositions are not the best. For the liturgy brings to the foreground the objective fact of salvation, and looks on the reactions of the subject only as a response to the realities that come from God, an effort to make them enter into his life. This effort is indispensable, but it would be ineffective in the way of salvation if it were cut off from the object, that is, from Christ, the Church and the sacraments. Thus the liturgy is concerned much less with introspection than with attention to God, to Christ the Redeemer, to the Church. And its therapy consists not so much in having the subject turn back on himself as in putting him into contact with the object.[3]

These observations will help us understand one of the reasons, and undoubtedly one of the most profound reasons, for the difficulty which many Catholics have encountered and still do encounter, even though they be fervent and desirous of an intense spiritual life, when they try to understand the liturgy and make it penetrate into their life.[4] And we shall understand too that it is no accident if the Catholics of our day who feel and express better than others the needs of their generation, have an ardent desire to rediscover the liturgy. And it is most often the same people who desire a better balanced life, who desire in particular that more importance be attributed to the objective, realist and communitarian reality than has been given it for some decades past, yet without denying or foregoing any of the progress achieved in the domain of the subjective and the individual.

Thus the essential problem confronting us today in the field of the liturgy is to know how to lead Christians, or lead them back, to reacting in a personal and subjective way in face of the objective data of the liturgy; how to lead them to make this Christian, ecclesial and sacramental world their own interior world, while safeguarding at the same time the harmony of subject and object and the preeminence of the object as determining and regulating element.

---

[3] Henri Bremond, after having analyzed the prayers of Duguet, a contemporary of Fénelon, observes, "The contrast we have just indicated between Duguet and Fénelon — bourgeois Christianity, mystical Christianity — is found again between the formulas of meditation and the liturgical formulas. One of the advantages of the latter, one of their glories, is precisely this, that they cut short these passionate introspections, of which Duguet's prayers offer us an example so pathetic and at the same time so disconcerting. The liturgy not only precludes the expression, and hence the exaggeration, of this rather morbid timidity, but even heals it, so to say, *in radice*. By keeping us from thinking so much about ourselves, the liturgy makes us live, effortlessly and unwittingly, the highest form of religion, which is disinterested adoration and pure love" (*Histoire littéraire du sentiment religieux en France*, X [Paris: Bloud et Gay, 1932], 288, note 2).

[4] For more details on this question, one may refer to the historical remarks, unfortunately too brief, of Jungmann in *The Mass of the Roman Rite*, I, 103–132, 141–151. See also the controversy to which I. Mennessier alludes in *S. Thomas d'A., La somme*, ed. rev. des jeunes, *La religion*, I, p. 327.

7 THE LITURGY AND THE CHRISTOLOGICAL AND TRINITARIAN DIALECTIC OF SALVATION: FROM THE FATHER, THROUGH CHRIST, IN THE HOLY SPIRIT, TO THE FATHER

The way by which God comes to us and we go to God is not left to our choice, but is pointed out to us by God Himself. What is that way?

Revelation teaches us that the God to whom we must go is God in three Persons, Father, Son and Holy Spirit; and it discloses to us the wonderful play of relations between this God in three Persons and each one of us. For it shows us that every good comes to us from the Father, through Jesus Christ His incarnate Son, and by means of the presence in us of the Holy Spirit; and that, similarly, it is by means of the presence in us of the Spirit and through Christ that everything must return to the Father.

Such is the Christological and Trinitarian dialectic of the history of salvation. The whole liturgy implies this dialectic, and becomes incomprehensible without it. We shall show in some detail the importance in itself and in the liturgy of this reality, which is too little known to Christians in our day.

1. Two Ways of Considering the Trinity; Advantages of the Earlier Way, that of the New Testament and of the Most Ancient Tradition

Everyone admits that it is impossible to understand anything about the liturgy without reference to Christ. But not everyone sees so clearly that it is no less necessary, in order to get to the bottom of things, to have reference to the Trinity. This is so much the more true today because so many Christians have a tendency to look on the Trinity not only as the most elevated and most impenetrable mystery of our faith, but also as the reality most abstract and farthest removed from our daily life, one of those realities which hold the least place in the psychology of the believer. For many people, God is the God of the philosophers, or at most the God of the Jews, rather than the Christian God, Father, Son and Holy Spirit.

From the unity of the divine nature to the trinity of the Persons or from the trinity of the Persons to the unity of the nature

This erroneous conception has a twofold cause, it seems. On the one hand, people are used to considering the mystery of the Trinity by starting out from the unity of the divine nature and coming only in a second psychological moment to the trinity of the Persons. On the other hand, when they look at this mystery, it is almost always in an ontological and intratrinitarian perspective, and not in function of the economy of salvation. But this demands some explanations.

The dogma of the Trinity comprises two terms: numerical unity of nature and real distinction of the three Persons, the mystery lying in the manner of reconciling these two terms. Because it comprises two terms, the dogma can be presented in two ways, both perfectly orthodox, but resulting in quite different attitudes toward the mystery. Writing in the last decade of the nineteenth century, the Rev. Théodore de Régnon drew the attention of theologians to this point.[1]

To formulate the mystery, one may start out from the unity of nature, and add only later, and almost like a corrective, the trinity of the Persons. Thus one will say that in God the nature is numerically one, but that in this one nature there subsist three really distinct Persons. It is the unity of the divine nature that is on the first level; it is the indisputable basis on which to rest; and this basis appears so much the more clear and certain because it is within reach of pure philosophical reasoning.

But, in this perspective, the trinity of the Persons remains in the background,[2] and there is danger of not giving it enough importance, at least in

[1] *Etudes de théologie positive sur la Sainte Trinité*, 4 vols. (Paris: Victor Retaux, 1892–1898).

[2] And it will tend to be the theologian's effort to show that this plurality of Persons is not incompatible with the numerical unity of the nature. The so-called psychological theory of the Trinity, proposed by St. Augustine rather as a psychological description, but later transposed by St. Anselm to the metaphysical level, and perfected by St. Thomas, has precisely the aim of demonstrating this possibility.

practice. There is danger of thinking about God only as a philosopher would, or as a Jew would, and not giving to each one of the divine Persons, and especially to the Father and the Holy Spirit, the place which belongs to them.[3]

This method of approaching the mystery of the Trinity prevailed in the West from the time of St. Augustine on. It became predominant especially with St. Anselm, who exercised a decisive influence over the later theologians as to the manner of considering the unity and the trinity in God.

St. Thomas, by defining the divine Persons as subsistent relations and by making a distinction, in the question of the processions, between the role played by the Persons (*principium quod*) and the role played by the nature (*principium quo*), did bring to light a "personalist" aspect which the Augustinian and Anselmian tradition had left in the shadow.[4] But for all that he did not change the climate and the orientation of the Western theology of the Trinity, for which it has remained a major preoccupation to know how to arrive at "three" from "one," to investigate the mystery of the trinity rather than the mystery of the unity.

To be sure, this presentation of the mystery is perfectly orthodox, and it offers certain advantages, including the advantage of forestalling the danger of Arianism right from the start. But this presentation is not that of the Scripture or, consequently, that of the liturgy. Hence it is a poor preparation for understanding fully the true Trinitarian dimensions of the view of the world proposed in the New Testament and the liturgy.

Actually, there is another way of formulating the mystery of the Trinity. Following an opposite direction, it starts from the plurality of the Persons, and only then proceeds to the assertion that the three really distinct Persons do subsist in a nature numerically one.

The problem is no longer to make three Persons proceed from a single nature, but to bring back the plurality of Persons to the unity of nature.[5] And the danger to be avoided is that of insisting on the real distinction to the point of forgetting the unity of nature and the perfect equality of the three Persons: in short, the danger of Arianism or subordinationism.[6]

---

[3] As far as the Son is concerned, He will always hold a conspicuous place in the believer's mind in so far as He is the incarnate Son, in so far as He is Christ. But the awareness of the Father and the Holy Spirit as distinct Persons will be very tenuous. In practice, the faithful will scarcely think of anyone but God — a God who will be the God of the philosophers or, at best, the God of the Old Testament — and Christ. In theology there will be a treatise "On the One God" — resembling strongly, whatever anyone may say, a philosophical theodicy crammed with texts from the Scripture and the Fathers — and a Christology ; as to the treatise "On the Trinity," it is much to be feared that its importance will not be seen.

[4] Cf. A. Malet, *Personne et amour dans la théologie trinitaire de S. Thomas d'A.* (Paris, 1956).

[5] The Greek Fathers, and the Latin Fathers before St. Augustine, who considered the Trinity in this second way, tried to solve the problem by affirming strongly, after the real distinction of the Persons, their inseparability and their unity of eternity, power, wisdom, action, etc. They had recourse, moreover, to helpful metaphors: the sun, its rays and its heat; a spring, the brook which flows from it and the lake which is formed by it; etc.

[6] And it was just so that some apologists of the second century and doctors of the second and third centuries, like Tertullian, Hippolytus,

On the other hand, one who considers the Trinity in this way will see very clearly that His God is not simply the God of the philosophers or of the Old Testament but the specifically Christian God, Father, Son and Holy Spirit.

Each of the two ways, therefore, has its advantages and its dangers. Whichever one a person chooses, he will have to be constantly on guard to bring to light the term which he has left in the shadow at first. And, whichever way he chooses, he will end up at the mystery.

It would be a mistake, however, to conclude from this that one may choose the one or the other presentation indifferently and without consequence for the manner in which he will live the mystery. For it is a fact that the Trinitarian awareness is more vivid in the person who adopts the second way. It is a fact also that the Scripture, the Greek Fathers, the Latin Fathers before St. Augustine, the liturgies and especially the Roman liturgy, almost always consider the Trinity in the "personalist" way, that which keeps the distinction of the Persons in the foreground.

Hence, for an understanding of the view of the world proposed by the New Testament, by the majority of the Fathers and by the liturgy as a whole, it is necessary to choose the second way. This is, so to speak, closer to the source and at the same time more irenic. It is the way in which the Trinitarian revelation was presented from the first to the faith of the believers and in which it is still presented today and lived in the liturgy.

The other system, on the contrary, is historically a derived system, predominantly apologetical in character. It made its appearance as a defense of the faith against the rationalist objections of Arianism, and it is in this perspective that it has developed.

The Trinity in itself or in its relations with the world

In its contemplation of the Trinity, the Scripture is more attentive to the distinction of Persons than to the unity of nature. It must be added that the Scripture is less concerned with knowing what the Trinity is in itself, in its metaphysical structure, than with knowing what are its relations with the created world, what role the three Persons play in the history of mankind, in the mystery of our salvation. In brief, the attitude is that of the historian rather than of the philosopher.

This does not mean, of course, that affirmations of a metaphysical order concerning the divine Persons are not found in the Bible;[7] still less that a certain number of such affirmations cannot be deduced legitimately from the explicit

Novatian, Origen and his school, came to give the Trinity a subordinationist explanation — which was an error, but an error on the level of the theological explanation of the faith and not on the level of the faith itself, in which they were all perfectly orthodox. By paying attention too exclusively to the distinction of the Persons, they emphasized that distinction at the expense of the unity of the nature. Subsequently, the Arians transformed this error into a heresy.

[7] For example, the preexistence of the Son, His divinity, His divine sonship.

statements of the Bible.[8] But, on the one hand, these affirmations are relatively rare in the Scripture, and they remain in the background, whatever may be their importance in themselves and for theology. And, on the other hand, the deduction from biblical data, however legitimate and even useful they may be, are not made by the Scripture itself.

Theological reasoning can look at things from a different viewpoint than the Scripture does. It has been our intention only to insist that for an understanding of the Bible it is indispensable to take the Bible's point of view.

The scheme *a, per, in, ad* in the New Testament

Thus the Bible, and the liturgy in its train, see in God the Persons, and in the Persons the role devolving upon each one in the history of salvation. An attentive reader of the New Testament, especially of St. Paul and St. John, will notice that this intervention of the divine Persons in the economy of salvation is presented according to a scheme which is not rigid or absolute, but which appears at least in supposition whenever there is question of that divine action in the world.

The scheme, which appears sometimes in its entirety and sometimes only in part, is the following : Every good comes to us from the Father, through Jesus Christ His incarnate Son and by means of the presence in us of the Holy Spirit; and similarly it is by means of the presence in us of the Spirit and through Christ that everything returns to the Father. "From the Father, through His Son Jesus Christ, in the Holy Spirit, to the Father" — *a Patre, per Filium eius Iesum Christum, in Spiritu Sancto, ad Patrem* — such is the descending and ascending movement in which the New Testament reveals the Trinity to us; such is the vast parabola of the mystery of salvation — "the going out from God and the return to God," *exitus a Deo et reditus ad Deum* — in which the Father reveals Himself essentially as the one from whom (*a quo*) and to whom (*ad quem*), the Son as the one through whom (*per quem*), and the Holy Spirit as the one in whom (*in quo*).

It must be noted also that the Son, in this context, is primarily the Son incarnate, Christ Jesus, considered in His Incarnation and His redemptive action, or at least in reference to them.[9] It is not only in a Trinitarian perspective, therefore, but in a Christological-and-Trinitarian perspective, that the Scripture looks at the world and history.

We cannot think of analyzing here even a portion of the texts of the New Testament which document what we have just said.

Let the inquirer merely read the beginning of the letter to the Ephesians, where the scheme appears in full: "Blessed be the *God and Father* of our Lord

---

[8] Theology has rightly deduced these affirmations by implying or stating explicitly that there is a correlation between the manifestations of the divine Persons *ad extra* and their intratrinitarian relations.

[9] This is equally true of the Word as St. John conceives Him. Cf. Jacques Dupont, *Essais sur la christologie de S. Jean* (Bruges: Abbaye de Saint-André, 1951), pp. 9–58.

Jesus Christ, who has blessed us with every spiritual, heavenly blessing in Christ . . . out of love having predestined us to be His adoptive sons *through Jesus Christ*, according to the good pleasure of His will, to the praise of the glorious manifestation of His grace . . . we have been predestined to contribute to the praise of His glory . . . in whom (Christ) you too . . . have believed, and have been marked with *the seal of the Holy Spirit*, who is the pledge of our inheritance . . . *to the praise of His glory*" (1:3-14). The same scheme is found complete in Rom. 8:3-17; 1 Cor. 6:19-20; Gal. 4:4-6; Eph. 2:4-5 and 18-22.

In other passages the scheme appears only in part: it has only the three terms *a, per, in* in Rom. 8:3-4; 15:15-19; 1 Cor. 12:4-6; 2 Cor. 1:21-22; 13:13; Eph. 4:4-7; more frequently still, it has only two terms, or even only one; this is the case in particular when there is question of the Father [10] as source or as end of the whole economy *ad extra*,[11] or of the incarnate Son as the one *per quem*, or of the Spirit as the one *in quo*.

In all these texts St. Paul employs these formulas in passing and without explanation. This proves how clear and normal the Christological and Trinitarian perspective was for the first Christians, even before the gospels were written. The fact is confirmed, moreover, by the original catechesis, as reported in the Acts of the Apostles (e.g., 2:32-33; 5:30-32; 15:7-11).

It would be rather naive to suppose that this way of considering the Trinity would dissipate the antinomies of the mystery for us. On the contrary, it offers for theological reflection a series of questions which are difficult, to say the least.

For example, is the formula *a, per, in, ad* to be explained by reducing it purely and simply to an appropriation? Many theologians seem to think so.[12] But perhaps their answer does not go to the basis of things. For, if it is true that the formula must be regarded as expressing only an appropriation on the level of efficient causality, it can still be given a "personalist" value on the level of exemplary causality. It seems that in this line of exemplary causality the formula *a, per, in, ad* expresses clearly the special relation which creatures have with the "properties" (*propria*) of each Person. But as soon as we try to determine more exactly these properties of each Person expressed in our formula by the prepositions *a, per, in, ad*, we must necessarily arrive at the mystery.

However this may be, it is in the perspective expressed by this scheme that the New Testament instructs the faithful on the mystery of the Trinity; and it is in this perspective that it conceives of their Trinitarian life and exhorts them to live it. The New Testament keeps reminding us that all the goods

---

[10] Often the Father is simply called God; cf. below, p. 118, note 28.

[11] Cf. Rom. 3:21-26; 5:8-11; 8:26-30; 2 Cor. 5:18-19; Gal. 4:4-7; Eph. 1:3-14; 2:4-10; Tit. 2:11-14.

[12] For example, P. Galtier, *Le S. Esprit en nous d'après les Pères grecs* (Rome, 1946); *L'habitation en nous des trois personnes divines* (2nd ed.; Rome, 1950).

with which we have been blessed come from the pure bounty of the Father; that Christ Jesus, Son of God made Man, is the supreme and necessary Mediator without whom no one can receive anything from the Father or approach Him; finally, that the Holy Spirit, merited by Christ and sent by the Father, dwells in us with His gifts, and that without Him no one would be united to Christ, nor would anyone be able to reach his last end, which is to return to the Father through Christ.

For the New Testament these data of revelation are to have a profound influence on the religious behavior of the faithful. These truths will animate their faith, hope and charity (cf. Rom. 8 in its entirety); will be for them an inexhaustible source of adoration, admiration and acknowledgment (cf. Eph. 1:3-14; 2:11-21; 3 in its entirety); will determine their method of praying, since, as St. Paul shows by his teaching and by his example, Christian prayer, especially that of thanksgiving, is addressed to the Father through His Son Jesus Christ, with the consciousness that it implies the active presence in us of the Holy Spirit (cf. Rom. 7:25; 8:26-27; 1 Cor. 1:4; 15:57; Eph. 1:3-14; 5:19-20; Col. 3:17; 1 Tim. 1:2).

These same data will constitute the strongest and deepest motives for the moral effort of the believer, whether the concern be with the general requirements of the Christian life (cf. Rom. 8:1-18), or with the duty of being kind and merciful (cf. Eph. 4:30-5:2), of preserving unity and charity among the brethren (cf. Eph. 4:1-16), or of fleeing adultery and immodesty: "Neither the effeminate, nor sodomites, nor thieves, nor the covetous, nor drunkards, nor the evil-tongued, nor the greedy will inherit the kingdom of God (—*ad Patrem*). And such were some of you; but you have been washed, you have been sanctified, you have been justified in the name of our Lord Jesus Christ (—*per Christum*) and in the Spirit of our God (—*in Spiritu*). . . . Do you not know that your body is a temple of the Holy Spirit who is in you (—*in Spiritu*) whom you have from God (—*a Patre*), and you are not your own, because you have been bought at a great price (—*per Christum*). Glorify God, therefore (—*ad Patrem*), in your body" (1 Cor. 6:10-20).

These few indications should suffice to show us that, even if we do not escape the mystery by considering the relations of the creature with God in the framework expressed by the scheme *a, per, in, ad,* still it cannot be denied that the awareness of these relations viewed in this framework is capable of giving the day-by-day Christian life an incomparable impetus and depth.

The scheme *a, per, in, ad* in the ancient tradition

The Christological and Trinitarian perspective of the New Testament is found again in the writings of the first Christian generations.

Here are the terms in which Clement of Rome in the year 96 describes to the Corinthians the establishment of the Church in the world: "The Apostles were sent to carry the good news by the Lord Jesus Christ (—*per Christum*);

Jesus Christ was sent by God (— *a Patre*). Christ comes from God, therefore, and the Apostles from Christ. Thus they proceed in an orderly way from the will of God. Having received their mandate, therefore, being made secure by the Resurrection of our Lord Jesus Christ and with faith confirmed by the word of God, in the assurance of the Holy Spirit (— *in Spiritu*), they went to announce the good news and the approach of the kingdom of God (— *ad Patrem*). Preaching through the countryside and through the cities, they appointed their first converts, whom they tested in the Spirit, to be bishops and deacons of future believers."[13]

And, in imitation of St. Paul, Clement exhorts the Corinthians to unity with these words: "Why are there contentions, passions, dissensions, schisms and wars among you? Have we not a single God, a single Christ, a single Spirit of grace poured out over us, a single vocation in Christ?"[14]

St. Ignatius of Antioch in the year 107 reminds the Ephesians of the meaning of the Christian life: "You are the stones of the Father's temple, made ready to be built into an edifice to God the Father (— *ad Patrem*), to reach the top by the engine of Jesus Christ, which is the cross (— *per Christum*), using as a rope the Holy Spirit (— *in Spiritu*); your faith then is the lever which raises you, and love is the road which leads you to God (— *ad Patrem*)."[15]

And this is no empty formula for Ignatius, since it is in this Christological and Trinitarian perspective that the ardent candidate for martyrdom sees the profound significance and the whole worth of his coming immolation: "After many prayers to God I have been privileged to see your holy faces. In fact, I have received more than I asked; for I hope to be in chains for Christ Jesus when I greet you, if the will of God considers me worthy to reach the goal. The beginning is good: may I obtain the grace (— *a Patre*) to reach my inheritance without hindrance. . . . Let me imitate the passion of my God (— *per Christum*). . . . My earthly longings are crucified; there is no longer in me any desire for the material. The living water (— *in Spiritu*) murmurs within me and says, 'Come to the Father' (— *ad Patrem*)."[16]

The same Trinitarian dynamism is found in the stirring prayer of St. Polycarp before the stake of his martyrdom, a prayer which certainly brings us an echo of the great "eucharist" which the bishop of Smyrna was used to pronouncing during the synaxis: "Lord, Father all-powerful, Father of Jesus Christ, Your beloved and blessed Son, through whom we have received knowledge of You . . . I bless You because You have esteemed me worthy of this day and this hour, and worthy to have a share among the number of the martyrs in the chalice of Your Christ, for the resurrection to life eternal of both soul and body, in the incorruptibility of the Holy Spirit. . . . For this and for all other benefits I render You praise and blessing and glory, through the eternal and heavenly high priest Jesus Christ, Your beloved Son, through

---

[13] I Cor., 42.
[14] Ibid., 46, 5–6.

[15] Eph., 9, 1.
[16] Rom., 1, 1 f.; 6, 3; 7, 2.

whom and with whom, together with the Holy Spirit, be glory to You now and in ages to come. Amen." [17]

Between 180 and 199 St. Irenaeus formulated the law of the universal return to the Father in this way : "This is the order and the plan for those who are saved . . .; they advance by these steps : through the Holy Spirit they arrive at the Son, and through the Son they rise to the Father." [18]

These few texts, which it would be easy to multiply, will suffice to show what influence this conception of the Trinitarian mystery had on the thinking and living of the first Christian generations.

In the fourth and fifth centuries this viewpoint was not forgotten, even when the struggle against Arianism obliged the Fathers to interpret the scheme *a, per, in, ad* more explicitly of the intratrinitarian life and to direct their attention to the Word rather than to Christ.

Here, for example, is how St. Athanasius formulates the general law of God's interventions in the world : "The Father does everything through the Word in the Holy Spirit." [19] And St. Gregory of Nyssa : "Whatever operation passes from God to the creature . . . takes its origin from the Father, is continued by the Son, and is achieved in the Holy Spirit." [20]

It is to this same Trinitarian dynamism that the Fathers appeal to defend the faith against those who deny the divinity of the Holy Spirit. The Spirit is truly God, they explain ; for it is because of His presence in us that we are conformed to the Word, and through the Word to the Father ; and this conformity, this participation in the divine nature, cannot come to us from a creature.

"The Spirit," says St. Athanasius, "is the ointment and the seal with which the Word anoints and signs everything. . . . Thus signed, we rightly become partakers of the divine nature, as Peter says, and thus the creature becomes a sharer of the Word in the Spirit, and by the Spirit we are partakers of God . . . whenever we say that we are partakers of Christ and partakers of God, we mean that that anointing and that sign which are in us are not of a created nature, but are of the Son, who joins us to the Father by the Spirit who is in Him." [21]

Such reasoning is common among the Fathers of that age. The minds of their contemporaries must have been deeply imbued with this scriptural way of considering the relations of the divine Persons with the world ; for the Fathers could start out from it as from a principle known and admitted by all, to argue against the errors of the heretics.

Of course, when we state that the New Testament and the ancient tradition consider the history of salvation and the whole Christian life according to the scheme *a, per, in, ad,* we do not mean that this scheme is found everywhere and

[17] *Mart. Polyc.*, 14.
[18] *Adv. Haer.*, V, 36, 2 (PG 7, 1223).
[19] *Ad Serap.*, I, 28 (PG 26, 596).
[20] *Quod non sint tres dii* (PG 45, 125).
[21] *Ad Serap.*, I, 23–24 (PG 26, 585).

always, as soon as there is question of the relations between God and man, of the benefits bestowed by God, of prayer, etc. It would be easy to cite biblical or patristic texts in which the author seems to mention only the one God, or else one or another Person in an isolated way.

But when these authors want to encompass the whole of the relations between God and Man in one view, and in a specifically Christian perspective, their synthesis is always constructed according to the scheme indicated. Christ, the Spirit, the Father, considered separately, are for them only elements of that synthesis, which is sometimes clearly expressed, sometimes merely understood.[22]

2. The Christological and Trinitarian Perspective in the Liturgy

The first part of this chapter has brought to light the indispensable data for anyone who wants to understand the importance of the Christological and Trinitarian perspective in the liturgy. For here, as in so many other points, the liturgy simply echoes the Bible and the most ancient tradition.

The first point to be noted is that the God of the liturgy is not simply the God of the synagogue or the God of the philosophers, but the Christian God, the God in three Persons.

To be sure, the liturgy pays attention to the unity of the divine nature and does proclaim it, especially by its use of the Old Testament texts in which there is question of God. Thanks to its use of these texts, it preserves all the riches of the idea of God proposed by the Old Testament.

But the liturgy never lets us forget that this God revealed by the Old Testa-

---

[22] Let it be noted that this way of presenting the Trinity, as long as it is limited to considering the Persons in the extratrinitarian relations, does not yet constitute a particular theory for explaining the faith, but is simply the statement of this faith as the Scripture states it.

It is possible to go beyond the biblical data and, basing one's theory on the principle of correlation between the manifestations *ad extra* and the intratrinitarian relations, to apply to the very life of the Trinity the scheme *a, per, in, ad*, given by the Scripture directly for the action of the Trinity in the world, and to try to explain that life as far as possible according to this scheme. This step is taken by what Père de Régnon has called the "Greek" theory as opposed to the "Latin" theory (these names are not happily chosen, and should be taken in a broad sense).

It was along these lines, in the very interior of the "Greek" theory, that the theory called "economical" developed. It is so called be-

cause it concludes from the "economy" of the Persons *ad extra* to their way of being *ad intra*. This theory was that of the doctors of the third century, in particular of Tertullian, Hippolytus, Novatian and, in the main, Origen and his school. These, however, did not succeed in escaping subordinationism entirely in their attempted explanation of the faith.

At any rate, when the liturgy employs the scheme *a, per, in, ad*, applying it only to the extratrinitarian relations — which is almost always the case in the Roman liturgy, if not in the Eastern liturgies — it does not depend at all on the "Greek" explanation and still less on the "economical" explanation, but is content to assume the scriptural perspective. Because he failed to take account of this fact, the observations of Dom M. Cappuyns ("Liturgie et théologie," *Le vrai visage de la liturgie, Cours et conférences des semaines liturgiques,* 14 [Louvain: Abbaye du Mont César, 1938], 194–209) lose much of their value.

ment in the unity of His nature is in reality a God in three Persons. The liturgical context, proximate or remote, always gives these texts a Trinitarian and Christian sense. It is thus that in the Roman liturgy, at least from the fourth century on, the psalms are christianized explicitly by means of the *Gloria Patri*. But even when this was not yet the custom, the liturgical context sufficed to give these texts a properly Christian meaning. In this precise sense it can be said that the worship of the one God does not exist in the liturgy.

But how does the liturgy consider this Christian God, this God in three Persons ? We know that the Bible brings its attention to bear first of all on the distinction of the Persons and only afterwards on the unity of their nature, and that it considers these Persons primarily in their relations with the created world and with the history of salvation. On the first point the liturgy has always followed the Bible faithfully ; on the second, however, its attitude has varied in the course of the centuries.

The most ancient texts remain strictly faithful to the biblical perspective. But, beginning with the Arian controversy, an undeniable shift of emphasis takes place in the liturgy. Though keeping as a general framework the scheme *a, per, in, ad,* applied to the divine interventions in the world, the liturgies answer the denials of Arianism by multiplying the texts which affirm the equality of the Persons within the Trinity. Alongside of, or even instead of, the *economical* perspective, which throws the spotlight on the Father, Christ and the Spirit in their relations with the history of salvation, an *ontological* perspective finds place, in which attention is brought to bear principally on the equality of the three divine Persons and the unity of their nature.

After having affirmed, as heretofore, that everything comes to us from the Father through Christ and thanks to the Spirit, and that everything returns to the Father by the same way, the liturgies now add that the Father, the Son considered independently of His Incarnation, and the Holy Spirit are one and the same God. It might be said that, starting with the Arian controversy, the complete formula of the liturgy becomes "from the Father, through Christ His Son, in the Spirit, to the Father, blessed Trinity, one God" (*a Patre, per Christum Filium eius, in Spiritu, ad Patrem, beata Trinitas unus Deus*).

It must be recognized that this preoccupation with apologetics is much less apparent in the Roman liturgy than in the Eastern liturgies. It is hardly shown except in the conclusions of the collects and in the doxologies, in the Nicene-Constantinopolitan and Athanasian creeds, in the preface of the Trinity — which is found as early as the ancient Gelasian sacramentary[23] — and especially in the Office and Mass of the feast of the Most Holy Trinity.

This feast is known to be of Gallican origin. The Mass is the work of Alcuin, who died in 804, and the feast is first found at Liége in the time of Bishop Stephen (903–920). Rome held out for a long time before adopting the feast in

[23] I, 84; ed. Wilson, p. 129.

the fourteenth century. Some prayers of the present Roman liturgy, addressed directly to the Trinity, are also of Gallican origin, such as the *Suscipe sancta Trinitas* and the *Placeat tibi sancta Trinitas* of the Mass, which appear in the missals in the ninth to the eleventh centuries.

As to the theological speculations on the Trinity, whether those of the "Greek" theory or those of the "Latin," we may say that they have left no trace in the Roman liturgy.[24]

Let us attempt now to illustrate and to support all that we have just said by passing in review the collects, the doxologies, the Mass, the sacraments and the sacramentals, and finally the liturgical cycles. In this study we shall consider especially the Roman liturgy.

The collects

The introduction and the body of the liturgical collects conform on the whole to the Christological and Trinitarian structure which is expressed by the scheme *a, per, in, ad,* applied primarily to the role played by the divine Persons in the history of salvation. This rule holds also for the conclusion of the most ancient collects. Only from the time of the struggle against Arianism are there an increasing number of conclusions in which the equality of the Persons is affirmed in a more directly intratrinitarian view. And only from the Middle Ages, and especially in still more recent times, have there infiltrated into the Roman liturgy some rare collects of a completely different type.

The ancient rule is that the liturgical prayer should be addressed to the Father through the mediation of Christ. The council of Hippo in 393, at which Augustine, then only a priest, assisted, formulated this rule unequivocally : "In services at the altar, let the collect be directed always to the Father" *(Cum altari assistitur, semper ad Patrem dirigatur oratio)*.[25] The force of this rule in antiquity is shown by the fact that the council took this step despite the danger that the Arians might take a pretext therefrom for attacking the Catholic faith.[26]

This orientation of prayer is based not only on the ancient tradition but also on the recommendations of St. Paul : "May the word of Christ dwell in you abundantly : in all wisdom teach and exhort one another by psalms and hymns and spiritual canticles, singing sweetly to God in your hearts; and whatever you do in word or in deed, do all in the name of the Lord Jesus; giving thanks to God the Father through Him" (Col. 3:16 f.). "Be filled with the Holy Spirit, speaking to one another in psalms, hymns and spiritual canticles, sing-

---

[24] We may say that in the Roman liturgy the opposition to Arianism is expressed not in polemical reasonings but in the simple affirmation of the faith in the unity of nature of the Persons and their equality.

[25] Mansi, III, 884.

[26] This danger was not illusory, as is proved by a fragment from an Arian author published by G. Mercati in *Antiche reliquie liturgiche Ambrosiane e Romane* (coll. *Studi e Testi,* 7; Rome, 1902), pp. 47–56. This text has been published also by Dom C. Mohlberg as an appendix to his edition of the *Sacramentarium Veronense,* pp. 201–202.

ing and making melody in your hearts to the Lord, always giving thanks for everything in the name of our Lord Jesus Christ to God the Father" (Eph. 5:18 f.). And with St. Paul the practice corresponded to the theory.[27]

From this we understand the ancient structure of the liturgical collect. The one who is praying addresses himself to the Father and, most often, in the very first words calls Him Father, God, Lord God, etc. He mentions one or another of His attributes: all-powerful, eternal, Creator. He recalls one or another of His interventions on our behalf: "You who have sent us Your Son, who in the Old Testament worked such and such wonders, who have adorned this saint with such and such a virtue, who at this time grant us such and such a grace." Right from the beginning, the collect recalls a moment of the history of salvation, where the Father appears as the one *a quo omnia*, from whom all things come.

It must be emphasized that the one to whom the liturgical collect is addressed is really God the Father and not only God, the divinity. And this is true not only when He is called Father and when there is mention in the text of His intratrinitarian relations with the Son (υἱός, *Filius*) and with the Spirit. It is true also when He is called simply God, or Lord (δέσποτα), or our Father, with attributes common to the three Persons, and when Christ is then mentioned with the specifically messianic title of Servant (παῖς, *Puer*), even if there is not the least allusion to the Holy Spirit. The liturgy herein is merely conforming to the original Christian usage as the Scripture makes it known to us.

For we find in the New Testament an unmistakable tendency:

1) to reserve the name of God to the Father;[28]

2) to call by the title "our Father" not the one God but God the Father, whose son (υἱός) is Jesus Christ, and of whom we are the adoptive sons;[29]

3) to consider as said of the Father that which the Old Testament said simply of God.[30]

It is known that the doxologies of the New Testament and the great Eucharistic prayer are built on the same plan as the Jewish prayers, which address God, enumerating His attributes and His interventions in history. But the New Testament and the earliest Christian tradition have christianized this scheme: the God to whom the prayer is addressed is now God the Father, whose Son is always mentioned.

This christianization is real even if the Son is simply called Servant (παῖς, *Puer*), Christ, Messias. For the plurality of the Persons in God was revealed

---

[27] Cf. Rom. 1:8–10; 8:34; and in general the beginning of the letters, such as 1 Cor. 1:4–9; 2 Cor. 1:3–6; Gal. 1:3–5; Eph. 1:3 ff.; Col. 1:3 ff.; 1 Thes. 1:2–3.

[28] Cf. Rom. 1:8–10; 8:5–35 to be compared with 1 John 2:1 and with Heb. 7:25; 1 Cor. 1:3; Gal. 4:6; Col. 3:16–17; 1 Tim. 2:5 to be compared with 1 Cor. 8:4–6; 1 Pet. 1:3.

[29] In St. Paul the identification of "our Father" with the Father of our Lord Jesus Christ, who is His Son (υἱός), is so frequent that it must be supposed where it is not made explicit. Cf. Rom. 1:1–9; 1 Cor. 1:3–9; 2 Cor. 1:2 ff.; Gal. 1:1–16; 2:19–21; 4:4–7; Eph. 1:1–3; Col. 1:2–3; 1 Thes. 1:1–10. See also 1 John 4:12–14.

[30] See, e.g., Heb. 1:5–8.

to the Apostles in a concrete way and not in an abstract way: they came to understand gradually that the Messias, the Servant of Yahweh, Christ, was Son of God by a very special right and that God, if He was our Father, was by a very special title the Father of Christ.

It is no wonder, then, that the ancient texts which speak of the Father and of the Son remain in this perspective of the God of the Old Testament and of His Servant, the Messias. It is no wonder, either, that prayers which at first glance seem to be addressed to the one God or to our Father were in fact addressed by the Christians to Him in whom they saw first of all the Father of Jesus Christ. The clearly Trinitarian context shows this for the prayer of thanksgiving of the first Christians after the deliverance of the Apostles (Acts 4:24–31), as also for the long prayer of St. Clement's letter to the Corinthians (58–61; cf. 46, 6).

Similarly, the two prayers of the *Didache*, 9, 2–4, and 10, 2–5, even though addressed to "our Father" and to the "holy Father," seem to be no more than an application of the rule laid down by St. Paul: ". . . giving thanks always in the name of our Lord Jesus Christ to God the Father."

We have even more reason to think that the *Deus* to whom many collects of the Roman liturgy are addressed without further specification, with the simple conclusion *per Christum Dominum nostrum*, is God the Father. Many collects of the ancient Roman liturgy — almost all in the Leonine sacramentary, many still in the Gelasian — and the modern Roman liturgy are so addressed.

In its central part, the collect expresses adoration, thanksgiving, compunction, or else it is a petition for graces. At the same time, the one who is praying sets forth in a more or less ample way the reasons for his petition or his thanksgiving; and very often this leads him to recall this or that moment of the history of salvation. Here again, the attention is directed primarily to the action of the Persons *ad extra*, and according to the scheme *a, per, in, ad*.

Finally, the collect has a conclusion. As Father Jungmann has rightly pointed out,[31] it is in the development of the conclusion of the collects (we must add: and of the doxologies) that, in the ancient era, the insistence on the equality of the divine Persons becomes manifest, as a reaction against Arianism.

In the Eastern tradition the conclusion of the collects almost always contains a doxology; not so in the Roman liturgy. But in both cases the conclusion always makes mention of Christ the Mediator.[32]

The simplest of these conclusions is the Roman formula *Per Christum Domi-*

---

[31] Joseph A. Jungmann, *Die Stellung Christi im liturgischen Gebet* (Münster in Westf.: Aschendorff, 1925). For the field which we are studying here, this work has largely cleared the ground, and we often rely on its conclusions.

[32] In the prayers of chapters 9 and 10 of the *Didache*, the mention of Christ the Mediator is found not in the conclusion of the prayer, but immediately before. This is the only such case that we know of.

num nostrum, which terminates all the collects, secrets and postcommunions in the Leonine sacramentary and figures largely in the present Roman liturgy. Its meaning is clear: Father, we thank You, we adore You, we petition You through Christ our Lord, that is, referring ourselves to Him, in union with Him, in His name, through His intercession, for He is our Head. It is simply the application of St. Paul's advice and of the New Testament doctrine of Christ our intercessor with the Father (1 John 2:1; Rom. 8:34; Heb. 7:25; John 14:16; 16:23).

St. Clement of Rome makes explicit in a magnificent way the meaning of this "Through Christ our Lord" in the conclusion of the great prayer in his letter to the Corinthians, 61, 3:

> "To You, who alone have power to do these good things
> and far greater things for us,
> we give thanks, *through the high Priest*
> *and patron of our souls, Jesus Christ,*
> through whom be glory and majesty to You
> both now
> and from generation to generation
> and age to age. Amen."

The same formula is found again in chapter 64 of the letter and, substantially, in the *Martyrdom of Polycarp.*[33] In chapter 36 of his letter, Clement explains this formula by showing what Christ's mediation means for us: "This is the way, dearly beloved, in which we found our salvation, Jesus Christ, the high priest of our offerings, our patron and helper in our weakness. Through Him we fix our gaze on the heights of heaven. Through Him we see as in a mirror (cf. 2 Cor. 3:18) the spotless and sublime likeness of God. Through Him the eyes of our heart are opened. Through Him our mind, at first obtuse and darkened, unfolds like a flower to the light. Through Him the Lord willed that we should taste immortal knowledge."

The conclusion "Through Christ our Lord," or, better, "Through Christ our high Priest," insinuates, therefore, that liturgical prayer is not possible, has no meaning or value, unless it is the Church's prayer united to Christ's, the very prayer of Christ present and acting in the Church. We can present ourselves to God only as hidden in Christ.

The conclusion of the liturgical collects is developed further when the mention of the Holy Spirit is added to that of Christ the Mediator.

We shall study the Greek formulas at the same time as the doxologies, because in the Greek tradition the collects end with a doxology which originally did not name the Holy Spirit.

---

[33] 14, 3. Jungmann, in *Die Stellung Christi im liturgischen Gebet,* pp. 126 f., points out the same formula in the fragment of a prayer, probably liturgical, of a papyrus of the second-third century, and notes the same idea in Tertullian's *Adv. Marc.,* IV, 9, and Clement of Alexandria's *Strom.,* VI, 6. (See also *Protrep.,* XII, ed. Otto Stählin, p. 84.) These are all indications that in the second-third century the formula must have been quite common.

As far as the Roman collects are concerned, the mention of the Spirit was introduced by a broadening of the ancient conclusion *Per Christum Dominum nostrum*. The broadening finally led to the most developed formula : *Per Dominum nostrum Iesum Christum (Filium tuum), qui tecum vivit et regnat in unitate Spiritus Sancti (Deus) per omnia saecula saeculorum.*

There is some disagreement over the precise meaning of the expression *in unitate Spiritus Sancti*, which recurs in the concluding doxology of the Roman canon. [34] Although not everything has yet been clarified on this point, the most probable explanation seems to lie along the lines proposed by Dom Botte : the broadening of the ancient conclusion would be explained as a reaction against Arianism.

To combat the Arian heresy, the Catholics are supposed to have named the three Persons in the conclusion of the collects, transferring attention from the extratrinitarian level to that of the intratrinitarian life and reign, and emphasizing no longer the distinction of the Persons only, but also their unity and their equality. After the traditional conclusion *Per Christum Dominum nostrum* (or *Per Dominum nostrum Iesum Christum*) they were supposed to have added a formula expressing the idea that Christ, the Son of the Father, lives and reigns eternally with the Father and the Holy Spirit. The formulas might vary in their details. It seems certain that the expression *cum Spiritu Sancto* preceded our *in unitate Spiritus Sancti*; it was around 420–430 that the passage was made from the former to the latter, and in the second half of the fifth century this change was accepted almost everywhere in the West, except in Spain.

Even if it remains difficult to explain the exact sense of the *in unitate Spiritus Sancti*, the meaning of which was no longer obvious from the beginning of the sixth century, it seems that the conclusion as a whole may be understood thus : "Through our Lord Jesus Christ, Your Son, who lives and reigns with You, in the unity of the divine nature which You have together with the Holy Spirit, for ever and ever." The resemblance to certain conclusions which recur in Arnobius the Younger, who lived at Rome and died about 450, confirms the interpretation here proposed. [35]

At any rate, this insistence on the unity and the equality of the Persons in the conclusions of a certain number of collects of the Roman liturgy has not changed the essential perspective of these collects. They still conform to the Christological and Trinitarian perspective of the history of salvation. The

[34] Cf. Joseph A. Jungmann, *Die Stellung Christi im liturgischen Gebet*, pp. 179 ff.; *The Mass of the Roman Rite*, II, 264–268; Bernard Botte, *L'ordinaire de la messe* (Paris-Louvain, 1953), pp. 133 ff.

[35] These texts of Arnobius the Younger have been pointed out by Dom Botte, *L'ordinaire de la messe*, p. 136: "Per ipsum Dominum nostrum Iesum Christum, qui regnat in unitate Patris et Spiritus Sancti in saecula saeculorum." "Qui regnat cum Patre et Spiritu Sancto in unitate deitatis." Nothing authorizes us to see in the formula *in unitate Spiritus Sancti* an expression of the Augustinian theory that in the Trinity the Holy Spirit is the unity between the Father and the Son.

broadened conclusion merely adds to this ancient perspective another perspective which is more directly and more completely Trinitarian.

The liturgical collects preserved their traditional structure as long as the rule was observed that they be addressed to the Father through the mediation of Christ. When it came about that some of the collects were addressed directly to Christ or to the Son, these inevitably took on quite a different character.[36] The ancient conclusion was no longer adapted to these new collects.

The new formula, *Qui vivis et regnas . . .*, makes its appearance in the Gregorian sacramentary, in a series of collects for the Masses of Advent. These collects are addressed to *Domine* or to *Deus*, which therefore designates no longer the Father but the Son. Starting with the fifteenth century, some begin with the words *Domine Iesu Christe*.

As for the medieval collects which are addressed directly to the Trinity, they are still further removed from the ancient tradition.

At any rate, this new type of collect occupies only a small place in the Roman liturgy. Of a total of about a thousand collects, secrets and postcommunions contained in today's Roman Missal, Father Jungmann counts only 64 of the new type.[37] Of these, moreover, 17 are ancient collects addressed to the Father, which were later understood as addressed to the Son.

The doxologies

The liturgical doxologies depend on those of the New Testament, which in turn have close bonds with the doxologies of the Old Testament and of the later Jewish tradition.[38]

In the New Testament a good number of doxologies are addressed to the Father alone (Rom. 11:36; Gal. 1:15; Phil. 4:20; 1 Tim. 1:17; 6:16; 1 Pet. 5:11; Apoc. 4:9–11; 7:12). Three are addressed to the Father through Christ (Rom. 16:27; 1 Pet. 4:11; Jude 25). Four or five are addressed to Christ alone (2 Tim. 4:18; Heb. 13:21; 2 Pet. 3:18; Apoc. 1:6; and probably Rom. 9:5). One is addressed to God and to Christ (Apoc. 7:10), another to the Father in the Church and in Christ (Eph. 3:21). These doxologies are occasioned by the consideration of the attributes of God (1 Tim. 6:16), of His creative action (e.g., Apoc. 4:11) and especially of His redemptive action.

It is from this source that the liturgical doxologies come into existence. They have always been particularly abundant in the Greek tradition, which terminates by a doxology not only the great Eucharistic prayer, but every liturgical prayer, as the Jews usually did. Very soon there were also independent doxologies.

The Roman tradition has not followed the custom of closing every prayer

---

[36] For the Greek liturgy, the first examples are encountered in the *Apostolic Constitutions*, VII, 43; VIII, 7. It is known that this compilation dates probably from the beginning of the fifth century.

[37] *Die Stellung Christi im liturgischen Gebet*, p. 103.

[38] Cf. A. Stuiber, "Doxologie," *Reallexikon für Antike und Christentum* of Theodor Klauser, IV, fasc. 26 (1958), 210–226.

by a doxology. It has at least preserved the universal custom of terminating the canon of the Mass with a doxology. Moreover, it has adopted a certain number of independent doxologies coming from the East, such as the *Gloria Patri*, the *Gloria in excelsis*, the *Te decet laus*, to which it has added the *Te Deum*, of Western origin. Finally, it has ended its hymns with doxologies of their own.

Like the collects, the doxologies conform to the Christological and Trinitarian perspective, but in varying degrees. In the liturgical texts that have come down to us, there are few traces of doxologies addressed solely to the Father. [39] They are almost always binary or ternary.

The doxologies, still more than the concluding formulas of the collects, bring us the echo of the struggle against Arianism.

Even before this controversy, there were doxologies in which the names of the divine Persons were simply coordinated. We have an example of them in the ancient Vesper hymn of the second-third century: "Joyous light of the holy glory of the immortal, heavenly, holy, blessed Father, Jesus Christ! Now at sunset, contemplating the evening sun, we praise the Father *and* the Son *and* the Holy Spirit." St. Basil, in reminding the Arians of this ancient text, lists a series of ancient authors, among them Denis of Alexandria, Julius Africanus, Gregory Thaumaturgus, who used similar doxologies. [40]

These formulas, which emphasize the equality of the Persons, seem to be derived from the baptismal formula of Matt. 28:19. But they remain the exception in the first centuries. It is only from the time of the Arian crisis that the Catholics will compose more of them.

Before that crisis, the type of doxology much more frequent was that in which the names of the Persons were connected by the prepositions "through . . . in . . ." Traces are found of ancient binary doxologies which rendered glory to the Father through Christ, without mentioning the Holy Spirit. [41]

In another formula, glory was given to the Father through the Son and through the Holy Spirit. Thus Justin writes, in a general way, "For everything

[39] Didache, 9 and 10. End of the prayer of the faithful in the papyrus of Dar-Balizeh, I verso, 10; ed. Quasten, *Monumenta eucharistica et liturgica vetustissima*, I, p. 40.

[40] *De Spiritu Sancto*, 29.

[41] *Didache*, 9, 4; Clement of Rome, 1 *Cor.*, 58, 2; 61, 3; 64; fragment of the anaphora of St. Mark (ed. Quasten, *Monumenta eucharistica et liturgica vetustissima*, I, p. 49); prayer for the blessing of fruits in the *Tradition* of Hippolytus according to the critical edition of Dix, p. 54.

It is likewise to this type of binary doxology that we must assign the Syrian version of the *Gloria in excelsis* (*Apostolic Constitutions*, 7, 47; ed. Funk, I, 454–456), which is a doxology to the Father through Jesus Christ. Certain authors have regarded this Syrian version as the most ancient, and have supposed that the Alexandrian version, to which the Latin *Gloria* is connected, was a development of it in an anti-Arian sense, with the explicit mention of the Holy Spirit. But as Dom Bernard Capelle has shown ("Le texte du *Gloria in excelsis*," *Rev. d'histoire eccl.*, 44 [1949], 439–457), it is the Alexandrian version "which has preserved substantially the authentic text of the *Gloria*." It is probable, however, that even in this version the mention of the Holy Spirit (καὶ ἅγιον πνεῦμα), inserted without any development amid the acclamations to Christ, is a later addition made in reaction against Arianism.

with which we are supplied, we bless the Maker of all things through (διά)
His Son Jesus Christ and through (καὶ διά) the Holy Spirit"; [42] and concerning the great Eucharistic prayer, "After which some bread and a cup of wine
mixed with water is carried to the provost of the brethren, and he, taking it,
gives praise and glory to the Father of all things through (διά) the name of the
Son and of the Holy Spirit." [43] And Clement of Alexandria writes, "To whom
(the Father) through His Servant (παῖς) Jesus Christ, Lord of the living and
the dead, and through the Holy Spirit, be glory." [44]

But the ordinary scheme of the doxologies in the East before the Arian
struggle was that which linked the names of the Persons by the prepositions
"through . . . in . . . ." Thus Origen recommends that prayer be concluded
by "praising the Father of all things through Jesus Christ in the Holy
Spirit." [45] In the sacramentary of Serapion the ordinary conclusion of the
collects is: "We thank You, we petition You . . . Through Christ (Your
Christ, Christ our hope, etc.; rarely: Your only-begotten Jesus Christ) in the
Holy Spirit, through whom be glory and empire to You both now and in all
ages forever. Amen." In book VIII of the *Apostolic Constitutions*, the conclusion of the collects is, with some variants: through Christ our God and
Savior, "through whom be glory and veneration to You in the Holy Spirit,
now and forever, world without end. Amen." It is likewise in the *Apostolic
Constitutions* that we find the most ancient text of the *Te decet laus*: "To You
praise is due, to You a hymn, to You glory, God and Father, through the Son
in the Holy Spirit for ever and ever. Amen." [46]

The meaning of these formulas is clear for anyone who refers to the scriptural scheme *a, per, in, ad*: we give thanks to the Father, or we petition Him,
through Jesus Christ, His incarnate Son, our high Priest, our Head and Mediator, and we do this in virtue of the Holy Spirit present in us, who enables
us to address ourselves to the Father in this way. This doxology "through . . .
in . . ." is the one that corresponds best to the Christological and Trinitarian
perspective of the New Testament. [47]

---

[42] *Apol. I*, 67 (PG 6, 429).

[43] *Ibid.*, 65 (PG 6, 428).

[44] *Quis dives salvetur*, 42, 20 (PG 9, 652).
The authenticity of the doxology of the
Martyrium Polycarpi, 14, in its present form is
very doubtful (cf. J. A. Robinson, "The
Apostolic Anaphora and the Prayer of St.
Polycarp," *Journal of Theological Studies*,
1920, pp. 97–105; J. W. Tyrer, "The Prayer
of St. Polycarp and Its Concluding Doxology,"
ibid., 1922, pp. 390–392). It combines the
ancient binary formula "to the Father through
Christ His Servant" with a ternary formula
of the coordinate type: "O God . . . I glorify
You through the eternal and heavenly Pontiff
Jesus Christ, Your beloved Servant (παῖς),

through whom be glory to You, with Him and
the Holy Spirit, now and in the ages to come.
Amen." The same combination is found in
the formula often used after the Arian controversy: "through whom and with whom"
(δι' οὗ καὶ μεθ' οὗ). In fact, it is for this reason
that the doxology of Polycarp is held suspect.
In the same *Martyrium Polycarpi* the binary
formula is kept in chapters 19 and 20, certainly
ancient, while a ternary formula is found in
chapter 22, certainly later, as also in the ancient Latin version.

[45] *De Oratione*, 33 (PG 11, 561).

[46] VII, 48, 3; ed. Funk, I, 456–458.

[47] In the doxology of the anaphora of Hippolytus, mention is made of the Church:

Until the middle of the fourth century this doxology was by far the most widespread in the East. But the Arian propaganda interpreted it in a subordinationist sense. The Catholics had no difficulty in replying that the divine Persons were here considered in their relations with the created world, not in their intratrinitarian relations. This was St. Basil's reply in his treatise on the Holy Spirit.[48]

The Arian danger was so pressing, however, that it seemed prudent to abandon the traditional formula and replace it by doxologies in which the Catholic doctrine would be expressed most clearly. As early as 350, the faithful of Antioch were singing the formula "Glory be to the Father and to the Son and to the Holy Spirit, now and forever, world without end. Amen" in a clearly anti-Arian sense. This doxology took hold. A little later, St. Basil introduced another of the same type: "Glory to God the Father . . . with ($\mu\epsilon\tau\acute{a}$) the Son and with ($\sigma\acute{v}\nu$) the Holy Spirit." In the fourth and fifth centuries these coordinate formulas multiplied throughout the East. Among the most widespread, aside from those we have just quoted, were: ". . . with whom ($\mu\epsilon\theta$' $o\mathring{v}$) may You be blessed together with the Holy Spirit"; "To You praise is due, to You a hymn, to You glory, Father, Son and Holy Spirit."

As for the ancient Roman liturgy, it adopted the type, and often the terminology, of the Greek doxologies composed, or modified, in reaction to Arianism. This is true of the *Gloria Patri*, in which the clause "as it was in the beginning" emphasizes further the anti-Arian character.[49] It is true of the *Te decet laus* in its later form, where the names of the Persons are no longer subordinated but coordinated.[50] It is equally true of the *Gloria in excelsis* in the Alexandrian version, with the explicit affirmation of the divinity of Christ and with the mention of the Holy Spirit.

The *Te Deum*, on the other hand, is of Western origin. Its author and its history remain clouded in obscurity. It is certain, at any rate, that the present text is the result of successive retouchings and additions. The Holy Spirit appears only in a short Trinitarian doxology inserted between the first part,

---

" . . . praising through Your Servant Christ Jesus, through whom be glory and honor to You, Father and Son, with the Holy Spirit, in the holy Church, both now and forever." Jungmann in *Die Stellung Christi im liturgischen Gebet*, pp. 132 f., points out certain liturgical remains which allow us to suppose that such mention of the Church was not exceptional in the ancient doxologies. Actually, it merely repeats St. Paul's formula: " . . . to Him be glory in the Church and in Christ Jesus down through all generations for ever and ever. Amen" (Eph. 3:21), to underline the fact that the Church, in as much as it is the body of Christ and the only place where the Spirit dwells in this world, is also the only

place where God the Father can be glorified. As St. Cyril of Alexandria says, "We are not made perfect in any other way but by being acceptable to God the Father, in the Church, Christ offering us, in as much as He is Priest" (*De adoratione et cultu in spiritu et veritate*, XVI [PG 68, 1016 B]).

[48] *De Spiritu Sancto*, 4–8 (PG 32, 77–105).

[49] For the history of the *Gloria Patri* in the West see Henri Leclercq in *Dict. d'arch. chrét. et de liturg.*, IV, 1525–1528; Petrus Siffrin in *Encicl. catt.*, VI (1951), 869 f.

[50] St. Benedict has his monks chant the *Te decet laus* at the Sunday night Office (*Rule*, ch. 11).

which is devoted to the Father, and the second, which is devoted to the Son:
"Father of boundless majesty; Your true and only Son, who is to be adored;
and the Holy Spirit, the Comforter." It seems that this ternary doxology has
been added to the original text with an anti-Arian intention.

The Western doxologies of medieval origin, which abound especially as
conclusions of hymns, are all situated in the anti-Arian perspective. In Spain
and in Gaul, some of them are even addressed to the Trinity, as is the case,
for example, in the Office of the Blessed Trinity. These are not numerous,
however, in the present Roman liturgy, where the more ancient anti-Arian
type predominates.

The Mass

The sacrifice of the Mass, as it appears in the anaphoras, is also conformed
to the traditional Christological and Trinitarian structure. In the texts still
in use, as well as in the more ancient formulas, we find again the scheme *a*,
per, *in*, *ad*. The Father appears as the principle *a quo* and the terminus *ad
quem* of the Eucharistic action. Christ appears as the high Priest through
whom we perform this action. The Holy Spirit appears as the one in whom,
that is, in and through whose presence, this action is performed here and
now.[51] Here again, the divine Persons are seen in their relations with the
history of salvation. Here again, the insistence on the equality of the Persons
will come only after the Arian controversy.

The most ancient complete text of an anaphora that has come down to us is
that of Hippolytus: "We render thanks to You, O God, through Your beloved
Servant Jesus Christ, whom in the last times You have sent to us as Savior
and Redeemer and the messenger of Your will; who is Your Word inseparable, through whom You made all things and in whom You were well-
pleased; whom You sent from heaven into the Virgin's womb; and who,
conceived within her, was made flesh and demonstrated to be Your Son, being
born of the Holy Spirit and the Virgin. Fulfilling Your will and acquiring
for You a holy people, He stretched forth His hands for suffering that He
might release from sufferings those who have believed in You. And when He
was betrayed to voluntary suffering that He might abolish death, break the
bonds of the devil, tread down hell, enlighten the righteous, establish the
ordinance and demonstrate the resurrection, taking bread and giving thanks
[making eucharist] to You, He said, 'Take, eat: this is My Body which is
broken for you.' Likewise also the cup, saying, 'This is My Blood which is
shed for you. When you do this you do My *anamnesis*.'

"Doing, therefore, the *anamnesis* of His death and Resurrection, we offer

---

[51] The idea of the sacrifice being performed
in Spiritu is a biblical idea. St. Paul supposes
it in Rom. 15:15 f. It is expressed likewise in
Heb. 9:14, if we read πνεύματος ἁγίου, but
also if we adopt the more probable reading
πνεύματος αἰωνίου, for, in the letter to the
Hebrews, "αἰώνιος means not only 'without
end, of infinite duration,' but also 'who has
divine power, divine energy'" (Ceslaus Spicq,
L'épître aux hébreux, I, 296, note 1; cf., however, II, 258 f.). See also St. Basil, *De Spir. S.*,
26 (PG 32, 184 f.).

You the bread and the cup, giving thanks [making eucharist] to You because You have found us worthy to stand before You and minister as priests to You. And we pray You (that You would send Your Holy Spirit upon the oblation of Your holy Church), that You would grant to all who partake to be united (to You), that they may be filled with the Holy Spirit for the confirmation of their faith in truth, that we may praise and glorify You through Your (beloved) Servant Jesus Christ, through whom glory and honor be to You with the Holy Spirit in Your holy Church now and world without end. Amen." [52]

This anaphora conforms to the traditional Trinitarian scheme. The Eucharistic action is conceived as an *anamnesis*, which brings before God in a real way a past event whose consequences remain effective in the present. This *anamnesis* is addressed to the Father, terminus of prayer and of praise and at the same time first source of all the benefits, past and present, which are here recalled or asked for. Christ is the Mediator of our thanksgiving, because He was the Mediator of our redemption, and because the Eucharistic action is the *anamnesis* of His death and of His Resurrection. Finally, the Holy Spirit is the one in whose presence the oblation of the holy Church is performed, the one whom the believers receive by communicating, and thanks to whom they are able to praise the Father through Christ. [53]

That the *schema* of Hippolytus is definitely traditional is proved by the fact that it is found again in the Eastern anaphoras, though with more or less important variations and developments, such as the much fuller description of the creation and of the history of Israel, and the insertion of the *Sanctus*. It is found in the Egyptian anaphora of Serapion as well as in the Syrian anaphora of book VIII of the *Apostolic Constitutions* and in the Byzantine anaphora of St. Basil, all three dating from the second half of the fourth century.

As might be expected, after the Arian crisis a certain number of Eastern anaphoras insisted on the unity and the equality of the Persons; this is particularly clear in the anaphora of St. John Chrysostom. Traces of theological speculation on the Trinity, especially on the Word, are even found here and there. But the Eastern anaphoras on the whole remain faithful to the traditional scheme.

As for the Roman canon, even if it lacks the linear logic and simplicity of the ancient Eucharist, and even if its different parts seem to lack unity and coherence, still it conforms to the classical perspective. If a person will reread the text, omitting the prayers of intercession (in the *Te igitur* the part from *in primis* on, the *Memento* of the living, the *Communicantes*, the *Hanc igitur*, the *Memento* of the dead and the *Nobis quoque peccatoribus*), he will have

---

[52] *The Treatise on the Apostolic Tradition of St. Hippolytus of Rome*, ed. by the Rev. Gregory Dix, pp. 7-9.
[53] The mention of the Holy Spirit in the anaphora is very ancient, as is shown by the text of Justin, *Apol.* I, 65, quoted above, p.

124. Likewise, there was always a general persuasion that in the Eucharist the faithful received the Holy Spirit (cf. Gregory Dix, *The Shape of the Liturgy* [Westminster (London) Dacre Press, 1954], pp. 266 f.).

no trouble in seeing that, with respect to the Father and to Christ, the Trinitarian dynamism according to the scheme *a, per, in, ad* is just as plain as it is in the anaphora of Hippolytus or in the Eastern anaphoras.

There is one difficulty, however. In the present text the Holy Spirit appears only in the final doxology: *in unitate Spiritus Sancti*; and this formula, as we have said, seems to be intended to emphasize the unity of nature of the three Persons, in protest against Arianism. Is there no mention, then, in the Roman canon, of the part played by the Holy Spirit in the history of salvation, and especially in the performance of the Eucharistic action? We may suppose either that this mention did exist at one time in an epiclesis which soon disappeared — to which Pope Gelasius I (492–496) would be making an allusion in his letter to Bishop Elpidius of Volterra: "How will the heavenly Spirit, invoked to consecrate the divine mystery, come . . ." [54] — or that this mention is implicit in the *Quam oblationem* or the *Supplices te rogamus*.

In the Gallican and Mozarabic liturgies, the anaphora has a structure analogous to that of the Roman canon. It differs from it, however, in some details, among them the fact that certain prayers vary with each Mass, as do the prefaces in the Leonine sacramentary. Originally, one of these prayers, called *Post mysterium, Post secreta* or *Post pridie*, constituted an epiclesis to the Holy Spirit. It was only beginning with the sixth century that the epiclesis in some of the Mass formularies is supposed to have been altered, attenuated or even suppressed. In the *Liber mozarabicus sacramentorum* of Férotin, it is still found very often. [55]

Did the Ambrosian canon, very similar to the Roman canon, include a mention of the part played by the Holy Spirit in the Eucharistic action? In the present text the Holy Spirit appears only in the final doxology, in the phrase *in unitate Spiritus Sancti*. But it is certain that St. Ambrose knew an invocation to the Holy Spirit in the course of the Mass, for he writes, "How can it be said, then, that the Holy Spirit does not possess entirely the nature of God, He who, together with the Father and the Son, is named by the priest in baptism, and is *invoked in the oblations* . . .?" [56]

The sacraments

Baptism

Together with baptism we shall study here the baptismal profession of faith, the rule of faith and the symbols, for all this is intimately linked with baptism.

---

[54] Thiel, *Epistolae Romanorum pontificum genuinae*, I, 486. On the question, much debated, of the existence of a consecratory epiclesis in the Roman canon, cf. S. Salaville, "Epiclèse," *Dict. de théol. cath.*, V (1939), 218 ff.; Jungmann, *The Mass of the Roman Rite*, II, 191–194; Righetti, III, 320 ff.

[55] Cf. S. Salaville, "Epiclèse," *Dict. de théol.*

cath., V, 216–217; S. Portier, "The Mozarabic *Post Pridie*," *Journal of Theological Studies*, 1943, pp. 182 ff.

[56] *De Spiritu S.*, III, 16, 112 (PL 16, 803). On the question of the epiclesis in the Milanese canon, cf. S. Salaville, "Epiclèse," *Dict. de théol. cath.*, V, 217–218; Borella in Righetti, III, 557 f.

Many documents show us how the ancient Church viewed baptism according to the traditional scheme *a, per, in, ad*. One of the clearest and most profound is this text of St. Irenaeus in his *Proof of the Apostolic Preaching*: "Here is what the faith attests for us, according to what the ancients, the disciples of the Apostles, have transmitted to us. First of all it obliges us to recall that we have received baptism for the remission of sins in the name of God the Father, and in the name of Jesus Christ, the Son of God . . . and in the Holy Spirit of God. . . . Therefore the baptism which regenerates us is conferred on us through these three articles [57] and guarantees our rebirth in God the Father, through His Son, by the Holy Spirit. For those who receive the Spirit of God are led to the Word, that is, to the Son; but the Son receives them and presents them to the Father, and the Father confers incorruptibility on them. Thus without the Spirit no one can see the Word of God, and without the Son no one can approach the Father; for the Son is the knowledge of the Father, but the knowledge of the Son is had through the Spirit. But it is the Son who, according to the Father's good pleasure, distributes the Spirit as a gift, as the Father wishes Him to, and to those to whom He wishes Him to give the Spirit." [58]

We cannot separate from baptism the profession of the faith which the Church required of the catechumen during the ceremony itself. This profession of faith is to be identified either with the original symbol or at least with a formula very similar, connected with that brief summary of the Christian faith which was called in antiquity the rule of faith.

At any rate, this profession of faith was concerned primarily with the Christological and Trinitarian truths, according to the usual scheme. And as it was intimately connected, in liturgical practice, to the administration of baptism, this act naturally received from it a very marked Christological and Trinitarian character. The clearest possible evidence of this is the description of baptism by Hippolytus in his *Apostolic Tradition*:

"And when he (*the one who is to be baptized*) goes down to the water, let him who baptizes lay his hand on him, saying, 'Do you believe in God the Father almighty?' And he who is being baptized shall say, 'I believe.' Then let him baptize him the first time, holding his hand upon his head.

"And after this let him say, 'Do you believe in Christ Jesus, the Son of God, who was born of the Holy Spirit and the Virgin Mary, who was crucified under Pontius Pilate, and died (and was buried) and rose the third day living from the dead and ascended into heaven, and sits at the right hand of the Father, and will come to judge the living and the dead?' And when he says, 'I believe,' let him baptize him the second time.

"And again let him say, 'Do you believe in the Holy Spirit in the holy

[57] In the context just preceding, Irenaeus speaks of the three articles of the creed, professing belief first in God the Father, second in Jesus Christ and third in the Holy Spirit.
[58] *Demonstr.*, 3; 7.

Church, and the resurrection of the flesh?' And he who is being baptized shall say, 'I believe.' And so let him baptize him the third time." [59]

This threefold interrogation corresponding to the three parts of the symbol, followed by the threefold reply of the candidate and the threefold immersion done without any other formula, was the only form of baptism in ancient times. [60] In the West St. Irenaeus [61] and St. Ambrose [62] likewise bear witness to it, and it is still found in the Roman rite described by the ancient Gelasian sacramentary. [63] It was thus that the ancient Church understood the Lord's command to baptize in the name of the Father and of the Son and of the Holy Spirit.

In the East we find no trace of a different usage before the middle of the fourth century. Then for the first time, it seems, the *Canons of Hippolytus* follow the threefold immersion, always accompanied by the threefold interrogation, with the formula "I baptize you in the name of the Father and of the Son and of the Holy Spirit, who is equal." [64] The obvious purpose of this addition was to underline the equality of the Persons. For the ancient baptismal formula was in danger of being interpreted in a subordinationist or Arian sense; St. Ambrose had already taken pains to counteract this interpretation. [65] The new formula forestalled this danger. Documented by several Eastern sources at the end of the fourth century, [66] it penetrated into the West in the eighth century. [67]

In this context it is easy to grasp the structure of the ancient Roman symbol, called the Apostles' Creed, whether in its more ancient form [68] or in its present form. It is divided into three parts, in each of which there is considered one of the Persons in His relations with the history of salvation according to the part He plays or the role appropriated to Him : for the Father, creation ; for Christ, the Son of God made Man, His Incarnation, His death, His Resurrection, His glorification and His future parousia; for the Holy Spirit, the Church with her means of sanctification, looking to the resurrection of the flesh and the completion of the whole history of salvation in life eternal. Such also is the interpretation of the rule of faith already given by St. Irenaeus. [69]

---

[59] See Dix edition, pp. 36 f. For the reading "in the holy Church" cf. P. Nautin, *Je crois à l'Esprit Saint dans la Sainte Eglise pour la Résurrection de la chair* (Paris, 1947), pp. 13–27. The papyrus of Dar-Balizeh, at the third article of its baptismal profession of faith, also has " . . . I believe . . . and in the Holy Spirit and in the resurrection of the flesh in the holy Catholic Church." Cf. C. H. Roberts and Bernard Capelle, *An Early Euchologium* (Louvain, 1949), pp. 32 f., 60 f.

[60] Cf. A. Stenzel, *Die Taufe* (Innsbruck, 1958), pp. 97 ff., 111 ff.

[61] *Demonstr.*, 7.

[62] *De sacr.*, II, 7, 20 (PL 16, 429).

[63] I, 44; ed. Wilson, p. 86.

[64] Text in Duchesne, *Origine du culte chrétien* (5th ed.; Paris, 1909), p. 50. It seems that the *Canons of Hippolytus* were written around the years 341–360; cf. Bernard Botte, "L'origine des Canons d'Hippolyte," *Mélanges Andrieu* (Strasbourg, 1956), pp. 53–63.

[65] *De sacr.*, VI, 2, 5–8 (PL 16, 455).

[66] Theodore of Mopsuestia attests to it between 381 and 392: *Catechesis* XIV, prologue; ed. Tonneau, *Les homélies catéchétiques de Théodore de Mopsueste* (coll. *Studi e Testi*), p. 403; and St. John Chrysostom around 390: *Catechesis* II, 26; ed. Wenger, *Huit catéchèses baptismales* (*Sources chrétiennes*), p. 50.

[67] Cf. Righetti, IV, 68 f.

[68] Dz 2.

[69] *Demonstr.*, 6.

This Christological and Trinitarian structure is found again without essential modifications in the later symbols, including both the Nicene creed [70] and the one called Nicene-Constantinopolitan, which is now said in the Mass. What the changes amount to, at most, is an insistence, against Arianism, on the divinity of the Son and of the Holy Spirit.

Only the creed called *Quicumque* or the Symbol of St. Athanasius, which dates from the fifth century, is composed in a quite different way: it has directly in view an exposition of the Catholic faith to confront the Christological and Trinitarian heresies.[71]

If the present-day ritual of baptism, especially of the baptism of adults, contains several texts which emphasize the unity and equality of the Persons (prayer *Omnipotens* at n. 3; admonition *Si vis* at n. 5; formula *Ego te baptizo*), still it remains faithful in many points to the traditional perspective (interrogation on the symbol at nn. 7 and 38; little exorcism at n. 8; prayer *Domine, sancte Pater* stressing the role of the Holy Spirit at n. 14; exorcisms at nn. 13, 19, 33, 37; prayer *Deus omnipotens* at n. 41).

Confirmation

The Christological and Trinitarian sense of confirmation results especially from its intimate connection with baptism. Confirmation has always been regarded as a sacramental rite giving a special infusion of the Holy Spirit with a view to perfecting, fortifying, sealing the action of God in the neophyte. Hence it has been given the names of seal, sign, consignation, confirmation. It emphasizes in a very particular way the role which the Holy Spirit plays in the Christian life as seal of the divine gifts, in whom every Christian perfection is realized. It is the liturgical translation of the biblical concept which considers the Spirit as the one *in quo*.

St. Ambrose echoes the whole tradition when he writes, "Then comes the spiritual sign (*signaculum*), about which you have heard the reading today, since after the font there still remains the reception of perfection (*post fontem superest ut perfectio fiat*) when, at the invocation of the priest, the Holy Spirit is infused." [72]

St. Cyprian had already laid down the rule that "those who are baptized in the Church are presented to the bishops of the Church, and thus, by our prayer and imposition of hands, they receive the Holy Spirit and are perfected with the sign of the Lord (*et signaculo dominico consummentur*)." [73]

Basically, the idea is already found in St. Paul: "Whatever God has promised finds its 'Yes' in Him (Christ), and for that reason we say our 'Amen' through Him to God's glory. But the one who has established us firmly along with you in communion with Christ, and who has anointed us, is God, who also stamped us with His seal and gave us the Spirit as a pledge in our hearts" (2 Cor. 1:20–22). The anointing of which St. Paul speaks is almost certainly

[70] Dz 54.
[71] Dz 39–40.

[72] *De sacr.*, III, 2, 8 (PL 16, 434).
[73] *Ep.* 73, 9, 2 (PL 3, 1115).

the baptism to which God has called us and by which He has established us and strengthened us in Christ. For greater security, like a seal placed on an envelope which contains precious things, God has added to this first gift the gift of the Spirit — almost certainly confirmation — which is the pledge of the total gift which He will give us in the life to come.

The Spirit, for St. Paul, of course, is the Spirit of Christ (cf. Gal. 4:6, clarified by Rom. 8:5–17).

It is this Pauline theology, in line with the Trinitarian scheme *a, per, in, ad,* which is at the basis of the liturgy of confirmation. St. Ambrose was right when he explained to the neophyte the Trinitarian dimension of the rite: "Remember, therefore, that you have received the spiritual sign, the Spirit of wisdom and of understanding. . . . Guard that which you have received. God the Father has signed you, Christ the Lord has confirmed you by giving into your heart the pledge of the Spirit, as you have heard in the reading from the Apostle." [74]

The liturgical formulas for the administration of confirmation have varied in the course of the centuries.

In the ancient Roman liturgy, the essential text, found in the Gelasian sacramentary [75] and referred to by St. Ambrose,[76] is the epicletic prayer which is said today at the beginning of the rite: "All-powerful, eternal God, who have seen fit to regenerate these Your servants through water and the Holy Spirit and have granted them the remission of all their sins, send them from heaven Your septiform Holy Spirit, the Comforter: Spirit of wisdom . . . . Fill them with the Spirit of the fear of the Lord and, in Your kindness, sign them with the sign of the cross of Christ for life eternal. Through the same Lord . . . ."

In the formula now used for the anointing, "I sign you with the sign of the cross and I confirm you with the chrism of salvation," it is hard to find the Trinitarian dimension of confirmation. As for the phrase "in the name of the Father and of the Son and of the Holy Spirit," which many theologians hold is not an essential part of the form, it emphasizes as usual the ontological aspect of the mystery of the Trinity.

Penance

The sacrament of penance as administered in the present Roman liturgy has kept hardly a trace of its Christological and Trinitarian signification, which was so obvious in the rites of the ancient liturgy.

The ancient liturgy showed clearly that the reconciliation of the penitent was accomplished essentially by the laying-on of hands and by imploring the coming of the Holy Spirit, in agreement with the biblical idea that there is a close connection between the remission of sins and the presence of the Holy

---

[74] *De myst.,* VII, 42 (PL 16, 402–403).
[75] I, 44; ed. Wilson, p. 87.
[76] *De myst.,* VII, 42 (PL 16, 402–403). The

first part of the formula accompanies the post-baptismal anointing in *De sacr.,* II, 7, 24 (PL 16, 430).

Spirit (cf. John 20:22 f.). The ancient conception was that sin drove the Holy Spirit out of the soul, and the reconciliation of the sinner was accomplished by the return of the Holy Spirit. It was to obtain this return that the hands were laid on and the prayers were said in the rite of reconciliation. The Fathers often make allusion to this point.

St. Jerome writes, "The priest offers his oblation for the penitent, lays his hand on him, who is in an attitude of submission, invokes the return of the Holy Spirit, and thus readmits to the altar the one who had been consigned to Satan for the death of the flesh that the spirit might be saved." [77]

St. Ambrose, though with a less clear allusion to the liturgical rite and with a greater emphasis on the invocation of the three divine Persons in a perspective which is rather ontological and anti-Arian, does make it understood that the Holy Spirit plays a special role in the reconciliation of penitents: "You see, therefore, that it is through the Holy Spirit that sins are pardoned. In the remission of sins, men are only His instruments, and they exercise no power in their own right. For they do not remit sins in their own name, but in the name of the Father and of the Son and of the Holy Spirit." [78]

The text from St. Jerome suffices to prove that the rite of reconciliation of penitents included an epicletic prayer to the Holy Spirit besides the imposition of hands. And this fact situates the rite in the traditional Trinitarian perspective.

This perspective is no longer found, as far as I can see, in the later formulas of penance, whether public or private. In the present rite the sole vestige, scarcely recognizable, is the gesture of the priest raising his hand slightly toward the penitent in the act of giving him absolution. This is the only trace of the ancient laying-on of hands and epiclesis to the Holy Spirit.

Holy orders

The prayers of consecration of deacons, priests and bishops are the ones which show us how the liturgy fits the sacrament of holy orders into the Christological and Trinitarian frame. In most of the rites, these prayers constitute real epicleses which implore the coming of the Holy Spirit, and they are accompanied by the usual laying-on of hands.

The consecratory prefaces in use today in the Roman rite come from the Leonine sacramentary; but we are acquainted with still more ancient formulas, the consecratory epicleses of the *Apostolic Tradition* of Hippolytus of Rome, the Trinitarian character of which is obvious.

Here, for example, is the text of the epiclesis for the consecration of a bishop: "O God and Father of our Lord Jesus Christ . . . who gave ordinances to Your Church 'by the Word of Your grace' (cf. Acts 20:32) . . . now pour forth that Power which is from You, of 'the princely Spirit' which You delivered to Your beloved Son Jesus Christ, and which He bestowed on Your holy Apostles who established the Church in every place to the endless

---

[77] *Dial. adv. lucif.*, 5 (PL 23, 159).   [78] *De Spir. S.*, III, 18, 137 (PL 16, 808–809).

glory and praise of Your Name . . . You who know hearts, grant upon this Your servant whom You have chosen for the episcopate . . . that by the high priestly Spirit he may have authority 'to forgive sins' according to Your command, ' to assign lots' (cf. Acts 1:26) according to Your bidding, to 'loose every bond' (cf. Is. 58:6; Matt. 10:1) according to the authority You gave the Apostles, and that he may please You in meekness and a pure heart, offering to You a sweet-smelling savor, through Your Servant Jesus Christ our Lord, through whom to You be glory, might and praise, with the Holy Spirit, now and world without end. Amen." [79]

The prefaces of consecration of priests and of deacons [80] are analogous to the one for the consecration of bishops, from the Trinitarian point of view. The same structure is found, moreover, in all the ancient texts, including those in the sacramentary of Serapion [81] and in the *Apostolic Constitutions*.[82] Here, for example, is how the scheme *a, per, in, ad* is expressed in the prayer of consecration of priests in the sacramentary of Serapion: "Lord, Father of Your Only-begotten, we pray that the Spirit of truth may come upon this man . . . that he may rule Your people and dispense Your divine word and reconcile Your people to You, uncreated God . . . You who by the spirit of Moses granted the Holy Spirit to those who had been chosen, give this man also the Holy Spirit by the Spirit of the Only-begotten in the gift of wisdom, of knowledge and of right faith, that he may serve You with a pure conscience through Your Only-begotten Jesus Christ, through whom be glory and empire to You in the Holy Spirit now and for all ages, world without end. Amen." [83]

Extreme unction

In the liturgy of extreme unction, the Christological and Trinitarian dynamism is only rarely expressed in the form itself of the sacrament, a form which has changed many times in the course of the centuries.[84] On the other hand, it appears clearly in the epicletic prayers for the blessing of the oil of the sick, both in the present Roman Pontifical and in the Gelasian sacramentary.[85]

Matrimony

The traditional Christological and Trinitarian perspective does not appear in the liturgy of marriage.

The sacramentals

For the question which concerns us here, there is no need for a long study of the sacramentals. Among the most ancient and most important formulas, a good number have preserved the form of an epiclesis, with a distinctly marked Trinitarian structure, down to our days.

[79] *Traditio*, 3; ed. Dix, pp. 4–6.
[80] *Traditio*, 8 and 9.
[81] 26–28; ed. Funk, II, 188–190.
[82] VIII, 5, 3–7; 16, 3–5; 18.
[83] 27; ed. Funk, II, 188–190.
[84] Cf. Righetti, IV, 243.
[85] I, 40: *Emitte* . . . ; ed. Wilson, p. 70.
[83] I, 44; ed. Wilson, pp. 85 f.

Among these sacramentals we may cite: the blessing of the baptismal font and of the baptismal water, both in the Eastern rites and in the Roman rite, in which this structure appears especially in the great preface, found as early as the Gelasian sacramentary;[86] the blessing of the oil of the sick, which we have just mentioned; the consecration of the μύρον among the Greeks; the consecration of an altar or of a church; the consecration of virgins; the *commendatio animae*, with the beginning of the prayer *Proficiscere*: "Take your leave, O Christian soul, of this world, in the name of God the Father all-powerful who created you, in the name of Jesus Christ, Son of the living God, who suffered for you, in the name of the Holy Spirit who has been poured out in you."

In the Middle Ages it became the general custom to give every blessing and begin every important rite by making the sign of the cross on oneself or on the objects to be blessed, and reciting the formula "In the name of the Father and of the Son and of the Holy Spirit." The Christological-and-Trinitarian character of these blessings and rites was not thereby lost, but it was weakened, to the advantage of the strictly Trinitarian aspect.

The sign of the cross made while invoking the three divine Persons signifies: we bless this object by the power, we perform this rite with the power, which, through the cross of our Lord, comes to us from the Father, from the Son and from the Holy Spirit, three Persons in a single nature.

The liturgical cycles

We shall find again in the liturgical feasts and cycles what we have noticed in the prayers and the rites: the fundamental elements are marked with the traditional Christological and Trinitarian character, but there has been added later a superstructure which emphasizes notably, or sometimes even makes predominant, the ontological and anti-Arian aspect. We shall confine ourselves here to a rapid glance at the Roman liturgy in its present state.

The most ancient cycle is that of Easter, the Paschal cycle, which now extends from Septuagesima to Pentecost. It attained its full development, essentially, in the seventh century.

The object of this period is the whole of sacred history, the whole mystery of Christ and of the Church, under the aspect of redemption. This redemption was made necessary, prepared for, prefigured, begun in the Old Testament. It was realized, radically, by Christ in His earthly life. Since the Ascension, it is realized and applied in the world by the Spirit whom Christ has merited for us and whom He has sent from His place at the Father's side, the Spirit who is the soul of the Church and gives life to every man through the sacraments received and the moral effort undertaken in the Church.

The Easter cycle is divided into three periods: from Septuagesima to Passiontide, from Passion Sunday to the Ascension, from the Ascension to Pentecost.

During the first period, the liturgy brings out the necessity of the Redemption, and also its preparation and its prefiguration in the Old Testament up to Moses. That is why the readings in the Office retrace the story of mankind from the creation to Moses. But the liturgy insists with equal force on the actualization of the Redemption for each one of the faithful through moral effort: those who are baptized and in the state of grace prepare themselves to participate more fully in the Redemption through the ascetical and liturgical life; the sinners prepare themselves for reconciliation through penance; and the catechumens prepare themselves for their entrance into the Church through the sacraments of the initiation.

In this first period, the person of the Father is in the foreground. Here again He appears as the one *a quo* and *ad quem*. It is He who created the world and man, made Adam the religious head of the human race, was offended by man's sin, but promised him a Redeemer and prepared the Redemption throughout the Old Testament. And it is to the Father that we must return, it is He whom we must satisfy through penance, fasting, prayer, almsgiving and good works.

In this period, Christ appears in the epistles and gospels of the Masses, but only on the second level, as the Teacher who, by His doctrine and His example, imparts to us the precepts of moral effort, of penance, of prayer, of good works.

In the second part of the cycle, from Passion Sunday to the Ascension, the perspective changes. In the foreground now is the accomplishment of the Redemption by Christ in His "Paschal mysteries": Passion, death, Resurrection and Ascension. The liturgy brings its attention to bear on the prefiguration of the Passion in Jeremias; on the historical events of the Savior's life, from the Passion to the Ascension; on the present application of the fruits of the Redemption to the faithful: reconciliation of penitents, initiation of catechumens, perfecting of the rest. In all this it is Christ, the incarnate Son, Redeemer and Head of mankind, in His Passion and in His glorification, who is in the foreground.

But the Father also is constantly present, as the one who is at the source of this whole history of Christ suffering and glorified, of this whole history which He has willed to be as it is, and which He directs infallibly to His own glory.

In the last period of the cycle, from the Ascension to Pentecost, it is the Spirit who comes to the foreground. The whole liturgy now expresses the idea that after the Ascension, the application of the Redemption to men is made *in Spiritu*, that is, thanks to the presence and the action of the Holy Spirit, who is the soul of the Church and inspires her sanctifying action, Her teaching and Her governing. Christ now appears primarily as the one who has merited the Spirit for us and gives us the Spirit that we may share His life; the Father appears as the one who, at the intercession of Christ, sends us the Spirit, and to whom the Spirit must finally lead us.

There is no need to enter into detail and to give examples in order to show that this is really the doctrinal framework of the whole Easter cycle. There is more advantage in pointing out how the attention of the liturgy in this whole cycle is brought to bear principally on the distinction of the divine Persons and on the role played by each one in the history of salvation.

The history of this cycle shows that it has grown gradually and has required long centuries to reach its present state. In its formation, however, the Church has been guided by a fundamental intuition which insures the unity of this whole period: to put into practice in the liturgy the idea expressed by St. Paul in the epistle read on Ember Saturday of Pentecost week, at the end of the whole cycle and as a sort of conclusion to it: "Justified, therefore, by faith, let us have peace with God through our Lord Jesus Christ, through whom, by faith, we have found entrance to this grace in which we stand, and we exult in the hope of the glory (of the sons) of God. . . . And this hope does not disappoint because the charity of God is poured forth in our hearts by the Holy Spirit who has been given us" (Rom. 5:1–5).

As for the Christmas cycle, which covers the whole period from Advent to the Epiphany, it also is constructed in the Christological and Trinitarian perspective, although the role of the Holy Spirit gets little attention here. This cycle has for its object the whole history of salvation, the whole mystery of Christ, but under the aspect of the manifested coming of the Lord: a coming prepared for and announced in the Old Testament, realized historically by the birth and life of Christ, accomplished each day in souls through the sacraments; a coming which will be complete only at the parousia, the object of our hope.

The same idea of the Christological and Trinitarian economy has inspired the liturgy in the creation of the feasts, and it explains why the liturgy does not include any particular feast of the Father, or of the Son, or of the Holy Spirit, considered in themselves and independently of the history of salvation.[87] As for the feast of the Holy Trinity, which appeared in Gaul in the eighth century, it is but the manifestation, in the field of liturgical feasts, of that need which was born of the anti-Arian reaction, to add to the ancient Trinitarian conception the explicit affirmation of the unity of the divine nature in the Trinity, considered in itself and in a perspective which transcends time and history.

Can anyone say that this shows a lack of liturgical spirit? No. Since the mystery of the Trinity includes two antithetical terms, every formulation of it that can be proposed has necessarily its advantages and its inconveniencies. The surest solution, therefore, is this: after having affirmed very clearly the real distinction of the Persons, to bring out their unity of nature so clearly that the believer will not be in any danger of forgetting it.

---

[87] At several periods, and again recently, an attempt has been made to have a feast of God the Father introduced into the liturgy. But Rome has always refused. Cf. Benedict XIV, *De servorum Dei beatificatione*, book 4, part II, ch. 31; M. Caillat, "La dévotion à Dieu le Père: une discussion au XVIIe siècle," *Rev. d'asc. et de myst.*, 20 (1939), 35–49; 136–157.

This is what the liturgy has done, in the conclusion of the collects and in the doxologies as well as in the feasts. This is what leads the liturgy to place at the end of the Easter cycle a feast which, by bringing the whole attention to bear on the unity of the Trinity, completes and crowns, so to speak, the whole Christian vision of the world and of history.

In instituting this feast, therefore, the liturgy has intended to give the Christian people a perfectly balanced idea of their relations with God. St. Ambrose was already expressing this need when he said to the neophyte, "In all that we have done, we have respected the mystery of the Trinity. Everywhere are found the Father, the Son and the Holy Spirit, one operation, one sanctifying action, even if there be, as it seems, some distinctive traits. . . . You have this that is special: it is God who has called you; while in baptism in a special way you have been crucified with Christ; and then, when you receive in a special way the sign of the Spirit, you see that there is distinction of Persons, but that the whole mystery of the Trinity is bound up together." [88]

And the Mozarabic liturgy says this prayer on the day of Pentecost: "Untiringly we pray Your omnipotence, O God, holy, all-powerful Father, that You fill us with the gift of Your Only-begotten . . . and of His Holy Spirit; that You may see fit to bring to perfection through the Holy Spirit those whom You created and then redeemed through the Son. Not that the operation of Your Trinity is separate or dissimilar, but in order that the unconfused equality of the distinct Persons in the one deity may appear obvious." [89]

Despite all solicitations, Rome held out for a long time, from the eighth to the fourteenth century, against accepting this feast into her liturgy. The conviction remained at Rome that a liturgical feast does not have for its object simply an abstract idea, but a fact, an event in the history of salvation; or perhaps an idea indeed, but one that is embodied in one or more events of that history.

The hesitations of Rome in former times to permit exceptions to this traditional rule are understandable. To make more and more exceptions means to offer Christian piety abstract notions, without much permanent effect, at the risk of forgetting the great biblical and liturgical perspective of the history of salvation, mystery of Christ and of the Church.

What the discovery and the penetration of this mystery viewed in this perspective can mean for the spiritual life of the believer is described for us by St. Cyril of Alexandria. For him, writes Père du Manoir, "the destiny of the Christian is to become, in the anointing and through the anointing of the Spirit, conformed to the image of the Son, the only Mediator, who leads us back to the Father. Such is the dominant motif of the spiritual doctrine of St. Cyril. His ascetical teaching and his mystique appear to us, let us repeat, essentially Trinitarian. The Father sends His Christ; with His Christ and

---

[88] *De sacr.*, VI, 2, 5, 8 (PL 16, 455).
[89] *Liber moz. sacr.*, ed. Marius Férotin (Paris: Firmin-Didot, 1912), n. 785.

through Him, He sends the Spirit; and it is in the Spirit, through the Son, that our ascending return to the Father is accomplished." [90]

Cyril himself wrote, "That our return to God is made through Christ the Savior means that it takes place through the participation and the sanctification of the Holy Spirit. The one who joins us with God and, so to speak, makes us one with Him, is the Spirit. In receiving the Spirit, we become participants and sharers of the divine nature; and we receive Him through the Son, and in the Son we receive the Father." [91]

The liturgy, if we know how to understand it and live it, is the best means for making us penetrate these marvelous realities and keep ourselves attuned to them.

[90] Hubert du Manoir, "Cyrille d'Alexandrie," *Dict. de spir.*, II, 2, col. 2682. For more details see the same author's *Dogme et spiri-* *tualité chez S. Cyrille d'Alex.* (Paris, 1944).

[91] *In Ioan.*, 11, 10 (PG 74, 544–545).

8 THE ONE LITURGIST

AND THE ONE LITURGY

We know now what is meant by the scheme "from the Father, through Christ, in the Spirit, to the Father." But it remains for us to specify the proper role which falls to Christ in the liturgical translation or application of that scheme. Exactly what does "Through Christ our Lord" mean in the liturgy? What does Clement of Rome mean when he speaks of "Jesus Christ, the high Priest of our offerings, our patron and helper in our weakness"?

1. The Heavenly Priesthood of Christ

When we speak of Christ's presence and action in His Church, we may be tempted to conceive of this presence and this action as a number of events that took place once and for all during the earthly life of the Man-God, but which belong to the present only in so far as they are objects of knowledge and of love. Here again is the danger of panpsychologism and of panmoralism. In short, we would see in Jesus only the wise Teacher who has taught us how to approach God, the admirable model whom we are to imitate, and, at best, the one who by dying on the cross has made it possible for us to obtain from God the graces necessary for our salvation.

If Christ meant nothing more for us, there would be no discernible difference between Him and a great saint. His presence and His action in the Church would be of the same order as the presence and the action of a philosopher among his disciples, of a saint among his devotees, of a founder among the members of his religious order. His presence and action would be merely of a psychological and moral order. But in reality they are of a physical order first of all, and then, as a consequence, of a moral order.

In order to understand the depth of this presence and this action of Christ in the Church, and especially in the liturgy, we must refer to the great synthesis of sacred history and of the Christian life proposed by the letter to the Hebrews.[1] The author of the epistle wants to show what is the meaning of history and of life. For that reason he not only views them, as do all the other writers of the New Testament, in the Christological and Trinitarian framework — though he does not insist much on the role of the Holy Spirit[2] — but above all he considers them under the aspect of sanctification and of worship. On the whole, the history of salvation and the Christian life appear to him as a vast liturgy.

It is known that the letter to the Hebrews is an exhortation addressed to a group of Jewish priests converted to Christianity. These priests, exiled from Jerusalem, are tempted to long for the splendors of the Jewish worship, in comparison to which the Christian worship may seem to them a disembodied spirituality. Thus the author strives to demonstrate and to illustrate in every way the superiority of the Christian economy over the Jewish liturgy from the viewpoint of sanctification and of worship.[3] To this end he presents the whole earthly life of the faithful as an immense procession toward the sanctuary where God dwells and where they hope to be admitted into His presence, to see Him, praise Him and offer Him their sacrifices.

At the center of this vision is the priesthood of Christ. A perfect priesthood, of which the others were but the shadow and the figure, it was exercised by Christ throughout His earthly life and above all on Calvary; it has found its fulfilment and its full efficacy with the glorification of Christ; and now it continues to be exercised on behalf of all the faithful.

The central theme, the capital point ($\kappa\epsilon\phi\acute{a}\lambda\alpha\iota o\nu$, Heb. 8:1) of this higher doctrine (cf. Heb. 5:11) which the author of the epistle wants to impart to his correspondents is that "we have such a High Priest, who has taken His seat at the right hand of the throne of Majesty in heaven, as liturgist of the sanctuary and of the true tabernacle, which the Lord, not man, has built" (Heb. 8:1–2). And this High Priest, "because He continues forever, has a priesthood which is not transitory, and therefore can assure perfect salvation to those who approach God through Him, as He is always alive to intercede in their behalf. Such a High Priest, in fact, fitted our needs: holy, innocent, undefiled, set apart from sinners and raised above the heavens; who has no need, as do the high priests, to offer sacrifices daily, first for his own sins and

[1] Cf. Ceslaus Spicq, *L'épitre aux hébreux,* especially I, 266–329.

[2] Cf. *ibid.*, I, 147 f. Very often the author speaks of the Father simply by the name of God; cf. *ibid.*, II, 446, under the words *Dieu* and *Esprit Saint* in the analytical index.

[3] Most of the characteristic terminology of the epistle is borrowed from the language of the liturgy: to approach, to present oneself, to offer, to sanctify, to expiate, to purify, altar, priest, etc.

then for those of the people; this He did once and for all when He offered Himself" (Heb. 7:24 ff.).

What does adherence to the faith and the practice of the Christian life mean in this perspective ? The author of the epistle answers the question in a very meaty text, whose terms are borrowed from the vocabulary of the liturgy: "You have approached Mount Sion and the city of the living God, the heavenly Jerusalem, the myriads of angels, a festive gathering (πανήγυρις) and assembly (ἐκκλησία) of the first-born inscribed in heaven, and God the Judge of all, and the spirits of the just who have reached perfection, and the Mediator of the new covenant, Jesus, and the sprinkled blood which speaks better than that of Abel" (Heb. 12:22 ff).

In this text and in those we have cited above are found the essential themes of the epistle. The Christian life is a liturgical procession of pilgrims who, by tending to perfection (τελείωσις), seek to approach the sanctuary and to appear before God. This sanctuary is nothing else but heaven, in which there are gathered around God in festive assembly (πανήγυρις) the angels by tens of thousands and the just men who have reached the end of their journey, that is, the perfection to which they were called (τετελειωμένων).

By their faith and their new life, the Christians also have attained in a certain way the goal of their liturgical pilgrimage; they also have approached, in a very real, though still imperfect, way, the holy Jerusalem and the heavenly sanctuary. And this has been possible for them and remains possible for them, thanks to Jesus, the High Priest and the Mediator of the new covenant. For Jesus has purified them from their sins and sanctified them by the sprinkling of His blood. He has introduced them even now into the sanctuary of Sion. He has united them really to the liturgical assembly of the angels and the saints, that assembly of which He Himself is the eternal High Priest, sitting at the Father's right hand, the liturgist always living to intercede on our behalf.

The worship, the purifications, the whole liturgy and the whole priesthood of the Old Testament were but the shadow and the figure (Heb. 8:5; 10:1) of this true priesthood, this true worship, this true sanctification, of which Christ is the liturgist and in which the Christians really participate. The Jewish liturgy has been abolished, therefore, and has given way to the one liturgy of Christ, to that liturgy which He performed in the course of His earthly life and which He is now continuing in heaven by drawing to it, by introducing into it already, the faithful who are still on their way to the goal.

2. Heavenly Liturgy and Earthly Liturgy

The author of the letter to the Hebrews, wholly occupied with the heavenly liturgy, hardly speaks of its relations with the liturgy on earth. He does apparently make some allusions to the earthly liturgy, however. It is in this sense, for example, that more than one commentator interprets the following text: "Since, then, brethren, we have confidence to enter the sanctuary, in virtue of the blood of Jesus, an entry which He has opened up for us, a new and living way beyond the veil, that is, His flesh, and since we have a High Priest in charge of the house of God, let us draw near with a sincere heart, in fulness of faith, our hearts sprinkled and cleansed from an evil conscience and our bodies washed with pure water. Let us hold fast to the unwavering profession of our hope — for He who has given the promise is faithful — and let us consider how to incite one another to charity and good works, not forsaking our own assembly, as is the custom with some; but rather let us exhort one another; and this all the more as you see the Day drawing near" (Heb. 10:19 ff.).

In this assembly (ἐπισυναγωγή) which the Christians are urged not to desert, some exegetes see the liturgical assembly. If this interpretation is correct, we might say that the author of the epistle sees in the liturgical assembly the obvious place where the Christians, their hearts purified of all guilt and their bodies washed by baptism, approach God even now under the aegis of Jesus the High Priest. He it is who has won this favor for us by His blood, and who gives us the firm hope of entering one day into the sanctuary of heaven. To that sanctuary He has preceded us, and to it we shall come, on condition that we keep our faith and our hope intact and translate them into good works.

Several commentators also see an allusion to the Eucharist in Heb. 13:10 and 6:4.

Even if the letter to the Hebrews does not indicate precisely the relations between the heavenly liturgy and the earthly liturgy, it does at least lay down the principles which permit us to define those relations, as the later patristic and liturgical tradition has actually done.

The fundamental principle we already know: there is only one liturgist, Christ, and only one liturgy, that of Christ now glorious.

Another principle is that the true and definitive world is the world of heaven, while the one we know here below is only its shadow, its figure, its imitation.[4]

This exemplarism is used here, however, especially to indicate the relations between Mosaic worship and heavenly worship (cf. Heb. 8:2-5; 9:11-24; 10:1). It does not seem possible to say with certainty that the author, in this context, is thinking also of the earthly worship of the Christians.

But it was normal that the Christians should ask what was the meaning of their worship in relation to the heavenly worship and to that of the Old Testament. And the answer was evident, flowing from the principles laid down by the epistle: If the Jewish liturgy was the shadow and the figure of the heavenly liturgy performed by Christ, the Christian liturgy on earth was also the shadow and the figure of that heavenly liturgy; with this difference,

---

[4] On this principle, which is fundamental in the epistle, cf. Ceslaus Spicq, *L'épître aux hébreux*, I, 72–76. The author of the epistle is here exploiting the Platonic and Philonian doctrine of exemplarism.

however, that in the second case the notions of shadow and figure involve something far more profound and more real: the work of sanctification of the Christians is that which Christ keeps achieving in them, their worship is that which Christ keeps celebrating through them and with them; in a word, their one liturgist is Christ Himself.

The earthly liturgy in its two aspects of sanctification and of worship reflects and realizes in its own way what the glorified Christ is doing in heaven. Under the veil of rites and symbols, it is the epiphany of the liturgy of heaven. Earthly liturgy and heavenly liturgy are one and the same reality; there is between them only a difference of fulness and of visibility, such as there was in the ancient concept between the image and the reality which it manifests.

These ideas have been abundantly developed by the patristic and liturgical tradition. This tradition has always been careful to show that in our liturgy it is always Christ Himself who acts under the veil of the rites and by means of human ministers; it is always Christ who is the principal minister of the liturgical action under all its forms: Mass, sacraments, sacramentals, divine praise.[5]

In connection with this statement that it is Christ Himself who offers the Eucharistic sacrifice, the testimony of Dom Dix is worth quoting: "I believe that with the exception of three series of Origen's *Homilies* I have read every sentence of every Christian author extant from the period before Nicaea, most of it probably eight or a dozen times or oftener. It is difficult to prove a negative from so vast and disparate a mass of material, but I have paid particular attention to this point for some years. I think I can state as a fact that (with two apparent exceptions which I will deal with in a footnote) there is *no* pre-Nicene author Eastern or Western whose Eucharistic doctrine is at all fully stated, who does not regard the offering and consecration of the Eucharist as the present action of our Lord Himself, the second Person of the Trinity. And in the overwhelming majority of writers it is made clear that their whole conception revolves around the figure of the High Priest at the altar in heaven.[6] This certainly is the conception of the early liturgical prayers. . . .

"The important thing to notice from our immediate standpoint is that when the pre-Nicene Church thought and spoke of the Eucharist as an action, as something 'done,' it conceived it primarily as an action of *Christ Himself*, perpetually offering through and in His body the Church His 'Flesh for the life of the world.' It is the perpetuation in time by way of *anamnesis* of His eternally accepted and complete redeeming act."[7]

Basically, the Church has always believed that the Mass is an earthly manifestation of that which was revealed to St. John when he saw "in the midst,

[5] Cf. Ph. Oppenheim, *Notiones liturgicae fundamentales* (Turin: Marietti, 1941), pp. 109-132, with bibliography.

[6] Dix cites, among others, Clement of Rome, Justin, Irenaeus, Tertullian, Clement of Alexandria, Origen, Cyprian.

[7] *The Shape of the Liturgy*, pp. 253-254.

where the throne was, amid the four living beings and the elders, a lamb standing upright, yet as if slain" (Apoc. 5:6), a lamb who is no other than that "High Priest who has taken His seat at the right hand of the throne of Majesty in the heavens, as liturgist of the sanctuary and of the true tabernacle" (Heb. 8:1–2), our "advocate with the Father" (1 John 2:1), "living always to make intercession" (Heb. 7:25) for us.

This concept of the Mass as thanksgiving of the glorified Christ is found again, even after Nicaea, in the Fathers and in the liturgy, even if here and there it is somewhat weakened by reason of the emphasis placed in the East, beginning with the fourth century, on the role of the Holy Spirit in the offering of the Eucharistic sacrifice.[8] Even in the liturgies which include a consecratory epiclesis asking for the coming of the Holy Spirit, the idea is expressed that it is Christ who acts at the essential moment of the sacrifice.

This is the case, for example, in the Byzantine liturgies of St. Basil and of St. John Chrysostom, in which the prayer called that of the *Cheroubikon* addresses Christ in these terms: "No one is worthy . . . to draw near, approach or minister to You, King of glory. For it is a great and tremendous thing even for the heavenly Powers to minister to You. But, by Your inexpressible and immeasurable love for mankind, without any change or loss You have become man, You have become our High Priest and You have given us the sacred liturgical rite of this unbloody sacrifice. . . . I beg of You . . . give me the strength . . . to stand at this holy table and to consecrate Your sacred and spotless body and Your precious blood. . . . Condescend to have these gifts offered to You by me, Your sinful and unworthy servant. For You are the offerer and the offered, the sanctifier and the sanctified" (the most recent text says: "the receiver and the one distributed"), "Christ, our God."[9]

Dom Dix, who insists a good deal on the difference between the two ways of conceiving the sacrifice, as the work of Christ or as the work of the Holy Spirit, recognizes that even after the fourth century the Eastern liturgies which emphasized the role of the Spirit have continued, "with a happy illogicality," to regard the earthly Eucharist as an act of Christ, High Priest of the heavenly altar, "who Himself offers, Himself prays, Himself consecrates, in the offering of His sacrifice."[10]

For our part, however, from a purely theological point of view, we do not see the contradiction which Dom Dix perceives between the idea that the consecration is the work of the Holy Spirit and the idea that it is the work of Christ. We need only remember the biblical theme that whatever Christ, henceforth associated in the glory of His Father, does in the world, He does by means of the Holy Spirit whom He sends from His place at the Father's side; so that the action of Christ and that of the Spirit are not two different

[8] Cf. *ibid.*, pp. 276–302. This insistence on the action of the Spirit leads to such a thing as St. Cyril of Jerusalem speaking of Christ as if He played only a passive role at the essential moment of the sacrifice.
[9] Ἱερατικόν, pp. 181–182.
[10] *The Shape of the Liturgy*, p. 292.

actions, but one single action, that of Christ in the Spirit or through the Spirit. At least in theory, then, one may very well underline the role of the Holy Spirit in the Mass without for that reason abandoning the idea that it is Christ, our High Priest seated at the Father's right hand, who is the principal minister of the Eucharistic sacrifice.

At any rate, the antiquity and the universality of the concept that it is truly Christ Himself who offers His sacrifice in the Mass is evident. The Council of Trent echoes this conviction when it says that in the Mass "it is one and the same victim who by the ministry of the priests now offers Himself and who then offered Himself on the cross." [11]

As for the precise manner in which the glorified Christ really offers every Mass that is celebrated, this is a question to which the theologians have given various answers, and it does not seem necessary for us to go into the matter here.[12]

We need not stop to demonstrate, either, that Christ is always the principal minister of the various sacraments. We know that this doctrine was made explicit in its essentials by St. Augustine, on the occasion of the controversy over the validity of the baptism conferred by the Donatists. It was then that he wrote the famous words: "Peter baptizes, but it is He (Christ) who baptizes; Paul baptizes, but it is He who baptizes; Jude baptizes, but it is He who baptizes." [13] The doctrine of the efficacy of the sacraments *ex opere operato* is founded wholly on this presupposition.

In the sacramentals also, in the rites instituted by the Church and in the divine praise, it is always Christ who is the principal actor. We have seen in a preceding chapter what the efficacy *ex opere operantis Ecclesiae* of these rites consists in, and its superiority to the efficacy of a private prayer.

What St. Augustine says of the prayer of the Christian in general applies by an eminent right to liturgical prayer, and even to all the rites established by the Church, which operate essentially after the manner of prayer: "God could not grant men a greater gift than to give them as their Head the Word through whom He made all things, and to unite them to Him as His members, in such a way that He would be Son of God and Son of man, God together with the Father and Man together with men; and that when we speak to God in prayer we would not separate the Son from God; and that when the body of the Son prays it would not separate its Head from itself; and that it would be the same Lord, Jesus Christ, Son of God, Savior of His body, who would pray for us and pray in us and be prayed to by us. He prays for us as our Priest; He prays in us as our Head; He is prayed to by us as our God. Let us recognize our voice in Him, therefore, and His voice in us. . . . He wanted to make the words of the psalm His own words also, when He hung

---

[11] Dz 940. It is known that this conviction gave rise to the iconographic theme of Christ celebrating the Mass Himself. Cf., e.g., G. Millet, *Monuments de l'Athos*, I (Paris, 1927), plates 64, 1 and 2; 118, 2; 168; 218, 2; 219, 3; 256; 257; 261; 262, 1 and 2.

[12] It has been studied recently by Ch. Journet, *La messe présence du sacrifice de la croix* (Paris, 1957), pp. 80–128.

[13] *In Io. Tract.* 6, 7 (PL 35, 1428).

on the cross and said, 'My God, My God, why have You forsaken Me?' He is prayed to, then, in the form of God; He prays in the form of a servant; there the Creator, here created. He took to Himself without change the creature which He was to change, and made us together with Himself a single man : Head and body. We therefore pray to Him, by Him and in Him; we say with Him and He says with us, we say in Him and He says in us the prayer of this psalm. . . . Let no one say, therefore, when he hears these words, 'It is not Christ who says them' or 'It is not I who say them.' Rather, if he recognizes himself as part of the body of Christ, he must say both 'Christ says them' and 'I say them.' Do not say anything without Him, and He will not say anything without you." [14]

Thus the Church's prayer is Christ's prayer, and Christ's prayer is the Church's. As Augustine says elsewhere, Christ and the Church "from two, become as one single person, head and body, husband and wife. . . . If they are two in one flesh, why not two in one voice ? Let Christ speak, therefore, because in Christ it is the Church who speaks, and in the Church it is Christ who speaks; the body in the Head and the Head in the body." [15]

It is with good reason, therefore, that the encyclical *Mediator Dei* cites the first of these texts from St. Augustine to explain how the Divine Office is by a very special title the prayer of Christ Himself. Of this Office it can be said that "by assuming human nature, the divine Word introduced into this earthly exile a hymn which is sung in heaven for all eternity. He unites to Himself the whole human race and with it sings this hymn to the praise of God." [16]

In the Mass, in the sacraments and the sacramentals, in the Church's prayer, Christ is always the principal actor. The Christians, His ministers and His faithful, are behind Him as His shadow; He carries them all in Himself, identifies them with Himself. The Father regards them as something of Christ. Only thus does he see them, hear them and love them. In the liturgy God does not see the action of men, but only the action of Christ who has incorporated men with Himself.

If now we recall the teaching of the New Testament, in particular of St. Paul and of the letter to the Hebrews, that Christ is also Head of the angels,[17] and if we advert to the statement of the Roman liturgy that the angels praise God through Christ,[18] we shall have no difficulty in understanding that He is the one "minister of the holy places and of the true tabernacle which the Lord has erected, and not man" (Heb. 8:2) in heaven; and we shall understand that He is at the same time the one liturgist of our earthly liturgy, who, under the veil of signs, under this sensible covering adapted to our nature,

[14] *Enar. in Ps.* 85, 1 (PL 37, 1081–1082).
[15] *Enar. in Ps.* 30, 4 (PL 36, 232).
[16] MD, n. 144 (Lat. 142).
[17] Cf., e.g., Col. 1:15–20 and Heb. 1:5–2:18. That Christ is Head of the angels is certain, aside from the question whether the grace of the angels is the grace of Christ.
[18] "Per quem maiestatem tuam laudant angeli."

renders present and active among us the heavenly liturgy which He is celebrating before His Father.

Always we come back to the great concept intensely lived by the ancient
Church and magnificently expressed by Tertullian when he called Christ
"*catholicus Patris sacerdos*," [19] the unique and universal priest of the Father.

3. Consequences for the Nature of the Liturgy

From these relations between earthly liturgy and heavenly liturgy there
follow a certain number of consequences which it will be worth while to make
explicit, since they will help us discover the true nature of the liturgy.

First of all, the worship rendered to God by the Church cannot be other
than a participation in the worship rendered by Christ to His Father. The
Church's worship is the worship which Christ renders to His Father in the
Church, using the Church as an instrument and associating it with His own
worship. With regard to Christ our liturgy is a manifestation, a continuous
epiphany of His heavenly priesthood; with regard to us, it is a present and
real participation of the Church in the priesthood which Christ continues to
exercise in the presence of His Father after having exercised it throughout
His earthly life.

All this supposes in the liturgical action an actual presence of Christ which
transcends the psychological level of knowledge and volition and is based
ultimately on the hypostatic union, on the fact of the mystical body and of
the "grace of the Head" (*gratia capitis*). Christ is present in the liturgical
reality in a physical way, whether in His person (Eucharist and sacrifice) or
at least in His sanctifying power working physically and really (other sacraments, sacramentals, Divine Office).

No one can understand the liturgy until he has grasped the fact that Christ
is present in it not as an abstract idea but as a living person and as a living
force emanating from a living person: "and therefore He can assure perfect
salvation to those who approach God through Him, as He is always alive to
intercede in their behalf" (Heb. 7:25) and to act through them and with them.

In the liturgy, Christ's priestly action becomes really present for us.
Time is surpassed and, as it were, suspended: Christ, His sacrifice, His
sanctifying power, His prayer, are present, really, physically, under the
veil of signs. Thus all men throughout the ages become contemporaries of
Christ by participating in the liturgy; not that they escape time and space
to return to the time of Christ; but Christ, always living and present, draws
them into the orbit of His priestly action, which henceforth transcends space
and time.

In this light we should see as the accurate expression of a reality beyond
dispute a certain number of statements about the nature of the liturgy which
are often taken in quite another way, as more or less poetical exaggerations

[19] *Adv. Marc.*, 4, 9 (PL 2, 376).

of liturgists living far from the real world and from the needs of the modern apostolate.

Thus, for example, there is no exaggeration in saying that the liturgy is the actualization and the prolongation in time and space of the priestly action which Christ began to exercise in His earthly life and which He continues to exercise at His Father's side. In fact, far from being an exaggeration of the liturgists, this notion of the liturgy simply repeats in other words the profound conception of *Mediator Dei*: "Along with the Church, therefore, her divine Founder is present at every liturgical function: Christ is present at the august sacrifice of the altar both in the person of His minister and above all under the Eucharistic species. He is present in the sacraments, infusing into them the power which makes them ready instruments of sanctification. He is present finally in the prayer of praise and petition we direct to God. . . . The sacred liturgy is consequently the public worship which our Redeemer as Head of the Church renders to the Father as well as the worship which the community of the faithful renders to its Founder, and through Him to the heavenly Father. It is, in short, the worship rendered by the mystical body of Christ in the entirety of its Head and members." [20]

On this passage Père Roguet comments quite rightly, "The Church does not *succeed* Christ; she does not substitute for Him. Not only did Christ institute the worship she renders to God, the sacraments she administers, but He is always present in them, through His assistance to the Church, through His presence in the community, through His sanctifying power. From this truth comes the greatness of the liturgy, work of the Church and work of Christ at the same time. The liturgy is therefore something quite different from a ceremonial or a memorial." [21]

Nor is there any exaggeration in saying that the liturgy is the continuation and the application to men, down through the ages, of Christ's redemptive action. This is a truth held by all the liturgists and recalled with authority by *Mediator Dei*: "It is an unquestionable fact that the work of our redemption is continued, and that its fruits are imparted to us, during the celebration of the liturgy, notably in the august sacrifice of the altar. Christ acts each day to save us, in the sacraments and in His holy sacrifice. By means of them He is constantly atoning for the sins of mankind, constantly consecrating it to God." [22]

Moreover, the liturgy itself more than once expresses this doctrine, for example in the secret of the ninth Sunday after Pentecost, quoted by the encyclical: "Grant us, we pray You, Lord, to take part worthily in these mysteries which we celebrate again and again, for every time that this commemorative sacrifice is offered, the work of our redemption is wrought." [23]

---

[20] N. 20.

[21] Edition of *Mediator Dei*, p. 10.

[22] N. 29.

[23] " . . . quoties huius hostiae commemoratio celebratur, opus nostrae redemptionis exercetur." MD, n. 79 (Lat. 78).

What we have been saying merely makes explicit, after all, the reality contained in those four words "Through Christ our Lord." There is but one Priest, one Mediator, one Liturgist, one liturgy; and, according to the plans willed and realized by God, this one liturgy encompasses the whole world of sanctification and of worship in which the relations between man and God take concrete form. "Through Him and with Him and in Him" — *per ipsum et cum ipso et in ipso.*

9 THE LITURGY AND
THE LAW OF SALVATION IN COMMUNITY

With this chapter we come to grips with one of the most difficult problems the liturgy poses for the modern mind: the relations between person and society, between individualism and communitarian spirit, in the inner domain of our relations with God.

Since the Renaissance, people have tended to accentuate the strictly personal character of their relations with God. They are anxious to safeguard their liberty and their spontaneity in the encounter with God, and they are afraid of everything that seems to them an intrusion coming from without, everything that seems to want a place between God and themselves: traditions, intervention of society, obligation to have recourse to a person or a thing.

Now the liturgy has the character of a social, communitarian activity. Those who take part in it must conform their attitude to that of the community, which expresses itself in forms that are ancient and often foreign to our modern mentality. Is that not enough to conjure up the specter of collectivism and legalism invading the personal sphere of religion?

We shall try to show that the communitarian character of the liturgy is not opposed to the legitimate demands of the individual in the religious sphere, and that on the contrary these demands cannot be fully satisfied except in close contact with the world of the liturgy.

1. Protestant Communitarian Sense and Catholic Communitarian Sense

It is a common thing to appeal to the social nature of man as evidence that he cannot find his full spiritual development except in a religion that is social in character. And there is truth in this, but only a partial truth. For while the social nature of man does undoubtedly postulate a religion that is social in character, it is not an adequate basis for determining to what extent and in what sense that religion must be social.

This demand of nature is satisfied, for example, by the communitarian element in Lutheran worship or Buddhist worship. But there is no common measure between the communitarian character of the Catholic liturgy and the communitarian element that could be logically admitted by a Lutheran or even imagined by a Buddhist.

For a Protestant, the social character of religion and of worship does not go beyond the psychological level. Sanctification does not consist in a physical [1] participation in the divine nature, but only in a feeling of trust in God's mercy. The sacraments are not instruments of grace, but mere symbols which arouse this feeling of trust in the believer. The priesthood is not a real participation in the priesthood of Christ, but a deputation, a mission entrusted to a pastor by a community, to instruct and stimulate that community. And the community itself is no more than the assembly of the faithful who experience this feeling of trust: no properly divine element is needed to constitute the community.

In such a perspective, worship is hardly more than a matter of preaching, and it is not by chance that the pulpit is the point toward which everything converges in a Protestant church. The community and the worship are not indispensable to the believer, since they have only the value of stimulants, and the believer can bypass them if he thinks he can find more efficacious means.

For a Catholic, on the other hand, the communitarian character of the religious life is situated primarily on the level of being. Sanctification is a transformation which affects being, for it is a participation in the being and the activity of God. The sacraments really produce what they signify, and all are ordained to the Eucharistic sacrifice, which requires a sacramental priesthood, a physical participation in the priesthood of Christ. This sacramental and hierarchical priesthood is one of the elements that go to make up the Church; and the believers do not constitute a community, they are not of the Church, except in so far as they are united to that hierarchy, framework of the mystical body of Christ. In the eyes of the Catholic, membership in the Church is not merely a psychological stimulant; it is a necessity of a physical order. Without this membership the individual is physically incapable of sharing in this divine life.

It can be seen how far we are from the Protestant position, and how inade-

---

[1] "Physical" here does not mean "material" or "sensible," but is opposed to "purely moral."

quate is the argument drawn from the social nature of man to account for so radical a dependence of the personal religious life on membership in a community.

2. Sacred History and Salvation in Community according to the Bible

Only revelation can inform us to what extent God has chosen to link the religious life of the individual to his membership in a society, and only revelation may be able to give us some idea why God has willed this to be so.

And in fact the Bible brings to light a very important aspect of the relations between God and man : in communicating His life to the world, God has not been content to draw to Himself a certain number of individuals, separately one from another, but He has founded a city of God, a people of God, a kingdom of God; so that the individuals cannot attain to being, on the supernatural level, or develop themselves, unless they have a close, physical bond with this community willed by God. Such is the law of salvation in community.[2]

To establish the reality of this law it would be necessary to study the themes of the people of God, the covenant, the kingdom of God, in the Old and the New Testament. This would amount to studying the whole theology of history according to the Bible. We shall confine ourselves here to recalling its main features, dwelling, when we need to, on certain points of greater interest to our purpose.

The idea of the solidarity of men in their relations with God appears from the very first pages of Genesis. The material world is created for man, and man in turn is created in order that friendly relations may be established between himself and God. For the sacred author, that state of grace and of friendship was to be the starting point for the development of mankind, and was to be transmitted by Adam to all men.

The Bible therefore looks on this solidarity of Adam and all men in good and evil as a fact willed by God. Between God and each one of us there is Adam, who not only begot the human race but also stands as its religious head. The Christian doctrine of original sin, and therefore of redemption, is intelligible only if one admits as freely willed by God this law of salvation brought to a community by the head of that community.

This law is applied in a manner still more visible to the religious society of Israel, as God conceived it and brought it to reality. Throughout Israel's history, God is not seeking so much to concern Himself with individuals as to form a people for Himself. It is to this people, as such, that He entrusts the extraordinary mission of being the instrument for the establishment of God's

---

[2] An immediate consequence of this law is that on the supernatural level there can be no conflict between the good of the society and the good of the individual. These two goods coincide formally. By God's free will, they constitute a single supernatural good, the good of the individual and of society, or, better, the good of the individual in society.

kingdom in the world: theirs is the mission of safeguarding the monotheistic faith, preparing the environment in which the Messias will appear, furnishing His first recruits for the messianic kingdom, and finally being the starting point from which that kingdom would set out for the conquest of the world.

For an Israelite, one cannot have any share in the messianic benefits, present or future, unless one is a member of the chosen people. If one does not belong to the chosen people by blood, by faith, by circumcision, by observance of the law and by the practice of worship, one is completely outside of the current of divine life.

The prophets, especially Jeremias and those following him, did find it necessary to remind the people that this communitarian salvation does not dispense the individual from any moral effort.[3] But this effort, this personal development, is understandable only in the context of the community. From the religious viewpoint, the society carries the individual, and he has value only in the people and thanks to the people.

To this people of God the Old Testament gives a very characteristic name, *Qahal Yahweh*, which will be translated Ἐκκλησία τοῦ Θεοῦ, *Ecclesia Dei* (Deut. 4:8–13; 23:1–9). It is the *assembly* of God, the *Church* of God, and this name indicates that by God's free choice the people of Israel has been chosen, called, separated from the others, gathered together and consecrated to God in view of a special mission.[4] The other expressions employed by the Old Testament to designate this people of God have basically the same meaning: God's possession, His inheritance and the object of His promises, a holy nation and a priestly people.

How will Israel perform its mission at the coming of the Messias? The prophets announce clearly that almost the whole nation will be struck blind and will prove unfaithful to the alliance. Only a little group, the "remnant of Israel," will rally to the Messias and form around Him a new religious people, which will be the successor and the heir of the old Israel.[5]

When the Messias comes, He carries out all of God's plans, plans which have remained the same since the day of creation and which consist not only in saving individuals, but in forming a people, a community, in which and through which the individuals will be saved. The Messias appears, therefore, as the new Adam, who lifts up mankind again and establishes it on a level even higher than the old; He appears as Head of this redeemed humanity (cf. Rom. 5:12–17).

The men who are redeemed all become associates of Christ. No one can share in the divine life if he is not united, mysteriously but really, to the Savior. This union is not only moral; nor can anyone say that it is physical, in the sense in which there is physical union between my hand and my body,

---

[3] Cf. Albert Gelin, *The Key Concepts of the Old Testament* (New York: Sheed & Ward, 1955), pp. 64 ff.; F. Spadafora, *Collettivismo e individualismo nel Vecchio Testamento* (Rome, 1953).

[4] Cf. Karl L. Schmidt, "Ἐκκλησία," *Theol. Wört. zum NT*, III (1938), 502–539.

[5] Cf. Salvatore Garofalo, *La nozione profetica del "Resto d'Israele"* (Rome, 1942).

for that would be incompatible with the real distinction which persists between the person of Christ and that of the believer. It is generally called *mystical* union : a physical union, if you will, but of a supernatural order. It is inconceivable, from the Christian viewpoint, that an individual should be able to have a real religious life without this mystical union with Christ.

No one can attain to this union except by entering the community founded by Christ to be His body, His people, His *ecclesia*. This Church of Christ is simply that people of God whose formation has been pursued throughout sacred history.

To designate the new Israel, the New Testament employs the same terms which had served to identify the old Israel.[6] This fact points up the profound unity between the two *assemblies* and shows, moreover, that the new economy is no less communitarian than the old.

As St. Peter says to the New Christians : "You are a chosen race, a royal priesthood, a holy nation, a purchased people, that you may proclaim the perfections of Him who has called you out of the darkness into His marvelous light; you who once were not a people, but are now the people of God; you who had not obtained mercy, but have now obtained mercy" (1 Pet. 2:9-10).

And St. Paul, to bring out the organic character of the Christian Church, compares it to a body, whose members cannot exist independently of one another. It is this body, he adds, that God has chosen to form, and not merely a collection of individuals : "Christ is Head of the Church, being Himself Savior of the body . . . (who) loved the Church and delivered Himself up for her, that He might sanctify her, cleansing her in the bath of water by means of the word of life; in order that He might present to Himself the Church in all her glory . . ." (Eph. 5:23 ff.).

Among the first Christians this ecclesial aspect of the new religion is manifested with marvelous force and freshness (cf. Acts 2:42-47; 4:32-35). They all understand that between God and the individual there is the community and hence the hierarchy, the sacraments, common prayer, and that it is impossible to be saved without entering into that community, without taking part in that liturgy.

Thus, in passing from the old to the new covenant, God's plans for mankind have not been changed, but have been fulfilled, and this in a way that surpasses infinitely anything that Israel could have expected. God continues to form His people around Christ, and it is only within this people that the individuals can find their salvation, their development, their perfection.

This divine policy will attain its aim only in the world to come. As described

---

[6] Christ speaks of "My Church" (Matt. 16:18), while St. Paul speaks of "the church of the Thessalonians in God the Father and in the Lord Jesus Christ" (1 Thes. 1:1; 2 Thes. 1:1). We find also : the new Israel, the Israel of God, the heirs of the promises, the true sons of Abraham (cf. Rom. 9-11; 1 Cor. 10:18; Gal. 3:29; 6:16); the holy people, the chosen people, the people beloved by God (cf. Rom. 8:27; 8:33; 1 Cor. 6:1-2; Phil. 4:21; Col. 3:12). For the theology of the people of God in the New Testament, cf. Lucien Cerfaux, *The Church in the Theology of St. Paul* (New York: Herder & Herder, 1959).

in the Apocalypse, heaven is not so much a collection of the individual elect as the triumph of a people, the eternal liturgy of the heavenly city made up of myriads of angels and the great throng of the faithful of the Lamb, who celebrate the cosmic liturgy all together and forever, singing, "You have redeemed us, O Lord God, in Your blood out of every tribe and tongue and people and nation, and have made us a kingdom to our God" (feast of All Saints, antiphon at Vespers; cf. Apoc. 7:9–12).

3. Church and Liturgy in the Perspective of Salvation in Community

That he may one day become a citizen of the heavenly Jerusalem, a person must first of all enter the Church, that people of God and hierarchical society which alone, through its priesthood and its sacraments, has the means of communicating divine life.

It is in this perspective of communitarian salvation that we can understand the power of the priesthood to transform an assembly of persons gathered for a liturgical celebration into an *ecclesia*, to make it the people of God and the mystical body of Christ, gathered around its Head who is present, in person or at least by His divine power, in the sacred rites or in the hierarchical ministers. The performance of the liturgy, whether it be the Mass, the sacraments or the Divine Office, is thus the performance of each Christian as member of the mystical body of Christ.

And this performance is an authentic perfecting of the person. If the Church, body of Christ and body of all the Christians, is the one place of salvation willed by God, how can anyone imagine that the communitarian character of the liturgy can be an obstacle to true piety and to the free development of our supernatural personality *as God wills it*?

Actually, as revelation teaches, what God asks of each man is not that he lead the religious life which seems best to him, but that he lead a religious life which will be a personal, sincere response to objective realities, according to rules which God Himself has established. Man cannot go to God by just any way at all, but only through Christ; and it is in the Church and in the sacraments that Christ gives Himself to him.

Hence the way to safeguard the spontaneity and the sincerity of religious behavior and to escape a deadly ritualism will not be to get rid of the liturgy or to reduce it to the minimum strictly required in order to remain orthodox. Rather, the only way will be to enter into the liturgy and to live it so deeply that all our thoughts, all our feelings and our whole life will be impregnated with it and transformed by it.

In other words, the Christian, who on the supernatural level is an essentially communitarian being, must have a religious psychology in keeping with his nature. His interior attitude when confronted with the history of salvation, the Church, the sacraments, must correspond to the realities. Otherwise he will never feel at ease in the world of the liturgy, and he will be tempted to become as little involved in it as possible.

If he does succeed in forming his religious sensibility according to the communitarian dimension of the liturgy, he will find it easy to live fully the dogma of the mystical body of Christ. He will not have to fear that he is reducing this reality, as too many do, to a purely moral and individual bond, even an individualistic bond, between Christ and the believer and among all the believers, independently and outside of the ecclesial reality willed in fact by God.

4. The Ritual Expression of the Communitarian Nature of the Liturgy; History and Present Status

The liturgy is the prayer of the Church, it is the prayer of a community. This communitarian character, very obvious in the early Church, has been somewhat obscured or weakened in the course of the centuries, especially in the Roman rite. This evolution was caused by the suppression of customs which had been a happy expression of the liturgy's collective dimension, by the fact that functions or prayers which originally belonged to the whole community were reserved to the clergy, finally by the introduction of rites which are rather of the nature of private devotion.

The Mass

The two works of Dom Dix[7] and Father Jungmann,[8] now classical works on the Mass, have brought to light the clearly communitarian character of the liturgy of the Mass, as well as its progressive obscuration since the fourth-fifth century, especially in the Middle Ages in the West.

The Mass, of its nature, is the action of the whole Christian community, and especially of the community assembled around this altar "here and now." This community, moreover, is hierarchically organized, each member and each rank having its own role to play. Each one remains in his rank, but all intervene actively in this drama which concerns them all. It was inconceivable to the ancient mentality that Christians should come to Mass as mere spectators or listeners. Still less was it conceivable that they should indulge in meditation or private prayer with no connection or only a loose connection with the common action that was going on.

Up to the fourth century, this essentially communitarian character of the Mass is manifested in a great number of rites. All the prayers, for example, are said aloud, so that everyone understands them. The chants are sung by the whole assembly, the readings are listened to by the whole assembly, including the celebrant: the celebrant does not read privately what is being chanted by the choir or read by the lectors. The prayers concern the whole assembly; they are said in the name of all, and not only for all the members of the community

---

[7] *The Shape of the Liturgy.*   [8] *The Mass of the Roman Rite.*

but also for all men or all classes of men. The priest never prays in his own name alone or for himself alone.

The Mass is celebrated in a language understood by the faithful. When they no longer understand the language hitherto in use, there is no delay in changing it, on condition that a literary language is adopted; this is what was done at Rome toward the middle of the fourth century. Since the Mass is not the priest's personal prayer, but the prayer of the whole community which takes part in it, it seems evident that it must be said in a language understood by all.

Before beginning a prayer the celebrant addresses the assembly with "The Lord be with you," "Let us give thanks to God," "Let us pray," "Peace be with you," or some such formula. At the end of the prayer said in their name, the people ratify it explicitly by the "Amen."

And this is still more manifest for the great Eucharistic prayer. Only the bishop or the priest who takes his place is allowed to say it. Only he can repeat the words of Christ whose representative he is. Yet here too the whole people is associated in the prayer and ratifies it by the final "Amen."

Similarly, at the communion, the one who receives the body and blood of Christ answers "Amen" to the formula said by the bishop or the deacon.

The people surround the altar and have no difficulty following the rites which take place there. It would not occur to anyone to have the altar at some distance from the assembly, still less to hide it.

All those present at Mass receive communion; for it is primarily through communion that one takes part in the sacrifice. Christ's body is brought to those who cannot come, that they too may participate in the Eucharist.[9]

In the third century the rite of the offering by the whole people makes its appearance: the faithful offer the celebrant the matter of the sacrifice. Thus all offer and all communicate, though only the priest consecrates. This custom is maintained in the West until the end of the eleventh century, and still longer in certain places.[10]

The communitarian character of the Mass is expressed likewise in the Roman custom of the *fermentum* : on festive days the pope sends to the priests celebrating in the churches of Rome and to the suburban bishops a fragment of the Bread he has just consecrated. The priests and bishops put this particle into their chalice, as a sign of unity. This rite persisted in Rome until the ninth century. It was practiced in other churches also.[11]

The Mass, then, is an action of the whole community, but of a community acting in hierarchical order: each member takes part, but in his own rank. Clement of Rome had to insist on this point against the anarchical tendencies of the Christians of Corinth: "We should do in an orderly way all that the Lord has commanded us to perform at stated times. He has commanded that

---

[9] Cf. Justin, *Apol.* I, 65 (PG 6, 428).   [11] Cf. *ibid.*, 404 f.
[10] Cf. Righetti, III, 248 ff.

the sacrifices be offered and the sacred services (λειτουργίας) be held, and not haphazardly and without order but at fixed times and seasons. And He Himself by His sovereign will has determined where and by whom He wants them done, that everything, being done in a holy way according to His good pleasure, may be acceptable to His will. Therefore those who make their offerings at the appointed times are well received and blessed, for they make no mistake in following the ordinances of the Master. To the high priest have been entrusted certain liturgical offices; to the priests has been assigned a special post; particular services are incumbent upon the levites; the lay person is bound by the rules laid down for the laity. Let each one of us, brethren, at his post, seek to please God with a right conscience and with reverence, not transgressing the rule established for his office (λειτουργίας)." [12]

This hierarchical aspect of the participation in the Eucharistic sacrifice found its highest expression in the ancient practice of the single Sunday Mass, which the bishop celebrated, surrounded by his priests, his deacons, the other clerics and all the faithful. In several passages, St. Ignatius of Antioch appears as the eloquent spokesman for this ideal:

"Follow the bishop, all of you, as Jesus Christ followed the Father, and follow the college of presbyters as you would the Apostles. Reverence the deacons, too, as you would the command of God. Let no one do any of those things which concern the Church, apart from the bishop. Let that Eucharist be held valid which is celebrated by the bishop or by him who has received authority from the bishop. Where the bishop appears, there let the community be, just as where Jesus Christ is, there is the Catholic Church. Without the bishop it is not lawful either to baptize or to celebrate the *agape*, but whatever he has approved is pleasing to God. In this manner whatever is done will be safe and valid." [13]

"Just as the Lord, being one with the Father, never did anything without Him either in His own person or through His Apostles, so you also must not do anything without the bishop and the priests. In vain will you try to make anything appear praiseworthy which you have done privately on your own account; only that which you do in common is praiseworthy. One prayer, one supplication, one mind, one hope animated by love, in the joy without blemish — such is Jesus Christ, whose excellence is beyond comparison. Hasten together, all of you, to one temple, to one altar, that is, to Jesus Christ, who is one and who, proceeding from the one Father, has remained one with Him and has returned to Him."[14]

"See to it, therefore, that you participate in one Eucharist only. For there is but one flesh of our Lord Jesus Christ, one chalice which unites us in His blood, one altar, just as there is one bishop, surrounded by the college of the presbyters and by the deacons, my companions in the ministry. In this manner whatever you do will be done according to God's will." [15]

---

[12] I *Cor.*, 40 and 41, 1.
[13] *Smyrn.*, 8 (PG 5, 713).
[14] *Magnes.*, 7 (PG 5, 668).
[15] *Philadel.*, 4 (PG 5, 700).

We can see from all this how foreign to the primitive Church are the Protestant tenets of the essential independence of the individual over against the community in his relations with God, and of the fundamental equality of function of all those who take part in a liturgical action. The conviction of the early Church is that on the supernatural level the person who does not belong to Christ's *ecclesia* is absolutely nothing. And the most expressive and most efficacious sign of this *ecclesia* is the participation of all the people in a single Eucharist.

This helps us to understand the profound significance of every liturgical action celebrated by a community united around its bishop or by a parish united around its pastor, who is the bishop's representative for the parish. It shows us also that the bishop is the liturgist *par excellence* of his church, and that one of the best means of making the priests and the people in our day appreciate once more the essentially communitarian and sacral nature of the Church is to begin by making them rediscover all the wealth of meaning of the *ecclesia* as liturgical assembly.

Unfortunately, beginning with the fourth century and especially in the Middle Ages in the West, the ecclesial dimension of the Eucharistic action has been gradually obscured in the liturgical rites and consequently in the minds of the Christian people.

In the East, as early as the fourth century, we find in the sacramentary of Serapion a series of prayers reserved to the priest, over and above the anaphora. In the fourth-fifth century, the offering made by the faithful is discontinued. Then the iconostasis is put up before the altar, and it keeps being enlarged until it ends up by hiding the altar completely from the eyes of the congregation when the central door is closed at the most solemn moment of the Mass. At the same time, the custom begins of having the priest recite the prayers of intercession in a low voice while the deacon and the people are singing; he raises his voice only for the conclusion (ecphonesis), that the people may answer "Amen." And above all, it becomes customary for the priest to recite the whole anaphora secretly, except for some ecphoneses.

In the West this evolution was even more notable. The evidence to be recorded is almost overwhelming:

A language no longer understood by the people continued to be used for the liturgy.

Low Masses became more and more frequent; at certain periods of the Middle Ages, solitary Masses of mere private devotion were multiplied in an extraordinary way.

For these low Masses a server was called upon; and not only did he take the place of the congregation when no one else was present, but he continued to make the responses alone even when there was a large congregation; so that the faithful were practically forbidden to use their right of taking an active part in the sacrifice.

Prayers which the celebrant is to say silently were introduced into the liturgy of the Mass, and also prayers of a private character, which he says in his own name and for himself alone.[16]

The canon was no longer said above a whisper.

In sung Masses the priest was at first authorized, later obliged, to recite privately the texts read or sung by the sacred ministers or by the choir.

As in the East, the offering made by the people was suppressed, and the communion of the people became more and more rare, or even, at certain periods, almost non-existent.

Or communion was given outside of the Mass, even to those who assisted at the Mass.

The schola reserved to itself the performance of all the sung parts, even those which ought to have been left to the people. It is true that the people were no longer capable of performing them, for the music had become too complicated. This was true of the classical Gregorian chants, but still more of the polyphonic Masses.

No longer having anything to do, the people began to occupy the time of the Mass with prayers which had only a remote connection with what was being done at the altar.

Finally, for a long time it was forbidden to publish translations of the missal, and especially of the ordinary of the Mass. Thus the laity were reduced to "assisting" at the Mass as at a spectacle.[17]

There is no need to insist further. True, many medieval abuses were eliminated or lessened by the reform of Pope Pius V or by other reforms. Still, a certain number of facts recalled above remain true: the liturgy is celebrated in a language which is not understood by the people, the chant is entrusted to specialists and not to the people, the canon is recited in such a way as not to be heard by the people.

It would be quite difficult now, of course, to modify this discipline. But at any rate it must be recognized that, to a great extent, it is this state of affairs which gives rise to the greatest liturgical problem of our day: how to bring the people back to participating actively in the Mass as in an action of the whole community.

The appearance which the Mass takes on today does not always help our contemporaries, imbued as they are with individualism and psychologism, to adapt their religious behavior to the profoundly communitarian character which the Eucharistic action always retains in spite of appearances.

[16] These prayers, of medieval Gallican origin, accumulated at the beginning of the Mass (all the prayers which precede the introit), at the offertory (from the *Suscipe sancte Pater* to the *Orate fratres* inclusive), and at the communion (from the *Domine Iesu Christe* to the *Corpus tuum, Domine* inclusive). Almost all these prayers are in the singular, and even those which are in the plural refer especially to the priest. On these "apologies," cf. Righetti, III, 144 f.

[17] For more details on this evolution cf. Jungmann, *The Mass of the Roman Rite*, I, especially from p. 74 to p. 159.

The sacraments

What has just been said about the Mass applies, on the whole, to the sacraments. These have a collective, ecclesial dimension; for, through the grace they communicate, the faithful are born to the supernatural life and grow in it as members of the people of God.

Thus, baptism is not only the supernatural regeneration of an individual and his adoption by God, but at the same time and necessarily his visible entrance into the Church, body of Christ, and hence his organic union with the other members of that body. Baptism unites us to Christ only in the Church and through the Church. Similarly, confirmation is at the same time a perfecting of the individual and a perfecting of his inclusion in the people of God.

Penance, while reconciling the sinner with God, reconciles him also with the Church, with the community which he has likewise offended and caused to suffer. The same may be said of extreme unction as complement of penance; and we may see in it also an act by which the earthly community prepares one of its members to appear before God, and sends it to the heavenly Jerusalem.

The ecclesial character of holy orders and of matrimony is quite clear, since the immediate end of these two sacraments is to guarantee Christian society its continuation, material and spiritual, and its hierarchical structure.

It would be easy for the historian to show how the ancient liturgy in the administration of these various sacraments brought out their communitarian aspect, while the present-day liturgy often obscures the communitarian aspect to such an extent that in many cases the faithful have almost lost sight of it.

For baptism and confirmation, we need only think of the ancient ceremony of the Christian initiation, celebrated once or twice a year, during the solemn vigils of Easter and of Pentecost, in the presence of the whole local community, presided over by the bishop, who as head of this *ecclesia* introduced the neophytes into it. In such a climate, the Christian initiation appeared truly as the act by which the mother Church brought new children into the world, the body of Christ added new cells, the militia of Christ enrolled its annual contingent.

In baptism as it is administered today, on the other hand, even the best Christians very often see nothing but the regeneration of an individual . . . and a family feast. They are unaware, or just barely aware, of its significance as integration into the community.

As for penance, it is certainly the sacrament which, for us, has the character of something private and secret in the highest degree. Everything, it seems, points to an affair between God and ourselves, in which the priest does play the role of an intermediary, but which is without any ecclesial dimension.

Actually, until the sixth to the eighth centuries, we find no convincing evidence — certain opinions to the contrary notwithstanding — of a private sacramental penance, while the discipline of public penance is the usual thing. It involves: the confession of sins, which is public at least implicitly [18] for notorious grave sins, which are submitted to the deliberation of the assembly presided over by the bishop, surrounded by the priests and the deacons, in the presence of the people; [19] the excommunication of the sinner, who "has deserved to be excluded from prayer in common and from our meetings and from any relation with us whatsoever"; [20] public penance, with the gesture of kneeling before the bishop, the priests and also all the faithful, to recommend oneself to their prayers; [21] finally, the public reconciliation granted by the bishop in the presence of the whole community, which is a reconciliation not only with God but also with the Church and all her members.

Basic to all this discipline, obviously, is the conviction that sin is an offense and damage done to the whole *ecclesia* at the same time that it is an offense against God. This is what made Origen say concerning fornication, "It is not permitted me to take a member of Christ and make it a member of a prostitute. Say to it (your evil desire): I have become a temple of God; it is not permitted me to introduce anything unclean, nor is it right for me to violate the temple of God. Add also: he who commits fornication sins against his own body; not only against this body which has become a temple of God, but also against that body of which it is said that the whole Church is Christ's body. He who soils his own body sins against the whole Church, since through one member the stain spreads throughout the body." [22] Thus the sin of one Christian and his reconciliation are things of supreme interest to the whole community.

Because all the members of this community, each in his own rank, could intervene in the judgment and the reconciliation of the culprit, Tertullian could say to the penitents, "These are brethren and fellow servants, who share with you the same hopes, fears, joys, sorrows, sufferings, because they have in common with you the spirit of a common Lord and Father. Then why do you regard them as strangers? Why run away from them as if they were going to gloat over your fall, when they themselves are affected by it? The body cannot rejoice at the sickness of one of its members. On the contrary, it is inevitable that the whole will suffer with that member and work together to heal it. The Church is in the one and the other; and the Church is Christ. When you cast yourself down, therefore, at the knees of your brethren, it is Christ whom you are embracing, it is Christ whom you are imploring. And when they mourn over you, it is Christ who is suffering, Christ who is praying to the Father. And it is always easy to obtain what the Son asks for." [23]

---

[18] Implicitly, since the fact of submitting oneself to the assembly's deliberation and decision as to notorious sins was equivalent to a public confession. Secret sins, on the other hand, were always confessed secretly to the bishop.

[19] Cf. Righetti, III, 129.
[20] Tertullian, *Apologetic.*, 39, 4 (PL 1, 469).
[21] Cf. Righetti, III, 131 ff.
[22] *In Iesu Nave*, V, 6 (PG 12, 851).
[23] *De poenit.*, X (PL 1, 1245).

In holy orders the communitarian character was still more manifest formerly than it is today, from the fact that the faithful really had a voice in the designation of candidates for the diaconate, the priesthood and the episcopacy. As for matrimony, its ecclesial aspect has always been apparent in the rites. It was even reinforced, from a certain viewpoint, when an obligatory form was prescribed and clandestine marriages were declared invalid.

Prayer

In the Roman liturgy the prayers on the whole have preserved the collective character imprinted on them by Christian antiquity. These prayers are in the plural and, through the mouth of the celebrant, it is the whole assembly that addresses God, as Church of God, people of God, family of God.[24] As early a writer as Cyprian pointed out that "our prayer is public and common, and when we pray we do not pray for an individual but for the whole people, because we, the whole people, are one." [25] And St. Ambrose, a century later, wrote, "The Church is the common right of all: it prays in common, works in common, is tempted in common." [26]

In the ancient Church the Divine Office was regarded as a prayer essentially choral, obligatory for the community as such, not for the individuals. By imposing it on all the clergy, even outside of choir, the Latin Church has given it more the character of a personal prayer. This is not an evil, provided those concerned do not forget that the Office is above all a collective prayer.

Thus the Church's whole liturgy is an application of the divine law of salvation in community, salvation which is not possible except in the Christian *ecclesia*, for, as St. Irenaeus says, "where the Church is, there is the Spirit of God, and where the Spirit of God is, there is the Church and every grace." [27]

Today it is the liturgical life of the parish that ought to be the normal expression of this communitarian spirit for the faithful. But modern conditions of existence are scarcely favorable to this parochial dimension of their Christian life. It is up to their pastors at least to call their attention to the great law of salvation in community.[28]

This rapid historical survey shows that the liturgy has long been in a state of tension by its effort to express at the same time the collective aspect and the individual aspect of its object. This tension, moreover, is more or less inherent in the very nature of the liturgy, since, in order to be effective, the liturgy requires that the reality proposed to all be really lived and assimilated by every member of the assembly and first of all by the celebrant himself.

[24] The expressions *ecclesia tua, populus tuus, familia tua* recur constantly in the collects of the Roman liturgy.

[25] *De dom. orat.*, 8 (PL 4, 524).

[26] *De officiis*, I, 29, 142 (PL 16, 65).

[27] *Adv. Haer.*, III, 24, 1 (PG 7, 966).

[28] It is only in this communitarian perspective that the necessity and the role of a liturgical law, established by the competent authority, will be accurately understood. Those who find it hard to accept this regimentation imposed on all are forgetting that this intervention of authority is a normal consequence of the law of salvation in community, in a community hierarchically structured.

But this effort of assimilation and interiorization very quickly tends to pull away from the original ecclesial context. Hence there is a danger of reversing the roles: the subject's individual behavior, instead of modeling itself on the liturgical reality, seeks to draw the liturgy into its own service and make it express the subject's own tendencies, forgetting that the liturgy is an essentially communitarian reality.

It is hard to maintain a perfect balance in this field. At any rate, the late Middle Ages and the baroque period have left us a rather embarrassing heritage of individualism, and we now experience an urgent need of a reaction, to bring into appreciation again a fundamental and too much neglected aspect of the liturgy.

10   THE LITURGY AND
THE LAW OF INCARNATION

In explaining what the liturgy is, we have more than once made allusion to the law of incarnation. Here we must dwell on it for a while, in order to understand better the concrete and human character of the liturgy as place of encounter between man and God through sensible signs and through men of flesh and blood.

1. The Law of Incarnation in the Relations between Man and God

The law of incarnation has two aspects. It signifies in the first place that God communicates His life to man by means of sensible realities, so that man must pass through these intermediaries to receive that life. It signifies in the second place that this communication, while leaving intact the substantial distinction between God and man, raises man to a divine way of being and acting, not only of a moral order but really of an ontological and physical order.

Hence the law of incarnation expresses a mysterious but very real theandrism, a union of the divine and the human, both in the end result of the relations between God and man and in the way which leads to it. The divine somehow becomes embodied in the human, in sensible human nature, to raise it to a divine way of being and of acting.

Christ, incarnate Word, Man-God, is the prototype in whom this law is verified in the highest degree and under all its aspects. And it is normal that this be so, since Christ is the concrete summing-up of the whole divine economy for men, the knot between man and God. In Him, human nature is assumed by the divine Person as soon as it begins to exist; it is wholly impregnated with the divinity not only on the level of knowledge and volition but, more profoundly, on the level of being. The hypostatic union is the most real and most perfect sanctification possible for a created being: no one can conceive of a closer union between the divine and the human. Theandrism is here at its source and at its summit, and all the other elevations to the divine order can be only imitations or participations.[1]

Now this communication, in Christ, is an incarnation. To be sure, the divine Word took on not only a human body but a complete nature, body and soul. But it was His body, the sensible and material thing, which veiled His divinity throughout His earthly life. Through His Incarnation God hid Himself from the world at the same time that He manifested Himself.[2] The contemporaries of Jesus could live alongside of Him without seeing the Man-God in Him. For many, His humanity was a screen which veiled His divinity, accessible only to the eyes of faith.

The fact that Christ chose to show Himself to the world in this manner which was so disconcerting for human reason, helps us to understand God's ways of acting towards men and the road men must follow to reach Him. Not only on those who lived with Jesus was this way of the Incarnation imposed; today it is still the only way that leads to the Father.

We might say that what the humanity of Jesus was for His contemporaries, the sacraments are for us: we can go to God only through these realities, sensible and spiritual at the same time, which are the sacraments. These are not mere symbols whose whole function would be to stimulate our faith and our charity; they are instruments, channels of grace, of that grace which confers on us a divine existence and a theandric life, prolongation and participation of the theandric life of Christ.

The whole sacramental world, therefore, is governed by the law of incarnation; and St. Thomas has reason to say that the sacraments are separate instruments of Christ, just as His humanity is the conjoint instrument of His divinity. And this holds likewise for the sacramentals, with only this differ-

---

[1] Cf., e.g., this magnificent collect for Christmas in the Leonine sacramentary: "Omnipotens sempiterne Deus, qui in Domini nostri Iesu Christi Filii tui nativitate tribuisti totius religionis initium perfectionemque constare; da nobis, quaesumus, in eius portione censeri, in quo totius salutis humanae summa consistit" (n. 1248; ed. Mohlberg, II, 159). Christ, who appears in the world on the day of His birth, is not only the source from whom all worship acceptable to God is derived (totius religionis initium), but also the summit of this worship and of all sanctification (perfectio, summa); for men, the thing to do is to be united to Christ and to share in His fulness (in eius portione censeri).

[2] Cf. Dionysius the Areopagite: "In the humanity of Christ, the Superessential is manifested in the human essence, yet remains hidden after this manifestation, or, to speak in a more divine way, remains hidden in the manifestation itself" (Ep. 3 [PG 3, 1069 B]).

ence, that they act *ex opere operantis Ecclesiae* while the sacraments act *ex opere operato.*

The entire Church is also subject to the law of incarnation. It can be said that the sacraments through which God gives Himself to us are not only things but also men. For there are men in the Church who have received the special and authentic mission from God of communicating the divine life to other men, so that it is indispensable to remain in contact with them in order not to be cut off from the current of life.

These men are those who constitute the hierarchy of the Catholic Church: the pope, the bishops, the priests. We are obliged to pass through them in order to reach God. They are necessary intermediaries between Him and us. Only they can celebrate the sacrifice, administer the sacraments, preside over the liturgical prayer. Here again the divine communicates itself through the human; and the human manifests the divine, and hides it at the same time, in the very act in which it manifests it.

It would be impossible to attach too much importance to these data of our faith. Believers and unbelievers are always exposed to the temptation of reducing Christianity to a philosophical system, a moral doctrine or a religious experience, whereas it is primarily a history; and the central event of this history is the Incarnation of the Son of God. To be a Christian is to accept this event, with all the consequences it entails for the relations between man and God.

2. The Incarnation and the Liturgy

These remarks have not taken us away from the liturgy. They were necessary in order to situate the liturgy in its proper frame. More than any other aspect of the Church's life, the liturgy prolongs the Incarnation: it is thanks to the sacraments and the worship of the Church, body of Christ, that men enter into contact and communion with the Incarnation of the Son of God, to the point of being transformed by it and raised to a theandric existence and activity, of which Christ is the prototype.

If the Incarnation of the Son of God has been and still is a scandal for many minds, it is understandable that the liturgy should be a stumbling-block also for a great number. Its whole exterior and sensible nature and its hierarchical structure — two characteristics which are direct consequences of the Incarnation — offend the idealism and the individualism of our contemporaries. Some of them belittle it with the disdainful question of the Jews, "Is not this the son of Joseph?" Must we seek God in this man? Must we tie the freedom of the spirit to all these material rites? Then what becomes of adoration in spirit and in truth? Those who speak thus, certainly would not have chosen the way of the Incarnation to save the world, at any rate not the Incarnation "in the condition of a slave" by which God appeared on earth "fashioned to the likeness of men and recognized by outward appearance as man" (Phil. 2:7).

If Christ's humanity was for many an impenetrable veil, what wonder is it that the visible element of a liturgy performed by men who are not so transparent to the divine light should be much more an obstacle and a scandal?

No doubt those ministers of the liturgy are partly responsible who instead of doing their best to facilitate the efforts of the faithful to penetrate into the liturgy, paralyze those efforts by their negligence or their own lack of appreciation. And to these ministers might be applied the words of Jesus, "For it must be that scandals come, but woe to that man by whom the scandal comes!" (Matt. 18:7).

But the liturgy can also say, with Christ, "Blessed is he who is not scandalized in Me!" (Matt. 11:6). For he who knows how to surmount the obstacle of the Incarnation will find the sources of living water and will recognize in the liturgy the epiphany of Christ. After having taken part in the Eucharistic sacrifice or in some other function, he can make his own the words of St. John: "What we have seen with our eyes,[3] what we have looked upon and our hands have touched of the Word of life[4] — and the Life was made known, and we have seen it, and now testify and announce to you the Life eternal which was with the Father, and has appeared to us — what we have seen and heard we announce to you also . . ." (1 John 1:1-3).

It is perhaps this question of incarnation that separates Protestantism most profoundly from Catholicism. The fact is that Protestantism implies a radical lack of appreciation of the law of incarnation, since it refuses to find place between the soul and God for a human intermediary on whom the soul depends in an essential way in its relations with God. It follows logically that Protestantism is opposed to the liturgy, and that every liturgical renewal in a Protestant community brings it closer to Catholic tradition, since a rebirth of the liturgical spirit means a rebirth of the spirit of the Incarnation.

---

[3] The Greek liturgy ordinarily chants after the communion of the faithful an antiphon which begins, "We have seen the true light, we have received the heavenly Spirit . . . ."

[4] At one time the faithful could say this literally, for it was in their hands that they received the consecrated Bread at communion (cf. Jungmann, *The Mass of the Roman Rite*, II, 378–380).

11 THE LITURGY AND THE LAW OF THE COSMIC UNIVERSALITY OF THE KINGDOM OF GOD: I. MAN AND THE INFRAHUMAN WORLD

When we say that there is a law of the cosmic universality of the kingdom of God, we mean that all creation, human, infrahuman and angelic, is ordained to a single end: the kingdom of God. That kingdom embraces all beings and the whole of each being; and the fact that they are all ordained to one and the same end establishes a certain solidarity and reciprocal dependence among them. They are all to constitute a single, universal symphony.

It is this law which explains that the cosmos is viewed in the liturgy as a universe, as a whole of which all the parts are linked together.

1. The Liturgy Addresses the Whole Man

Revelation takes man as a whole

Revelation teaches us that the whole man, body and soul, is a subject of the kingdom of God. Creation, elevation to the supernatural state, the fall, the Redemption, asceticism, glorification concern not merely souls, but men. At every one of these stages it is the human being, with all his physical and psychological faculties, who is involved and who acts.

It is in this light that we must consider the dogmas of the Incarnation and the Resurrection. Because He wanted to save the whole man, the Word was

170

not content to assume a soul or a body, but He became man, He assumed a complete human nature. Nor will man be fully saved and fully happy until the divine life has transformed his whole being, body and soul. The dogma of the resurrection of bodies is like a desire of our nature, and it was in this perspective that the Fathers of the first centuries defended it against the pagans, who found it so hard to admit.[1]

It is in this light also that we can understand the continual struggle carried on by the Church against any form of asceticism founded on the idea that matter, and the body in particular, is something evil in itself.[2] From this point of view, there is nothing more foreign to the true Christian spirit than the exaggerated spiritualism of the Orphic, Platonic and Neoplatonic tradition, with its tendency to disembody man and to regard the body as a prison for the soul, and the senses as chains which prevent the soul from flying freely back to its original state as a pure spirit.

For the Christian, the body is not an enemy, but a part of the subject and an instrument. Bodily mortification and the very desire for death are only means to which recourse is had temporarily to keep the part in the service of the whole and, in the final accounting, to assure to the body itself its glorious resurrection. The Christian does not seek to destroy his body and his senses, but to make them tractable instruments in the service of the divine life that is given him — given him, who is a substantial composite made up of a soul and a body. He seeks to withdraw his body and his senses from the influence of sin in order to submit them to that of grace.

St. Augustine himself in the first period of his conversion misjudged the distance between Neoplatonic spiritualism and the authentic Christian spiritualism. Later on, when the Christian sense had been sharpened in him, he discovered man in Christ, and in man he discovered the body and the senses, and in the Church the sacraments and the liturgy. Thus, at the end of his life, more than once he puts his readers on guard against the inaccuracy of his first statements on this matter.

"I regret," he wrote in regard to his book *On the Happy Life*, ". . . having said that, in this life, happiness resides only in the mind of the wise man, and the condition of his body matters little. In reality, the perfect knowledge of God, that is, the maximum that man can have, is hoped for by the Apostle in the life to come, which alone should be called the happy life, for there the body too, incorruptible and immortal, will be subject to its spirit without trouble or resistance."[3]

Elsewhere he explained carefully the difference between the contempt of the body recommended by the philosophers and that practiced by the Chris-

---

[1] Cf., e.g., Athenagoras, *De resurrectione mortuorum*, 15 (PG 6, 1004-1005); Irenaeus, *Adv. Haer.*, V, 6 (PG 7, 1136–1139); Tertullian, *De resurrectione carnis*, 53 (PL 2, 872–875).

[2] Cf., e.g., Clement of Alexandria, *Strom.*, book III in its entirety (PG 8, 1097–1213).

[3] *Retract.*, I, 2 (PL 32, 588); cf. I, 4, 3 (PL 32, 590).

tians and especially by the martyrs: "The Christian martyrs acted prudently, therefore, and did not despise their bodies. Such a philosophy would have been perverse and worldly. It is the philosophy of those who do not believe in the resurrection of bodies. They consider themselves great despisers of the body, because they regard bodies as prisons in which they think souls have been shut up for having sinned in a previous life.

"But our God has made both body and soul. He is Creator of both, Redeemer of both, Author of both, Restorer of both. The martyrs, therefore, did not despise or persecute the flesh as an enemy. 'For no one has ever hated his own flesh' (Eph. 5:29). Rather, they took care of it precisely when they seemed to be neglecting it. When, still in the flesh, they endured temporal torments with faith, they were procuring eternal glory for that very flesh also." [4]

This example of St. Augustine is worth citing, for the Neoplatonic temptation is only too real, even today.

Let us add that, according to revelation, the divine life does not stop at invading the whole man, but also sanctifies all his good activities, in particular his creative activity and his effort to subject the world to himself and to organize it. The words of Genesis (1:28), "Be fruitful and multiply; fill the earth and subdue it," contain in germ the justification and even the sanctification of all these individual or social activities by which man cooperates with God in the creation and the organization of the world.[5]

The liturgy also takes man as a whole

The liturgy once more adopts the perspective of the Bible. The liturgy also addresses the whole man, in the concrete unity of his being. It is the whole man, body and soul, who is sanctified by God and who renders worship to Him. And those who take part in a liturgical function should unite themselves to it not only in their soul but also, in certain ways, in their body. First, they must be really present in the place where this function is celebrated.[6] Then, they must assume the attitudes prescribed by the rites themselves or by the customs accepted in the Church and imposed by the rubrics. It is therefore the law of the cosmic character of salvation which in the last analysis justifies the rubrics or the prescriptions of the ceremonial which impose this or that attitude on the ministers and the faithful at the various moments of the liturgical celebration.

Moreover, there is interdependence between the attitude of the soul and that of the body: the interior sentiment tends naturally to express itself outwardly, and the mere fact of taking the attitude corresponding to a given

---

[4] *Sermo* 277, 3 (PL 38, 1259).

[5] This is the basis of the theology of labor, of technology, of earthly realities. Cf., e.g., G. Thils, *Théologie des réalités terrestres*, 2 vols. (Paris, 1946–1949); Yves Congar, *La théologie du travail* (Paris, 1955).

[6] Which explains, among other things, why one cannot satisfy the precept of assistance at Mass except by bodily presence. The anomaly of marriage by proxy seems to be justified by the fact that the nuptial blessing is not the sacrament of matrimony, but that this sacrament is a contract which consists only in the exchange of consent by the partners.

sentiment generally favors the production or the growth of that sentiment. It is normal, then, for the Church to regulate carefully the gestures and the attitudes of those who take part in her worship.

If our body must play a part in the liturgy, the liturgy in turn is concerned with the body's welfare. It implores simultaneously the health of the soul and that of the body, always considering the body, of course, in its relation to the soul and to the last end of the whole man. If the Lenten liturgy emphasizes the mortification necessary for the equilibrium of the human composite, numerous postcommunions, on the other hand, ask God to extend to our body the effects of the Redemption, basing their petition on the biblical and traditional idea that the Eucharist is a remedy bestowing bodily as well as spiritual incorruptibility and immortality.

The postcommunion of the eleventh Sunday after Pentecost makes this petition: "By partaking of Your sacrament, we pray You, Lord, may we experience help for soul and body, that both may be saved and we may glory in the perfection of the heavenly remedy." [7] And in many other cases, the liturgy asks, for example, that the participation in the sacrifice be "a renewal of soul and body," [8] that it assure "the health of soul and body," [9] "salvation of soul and body," [10] that it be "a safeguard and a remedy for soul and body." [11]

In all the liturgies, ancient or modern, there are collects and Masses for the sick,[12] as well as numerous blessings and anointings for different kinds of ailments.[13] The sacrament of extreme unction also asks of God, as a secondary end, the health of the body.[14] And the funeral rites testify clearly to the solicitude with which the liturgy surrounds the Christian's body.

This solicitude for the body, which is explained ultimately only by the hope of the resurrection in glory, extends especially to the senses. It will be enough to recall here how in the present Roman rite the senses are sanctified during baptism and extreme unction, the first and last interventions of the liturgy in man's life.

Since ancient times, the catechumen has received the sign of the cross on his forehead. Taking up an Eastern and Gallican custom, the ritual for the baptism of adults develops this rite by having this *signatio crucis* made on all the senses: "With his thumb the priest traces the sign of the cross on the

---

[7] "Sentiamus, quaesumus, Domine, tui perceptione sacramenti, subsidium mentis et corporis: ut, in utroque salvati, coelestis remedii plenitudine gloriemur."

[8] *Reparatio* . . . postcommunion of the eighth Sunday after Pentecost.

[9] *Sanitas* . . . secret of Wednesday of the fourth week of Lent.

[10] *Salvatio* . . . postcommunion of occasional prayers, n. 19.

[11] *Tutamentum* . . . *medela* . . . canon of the Roman Mass, third prayer of the priest before communion.

[12] Cf., e.g., the Gelasian sacramentary, III, 69–71; ed. Wilson, pp. 281–283. In the present Roman Missal is found a Mass "for the sick," with special prayers "for one on his death-bed."

[13] Cf., e.g., *Rituale Romanum*, title IX, ch. 4, nn. 6–8, and also ch. 3, n. 7: blessing of candles against maladies of the throat on the feast of St. Blaise.

[14] Roman Ritual, order for administering the sacrament of extreme unction, n. 12, that is, the three final prayers.

forehead of each, saying, 'I sign you on the forehead that you may accept the cross of the Lord.' On the ears: 'I sign you on the ears that you may listen to the divine precepts.' On the eyes: 'I sign you on the eyes that you may see the glory of God.' On the nostrils: 'I sign you on the nostrils that you may perceive the sweet fragrance of Christ.' On the mouth: 'I sign you on the mouth that you may speak the words of life.' On the breast: 'I sign you on the breast that you may believe in God.' On the shoulders: 'I sign you on the shoulders that you may take upon you the yoke of His service.' On the whole body, without touching it, he traces the sign of the cross and says: 'I sign you in your total being in the name of the Father and of the Son and of the Holy Spirit, that you may have eternal life and may live for ever and ever. Amen.'" [15] It is evident that the aim of this rite is to sanctify man's various senses, which will play so important a role in his ascent to sanctity and in the worship he will render to God.

And it is logical that, when the Christian prepares to leave this earth, his senses receive a sacramental anointing, to wipe out the sins of which they have been the instruments: "Through this holy anointing and His most tender mercy, may the Lord pardon all the sins you have committed by the sense of sight . . . by the sense of hearing . . . by the sense of smell . . . by the sense of taste and the power of speech . . . by the sense of touch . . . by the power of walking. Amen." [16]

In all these rites the liturgy echoes the true Christian mind in its rejection of all spiritualism of a Neoplatonic or Gnostic character. Tertullian had already pointed this out in his lapidary style: "The flesh is the hinge of salvation. In the process of salvation, when the soul is reconciled to God, it is the flesh that makes it possible for the soul to be so. That is: the flesh is washed that the soul may be cleansed; the flesh is anointed that the soul may be consecrated; the flesh is signed with a seal that the soul may be protected; the flesh is covered with a shadow in the laying-on of hands that the soul may be illuminated by the Spirit; the flesh is fed on the body and blood of Christ that the soul may also be nourished on God. Hence the two elements cannot be separated in the recompense, when they have been united in the work." [17]

The liturgy brings all of man's faculties into play

The liturgy addresses the body simultaneously with the soul. Let us add that it addresses all of man's faculties and brings them into play in a singularly

---

[15] Roman Ritual, baptism of adults, n. 11.

[16] Roman Ritual, extreme unction, nn. 8–10.

[17] *De resurrectione carnis*, 8 (PL 2, 806): "Caro salutis est cardo. De qua cum anima Deo alligatur, ipsa est quae efficit ut alligari possit. Scilicet caro abluitur, ut anima emaculetur; caro ungitur ut anima consecretur; caro signatur ut anima muniatur; caro manus impositione adumbratur, ut et anima spiritu illuminetur; caro corpore et sanguine Christi vescitur, ut et anima Deo saginetur. Non possunt ergo separari in mercede quas opera coniungit." Earlier, St. Irenaeus, against the gnostic claim that "salvation is something which concerns only souls, and that the body, being taken from the earth, cannot participate in salvation" (*Adv. Haer.*, I, 27, 3 [PG 7, 689]), strongly affirms that the flesh also participates in life (*Adv. Haer.*, V, 3, 3 [PG 7, 1131–1132]).

harmonious fashion. Every liturgical action, but especially the Mass, and above all the solemn or the pontifical Mass, demands of those who take part in it a continual attention and cooperation, both in the order of knowledge — sight, hearing, imagination, understanding — and in the order of volition — emotions and will. The senses and the faculties are never left inactive for long.

The reason is that the liturgy has the character primarily of an action being done and not of a meditation. This is true if by meditation we mean an individual exercise in which a person concentrates on God or the divine realities in a wholly interior way. And it is still more true if a person seeks in meditation to suspend all exterior activity of the faculties, and even all interior activity of the discursive type, to become absorbed in a simple contemplation of God, in a purely intuitive act. If that is approximately what we understand by meditation, we must recognize that the liturgy is not primarily a meditation but a sacred action; not a θεωρούμενον or a θεωρία but a δρώμενον, the ancients would say.

In the present liturgy, the times intended for meditation in the sense we have just indicated are extremely rare, if they exist at all. In the ancient Roman liturgy, there were times during the fore-Mass when the people and the sacred ministers, at the deacon's invitation, "Let us kneel," stopped for a while to meditate and to pray silently, until the deacon told them, "Arise," and the celebrant began the common prayer aloud: "Let us pray." But this private prayer was very brief, and the intentions for it had been suggested beforehand by the celebrant: "Let us pray for the Church of God . . ., for our pontiff . . ., for the priests and the deacons . . ." etc. Today this form of prayer, with invitatory, silent prayer of the community, collect pronounced by the celebrant, is customary only on Good Friday and in the Easter Vigil. Traces of it are preserved in the Ember Day Masses, at ordinations and elsewhere. It is to be hoped that they will recover their full value by the reestablishment of the silent prayer after the *Flectamus genua.*

Perhaps the monastic Office at one time had periods of silence between the psalms, to permit a meditation and an individual prayer. At any rate, in the Mass of the faithful there are no grounds for supposing that such periods of pause for private prayer ever existed.[18] The Mass is the sacred *action* above all others, something that is *done*; we need only recall some traditional expressions: *eucharistiam facere, sacrum facere, oblationem facere,* εὐχαριστίαν ποιεῖν, μυστήρια τελεῖν, προσφοράν ἐπιτελεῖν.

From these remarks one should not conclude that it is inadvisable, or perhaps impossible, for the sacred ministers and the faithful who take part in a liturgical action to be recollected and to concentrate interiorly, perhaps to reach a passive and mystical state. But, in order to arrive at that union of

---

[18] The interruption which now takes place in the reading of the diptychs, formerly done the Roman canon at the *Memento* of the living aloud by the deacon. The change came with and that of the dead is intended to replace the appearance of low Masses.

the soul with God, the Christian is invited, not to isolate himself as much as possible from the common prayer and from the action which is taking place, but on the contrary to take an active and attentive part in the mysteries which are being celebrated and which are appealing, with a gentle insistence, to all his senses and all his faculties.

Let us recognize, however, that there is a problem here, which we shall examine in the chapter devoted to the relations between spirituality and liturgy: Are there not good grounds for accusing the liturgy of being too "distracting" and not favorable enough to the "recollection of the senses," of being on the whole a rather superficial means of union with God, useful only for beginners?

The liturgy offers the intellect abundant, wholesome nourishment. To be sure, it hardly ever serves its intellectual food in the scholastic manner, that is, with the intellectual preoccupations of scholastic theology, which appeared, after all, at an epoch when liturgical prayer, on the whole, had long been fixed in its forms.[19]

But the liturgy nonetheless contains very rich nourishment. No prayer is richer in doctrine than liturgical prayer, in which the vast design of the history of salvation is reflected again and again, in which everything is viewed in this framework, in which all of man's sentiments towards God appear as a response to the divine advances, to the objective data of revelation. It is those data that remain always in the foreground of attention, and they must be clearly grasped by the mind before they will arouse "pious affections." There is nothing more foreign to the Roman liturgy than sentimental outpourings, the result of a superficial contact with an object of which only the emotional aspect is noticed.[20]

Still, because it considers the mystery of Christ not in an abstract and speculative way but in a concrete, intuitive, historical way, liturgical prayer does allow plenty of room for man's affective and volitional reactions, which it expresses under many forms and with many gradations: admiration, desire, supplication, compunction, thanksgiving, etc. In its effort to involve the whole man, the liturgy never stops short of this stage.

[19] Scholastic theology strove to examine the data of revelation from a point of view chiefly ontological and metaphysical. In the present Roman liturgy the Office of Corpus Christi — a very beautiful one, moreover, and composed with a remarkable liturgical sense — is undoubtedly the only one to bear some discrete traces of this scholastic way of thinking.

[20] The exceptions to this rule are extremely rare. One might mention the hymns *Iesu dulcis memoria* and *Iesu decus angelicum* of Vespers and Lauds of the feast of the Holy Name of Jesus. These hymns, taken from the *Iubilus rythmicus de nomine Iesu* by an unknown author of the end of the twelfth century or the beginning of the thirteenth, were introduced into the liturgy by Innocent XII in 1721 when he extended this feast to the whole Church. One might also cite the Mass and the Office of the two feasts of the Seven Sorrows of the Blessed Virgin Mary, which date from the seventeenth century. All these pieces correspond to a type of religious sensibility in which the *ego* of the subject takes up much more space than the objective consideration of the dogmatic reality. Nothing is more eloquent in this regard than the contrast between the feast on September 15 and the feast of the Exaltation of the Cross celebrated the day before.

To be convinced that the liturgy is ready to sanctify all honorable human activities, both individual and social, a person need only notice that the liturgy has provided blessings for all the circumstances of life and for all the forms of work, of art, and even, in our day, of sport.

The theme of these blessings is always approximately this: "Grant, Lord, that those who engage in the activities connected with these things here, may be protected by You in body and in soul, may make good use of these things and may conduct their activity conformably to Your will, that they may come to love You, serve You and finally enjoy You in eternity."

Almost every year witnesses the appearance of new formulas of blessing, as if no human invention must escape the sanctifying influence of the Church's prayer. Here, for example, is the prayer which accompanies the formula for blessing the implements of Alpine climbing: "Through the intercession of St. Bernard, whom You have given as patron to Alpine dwellers and travelers, protect, O Lord, these Your servants, and grant that those who climb these peaks may come to the mountain which is Christ. Through the same Christ, our Lord." [21]

This effort of the liturgy to give a Christian value to all the aspects of human activity is particularly evident with regard to the esthetic sentiment, artistic activity and works of art. The fact is that the liturgy has drafted into its service architecture, painting, sculpture, music, even the dance. If the primitive Church excluded, to some extent, figured representations, statues and also music,[22] this was by reason of the excessive use of them by the pagan cults at that time. It was necessary to give the new Christians a very clear understanding of the difference between Christian worship and pagan worship. Later, the liturgy called upon the arts repeatedly.

No doubt there is a danger, by no means imaginary, in this recourse to art: the danger of letting oneself be lulled into an esthetism devoid of any true religious vitality. But that is no reason for denying that art can contribute in a large measure to that elevation of man at which the liturgy aims, and this precisely because of the profound unity of the human composite, which is material, sensible and spiritual at the same time.[23]

This aptitude of the liturgy for involving the whole man is likewise the source of its extraordinary effectiveness in teaching. In the liturgical action the mystery penetrates the whole man and finds entrance into him by all his senses and all his faculties, almost without his noticing it. Every age, every culture, every state of mind finds plentiful nourishment in the liturgy, each in its own way and according to its own capacity.

This broadly human character of the liturgy explains also, at least in good part, the fact that all the great epochs of history and all the peoples who have

---

[21] Roman Ritual, title IX, ch. 8, n. 20.

[22] It seems, however, that the singing of simple, popular hymns was allowed.

[23] In his various works on the liturgy, Romano Guardini has dwelt on the idea of the liturgy as "disinterested activity" and on the concept of "liturgical play."

made use of the liturgy have been able to leave their imprint on it as evidence of their particular needs. Thus, along with the principle of permanence and of conservation, there is also in the liturgy a principle of development and continual adaptation which allows it to remain a living thing and not be handed down from generation to generation as a mere museum piece. This openness was most notable at the time when numerous particular liturgies developed, both in the East and in the West. It has been conspicuously limited since the aim of unification began to prevail, especially in the West.

Actually the present Roman liturgy, which seems to us so far removed from the real state of mind of the congregations to which it is addressed, is no longer the ancient Roman liturgy, but that liturgy modified and developed by numerous Gallican and Germanic accessions of the Middle Ages. Whether a person is glad of this fact,[24] or whether he cannot forget the reverse side of the medal,[25] the fact is there, and it proves the vitality of the liturgy. The encyclical *Mediator Dei* has insisted on the normality and the legitimacy of a certain evolution of the liturgy to adapt itself to the needs of each epoch.[26] And the reforms now under way, inspired largely by pastoral considerations, seek only to permit a better and more complete participation of the actual man, the man of today, in the Church's official worship.

It is again this human openness of the liturgy which explains the resemblances, often striking, between certain rites of Christian worship and more or less parallel rites of the pagan cults. It explains also the fact that the ancient Church adopted and christianized rather a large number of religious customs of the Greek and Roman environment. There is nothing out of the way in this: if human nature is always the same, it is only to be expected that the outward forms in which it is incarnated and manifested will always be approximately the same. Thus the Christian liturgy has done no more than adopt, at least in some respects, certain rites already created and used by men; but it has renewed them and deepened them by giving them a Christian meaning.

2. The Liturgy Makes the Infrahuman World Participate in Worship
The unity between man and the infrahuman world in revelation

Revelation teaches us that in the divine plan there is a strong bond between man and the world inferior to man. The infrahuman world is to contribute to the establishment of the kingdom of God; but it fills this role only in reference to man, in as much as it helps man reach the place God has assigned

---

[24] As Theodor Klauser, *Petite histoire de la liturgie occidentale* (Paris, 1956), pp. 59–63. After showing how our knowledge of the part played by the Franco-Germanic church has increased, the author concludes, "The meaning of all these historical discoveries with regard to our attitude toward the Roman liturgy is clear: It is Roman, but it is also ours (*Romana est, sed etiam nostra*)."

[25] As Ildephonse Herwegen, *Antike, Germanentum und Christentum* (Salzburg: A. Pustet, 1932). Cf. Joseph A. Jungmann, *The Mass of the Roman Rite*, I, 74–141.

[26] Nn. 49 ff. (Lat. 48 ff.).

him in this kingdom. The infrahuman world is wholly at the service of the divine life in man.

Some essential characteristics of this doctrine are already present in the first three chapters of Genesis.

In its story of the creation, the first chapter brings out the transcendence of God, but also, thanks to the scheme of the six days and of the distribution of the creative action over those six days, the unity and order of the cosmos: God's whole work culminates in the creation of man; man is, by right, the master of the world, and his labor is supposed to enable him to exercise this sovereignty effectively (Gen. 1:28-30); the inferior creatures, finally, constitute the theater in which his story will unfold and the accessories which will help him attain his end. But the end itself is not specified in the first chapter.

The second and third chapters teach us more. Here again the plants and the animals are at the service of man, their lord and master, who himself is subject to God.[27] But the author goes further, and lets it be clearly understood that human life has for its end the friendly relations with God, the paradisiac state, which Adam and Eve enjoyed before the fall.

Original sin disrupted not only the bonds of grace between man and God, but also the balance between man and inferior creatures. Man does keep the right and the duty of subjecting to himself the world which surrounds him; but he will succeed in this task only slowly and with difficulty, as Genesis itself points out in telling the primitive history of mankind.[28] The idea which these narratives want to put across is that man's relations with earthly creatures depend in large part on his relations with God.

This fundamental idea is found again in many passages of the Old Testament, with numerous developments and colorings.

God is the Creator and the absolute Master of the material world. This theme, constantly recalled, is sung most lyrically in the book of Job, 38-41.

This material world is at the service of man, first of all to provide his sus-

---

[27] Cf. Gen. 2:8-9 and 15-20. The question is discussed whether to admit a genetic connection between the body of the first man and the body of animals. From the theological point of view, such evolutionism is admissible on certain conditions: first, that it be extended only to the body and not to the soul; then, that the theory suppose an extraordinary intervention of God at the decisive moment, transforming the animal body in such a way as to make it capable of receiving a human soul, therefore transforming it into a human body. On the metaphysical level, this transformation reaches into the very essence of the body, even if it be of small extent on the morphological level.

In such a perspective the connection between man and the infrahuman world, and hence the unity of the cosmos, and divine Providence itself, appear still more wonderful: all the lower creatures, mineral, vegetable and animal, tend and cooperate, in a vast organized process, to the formation of the human body, which is then endowed by God with a spiritual soul; and this human composite enters into participation in the divine life.

[28] Cf., e.g., the invention of the crafts and occupations according to Gen. 4:17 ff., which belongs, like Gen. 2 and 3, to the Yahwist tradition. That man, even after his fall, still has the right and the duty to subject the earth to himself, is pointed out expressly by the priestly tradition in Gen. 9:1-7.

tenance; and the offering of firstfruits will have for its aim the acknowledgment that all these goods placed at man's disposal come to him from the Creator's generosity (Lev. 23:9–21; Deut. 26:1–11).

The material world is to serve man also by raising his mind to the knowledge of God, of His existence and of His attributes (Wis. 13:1–9).

It is to serve him, again, by helping him praise and adore God, of whom it is a manifestation. Many of the psalms and hymns praise God for His creation and invite the creatures themselves to join in this song (Ps. 8; 18A; 28; 95:11–13; 97:7–9; 103; 146:8–9; 147; 148; canticle *Benedicite*, Dan. 3:56–88). In these hymns it is truly the whole cosmos that becomes an instrument of God's glory.

Moreover, the Old Testament develops the theme of Gen. 3:17–19: if man rebels against God and makes evil use of creatures, God makes those same creatures serve for man's chastisement, to incite him to penance. One of the most potent weapons in the hands of God is famine, caused by drought or by invasions of locusts; and He uses it against Israel at times of infidelity (2 Kings 8:35–40; Joel 1:1–20) or against the pagan peoples (Deut. 32:31–33; Wis. 11–12). On the other hand, He rewards faithfulness by the fertility of the soil and the abundance of flocks (Lev. 26:3–12; Joel 2:25–26; Amos 9:13–15), and goes so far as to suspend the ordinary course of nature in order to accredit His witnesses, the wonder-working prophets.

The conviction that there is an intimate connection between man and nature is so strong in the Old Testament that the second part of the book of Isaias foretells, for the messianic people, the people of the last times, a new heaven and a new earth: the new spiritual creation demands a new material creation, a universe in which the original harmony of paradise will be found anew.[29]

This whole teaching of the Old Testament is taken up again and made more profound in the New Testament. And this deepening is due primarily to the almost unbelievable fact of the Incarnation: to save men, who "have blood and flesh in common," the Son of God "likewise shared in these" (Heb. 2:14). The Word takes on a complete human nature, and Christ becomes the prototype and the head of all creation, the knot which ties man and the sensible world to God. In Christ's human body, matter is united to God and placed at the service of God to an extent that is unparalleled.[30] The Incarna-

---

[29] Is. 65:17–25. The comparison of Is. 65:25 with 11:6–9 suggests that these verses 6–9 also describe a return to the state of paradise and are not merely a symbolic tableau of the relations among men, as Jean Steinmann would have it in his *Le prophète Isaïe* (Paris: Ed. du Cerf, 1950), pp. 169–170. Steinmann's assertion that vegetarianism appears in the Bible only after the author of the first part of Isaias would have to be proved. On the new

creation see also Is. 24:18–23; 32:15–18; 35:1–9.

[30] Cf. St. John Damascene: "The Father's gracious will, in His only-begotten Son, has effected the salvation of the entire cosmos and restored the unity of all things. For since man is a microcosm, the knot that ties together all substances visible and invisible, because he himself is both, it was most fitting that the Lord and Creator and Ruler of all things

tion consecrates not only man but the whole cosmos, as the martyrology for Christmas says.

There is nothing extraordinary, therefore, in the fact that Jesus, as the gospels testify, appears in perfect mastery over the material world. He is master of it, and He uses it freely, for all creatures are good; [31] but at the same time He invites man to free himself of it inwardly, because of the slavery in which it involves those who become its servants.[32]

For Christ, nature is a flawless mirror which shows us the Father. In His parables and His comparisons He uses it to raise the minds of His hearers to God or to illustrate the laws of the divine economy in the world. And when He institutes baptism and the Eucharist, He chooses the most common material creatures to be the instruments for transmitting His divine life to man.

St. Paul affirms clearly the original unity and harmony of the cosmos. Disrupted by man's sin, they have been reestablished by Christ. This restoration will be complete only in heaven, with the resurrection.[33]

Finally, the Apocalypse shows how material creatures, directed by the angels, serve for the punishment of God's enemies and the glorification of His faithful servants, and how they all participate in the heavenly liturgy (Apoc. 5:13).

Thus, from one end of the Bible to the other, we are taught that the material world does not remain alien to the history of salvation, but that it is at the service of man, and especially of the Man-God, to contribute to the establishment and the development of God's kingdom.

The unity between man and the infrahuman world in the liturgy

The liturgy in its turn makes ample use of material creatures. It restores to them their original destiny, which is to help man attain his supernatural end; and it transfigures them by making them instruments of divine grace. In our earthly liturgy, however, this restoration remains incomplete; for we live in a world where sin still reigns, with all its consequences. Moreover, this transfiguration remains hidden, visible only to the eyes of faith, because the whole liturgy is performed in mystery and under the veil of signs.

It is in the Eucharist that material creation finds its noblest use. The

should desire that in His only-begotten and consubstantial Son the unity of divinity with humanity be realized, and by means of this the unity of divinity with all things, so that God would be all in all" (*Hom. de Transfig. Dom.*, 18 [PG 96, 572 f.]). In such a perspective as this, the modified evolutionism mentioned in note 27 above is seen as a preparation not only for the human body but even for the Incarnation.

[31] Cf. Mark 7:14 f.

[32] Cf. Matt. 22, parable of those invited to the wedding feast, who go off, "one to his farm . . . another to his business . . . . "

[33] Cf. Rom. 8:19–22; Col. 1:15–20. On this theme of unity ruptured and restored, see Lucien Cerfaux, *Christ in the Theology of St. Paul* (New York: Herder & Herder, 1959), pp. 419 ff. The theme of the reestablishment of the unity of the cosmos under the sovereignty of Christ is developed especially by St. Irenaeus. who includes it in his theory of "recapitula tion."

changing of bread and wine into Christ's body and blood is the most extraordinary elevation and transfiguration of the material world to the service of the divine life. Aside from the assumption of a human body by the Son of God, there is no more wonderful example of the importance of the role played by this material world in the divine plan.

The bread and the wine, whose whole substance is changed into the substance of Christ's body and blood, serve as a substratum or a vehicle for the real presence of Christ. Thus they are intimately associated to that whole current of divine life for men, of joy for the angels and the saints, and of glory for God, which is the effect of the Eucharistic sacrifice. Thus the Mass realizes, as perfectly as possible before the time of the new heaven and the new earth, the redemption of material creation, that liberation from the slavery of sin and corruption of which St. Paul speaks.

In three of the other sacraments — baptism, confirmation and extreme unction — something analogous takes place, but in a much lower degree. In these sacraments the "matter" consists of a truly material element, water or consecrated oil. Here again, therefore, sensible creatures are the instrument of divine grace.

Many of the sacramentals — exorcisms, consecrations or blessings — aim likewise at bringing nature back to the service of the divine life. This restoration, of course, is not as profound as it is in the case of the sacraments; but it has its own importance, by reason of its extension to an almost infinite number of things and situations.

What is the meaning of an exorcism made over a material object? Through sin, man has given the devil the possibility of using material creatures to thwart the development of the kingdom of God. In extreme cases this seizure by the devil can go as far as possession properly so called. The exorcism is a prayer which the Church addresses to God; its aim: that the devil be driven out of the thing, if there is really possession, or, more simply, that the divine protection be attached to this thing in favor of the person who will use it with the required dispositions. This protection of God over a material object means that it will be withdrawn from the devil's power, and furthermore that actual graces will be granted the person who uses it properly.[34]

Similarly, the consecration of a church, of a chalice or of any other thing, brings it about that in virtue of the Church's prayer God accepts that thing as reserved to His service and grants particular graces to those who make use of it with good dispositions. And the simple blessings of sensible creatures have also the effect of God's granting them at least a temporary protection which will help men use them properly towards their salvation. Read, for example, the very meaningful blessing of bees in the Roman Ritual.[35]

[34] Cf., e.g., in the Roman Ritual the exorcisms over the water to be blessed (IX, 2), over the oil to be blessed (IX, 7, 8), over the water to be blessed on the vigil of the Epiphany (IX, 9, 28).

[35] IX, 5, 6. Cf. the prayers used in the blessing of oil (IX, 7, 8), of wine for the sick (IX, 7, 3), of animals (IX, 5, 3), etc.

Thus the many sacramentals translate into our concrete life the Christian view of the universe, which can be summed up in these few points: unity of the cosmos; extension to the universe of the fall and of the devil's empire, but also of the Redemption as liberation from Satan's power; central place of man as microcosm and point of convergence of the universe; sacred worth of the material world, God's gift to man and the instrument placed at man's disposal for going to God.

Anyone can see how such a conception is opposed to pantheism, polytheism, magic, naturalism and every secular explanation of the universe.

Finally, only a reminder is needed of the fact that the inferior creatures also have their place in the divine praise. We have seen already that the psalms and hymns of the Old Testament often amplify the theme "All you works of the Lord, bless the Lord." [36] And another way for the liturgy to associate nature to the divine praise is to have recourse to its symbolism, or, more exactly, to its exemplarism. Thus the hymns of the hours exploit the symbolic value of the alternation of light and darkness.

There are many ways, then, in which the infrahuman world, placed at the service of man, attains its final end in the liturgical action, which is to lead to the knowledge, adoration, and glorification of God. To all material creatures the liturgy lends a consciousness and a voice, the voice of the Church, or rather the voice of Christ Himself.

[36] *Benedicite omnia opera Domini Domino.* Cf. p. 180 above.

12

THE LITURGY AND THE LAW OF

THE COSMIC UNIVERSALITY

OF THE KINGDOM OF GOD:

2. THE SAINTS AND THE ANGELS

The liturgy is addressed to the whole man, that is, to that composite of flesh and spirit who lives in close contact with his material environment, but also to that social being who cannot be abstracted from the community to which he belongs.

We have seen in a preceding chapter how the Bible and the liturgy consider man less as an individual than as member of a people, in necessary relations with other men. We must add here that, for the Bible and the liturgy, these social relations are not limited to the present life, and that a close bond unites the faithful who are still journeying on earth to all the just who are already assembled before God and also to the multitude of the angels.

1. The Liturgy and the Saints

The idea that there is even now a close connection between the members of the earthly Church and those of the heavenly Church is expressed in a marvelous epitome by the author of the letter to the Hebrews: "You have approached Mount Sion and the city of the living God, the heavenly Jerusalem, the myriads of angels, a festive gathering and assembly of the first-born inscribed in heaven, and God the Judge of all, and the spirits of the just who have reached perfection, and the Mediator of the new covenant, Jesus, and the sprinkled blood which speaks better than that of Abel" (Heb. 12:22–24).

We have already commented on this text,[1] and there is no need to return to it, but we had to recall it at the beginning of this chapter in which we are simply going to illustrate the text by showing what place the saints and the angels occupy in our earthly liturgy.

Communion with the souls in purgatory

In speaking of the saints, we are thinking not only of the elect who have already entered into the glory of heaven, but also of those who are being purified in purgatory, for they too are truly saved and are certain of attaining to the beatific vision. We are in communion with both. This we learn from the dogma of the communion of saints, from which are derived a number of truths of great importance for the liturgy : the lawfulness and the usefulness of the veneration of the saints, in particular of the Blessed Virgin Mary ; the reality of the intercession of the saints on our behalf ; the efficacy of the Mass, of the Church's prayer and of good works in helping the souls in purgatory.

It is not within our scope to go back and trace the history of the veneration of the saints and of the liturgy of the departed,[2] but only to point out its meaning.

Right from the beginning, the Christians were convinced that they remained united to their dead brethren in the communion of the Church ; and, from the second century at least, this conviction was expressed in the custom of celebrating the Mass for them, whether at the time of their burial or on the anniversary of their "deposition" or, if they were martyrs, of their martyrdom. Before 138, Aristides wrote in his *Apology*, "If one of the faithful dies, obtain salvation for him by celebrating the Eucharist and by praying next to his remains."[3] And in the apocryphal *Acts of John,* dating from about 160, the Apostle St. John is represented as celebrating the breaking of bread over the tomb of a Christian woman named Drusiana, who had died three days before.[4] For Carthage, the custom is certified by Tertullian, then by St. Cyprian.[5]

In the fourth and fifth centuries the evidence abounds.[6] The Leonine and Gelasian sacramentaries already have proper formularies of Masses for the dead.[7] At these Masses, the departed for whom they were being celebrated

---

[1] Cf. p. 142 above. For the explanation of this passage, reference may be had also to Ceslaus Spicq's *L'épître aux hébreux*, I, 227 ff., 280 ff., 311 ff.; II, 214 ff. 405 ff.

[2] Cf., e.g., Righetti, II, 304 ff., 360 ff.

[3] Fragment edited by H. J. M. Milne, "A New Fragment of the *Apology* of Aristides," *Journal of Theological Studies*, 1924, pp. 73–77. Milne's own translation differs from the one given above.

[4] *Acta Ioannis.* Cf. in Jesús Solano, *Textos*

eucaristicos primitivos, I (Madrid, 1952), 721.

[5] E.g., Tertullian, *De monogamia*, 10 (PL 2, 942); *De exhortatione castitatis*, 11 (PL 2, 926); St. Cyprian, *Ep.* 1, 2; 12, 2; 39, 3; ed. Bayard, I, 3, 34, 99.

[6] Cf., e.g., *Const. apost.*, VI, 30, 2–7; ed. Funk, I, 381–383.

[7] Leonine sacramentary, nn. 1138 ff.; ed. Mohlberg, II, 144–146. Gelasian sacramentary, III, 92–105; ed. Wilson, pp. 301–313.

were named aloud. This practice gave rise later to the diptychs or lists of the dead, which the deacon read during the Mass offered for their benefit. Still later, this reading of the diptychs evolved into a general memorial of the departed, made at all the Masses, the Roman canon's *Memento* of the dead.

Such customs are common to all the liturgies, and their meaning is evident. The Mass is an act from which those who have died in communion with the Church can draw profit. Thanks to the Mass, they are purified of the last consequences of their sins and admitted into the society of the elect.

The names of the departed are publicly recited at the Masses celebrated for them, says St. Epiphanius, "in order that those present may be fully convinced that the dead still live, that, far from being annihilated, they do exist and live in God's presence; and also for the proclamation of that sublime dogma, according to which those who pray for the brethren have hope for them, as for those who have departed on a long voyage. . . . We make a memorial of the just and of the sinners: of the sinners to implore the Lord's mercy on them." [8]

And St. Cyril of Jerusalem writes, "After which we pray also for the departed holy fathers and bishops and in general for all those among us who have died, believing that this will be of great help to those souls for whom the prayer is offered while the holy and tremendous victim lies before us. . . . In the same way we offer prayers to God for the departed, even if they were sinners . . . for our sins we offer Christ immolated and thus make the most kind God propitious to ourselves and to them." [9]

These rites obviously imply a belief that not all the faithful have access to the beatific vision as soon as they die, but that a certain number must first be purged of the consequences of their sins. The rites imply also that we can come to the aid of these deceased by offering the Mass for them. In other words, they imply the doctrine of purgatory and of our spiritual communion with those who are detained there, a communion which is realized to the maximum in the Eucharistic sacrifice.

This twofold doctrine underlies also the numerous rites on behalf of the dead which sprang up very quickly in all the liturgies. We may cite, for example, the vigil of the dead, which became customary in a good number of churches in the fourth century; the rites of burial, which have varied a great deal from one epoch to another and from one place to another; the Office of the Dead, celebrated at Rome at least from the end of the seventh century; the commemoration of all the faithful departed, on one or another day of the year, adopted by all the liturgies and given definitive shape in the West by St. Odo of Cluny.[10]

Thus, since its beginning, the liturgy has expressed in concrete form that

---

[8] *Adv. haer.*, 75, 8 (PG 42, 513). Cf. *ibid.*, 75, 3 (PG 42, 508).

[9] *Catech. myst.*, V, 9–10 (PG 33, 1116–17). [10] On all these rites cf. Righetti, II, 360–399.

spiritual, mysterious but real brotherhood in virtue of which we remain united to all those who have departed from this world at peace with God. It is a feeling deeply rooted in the heart of man that the legitimate bonds which unite us to one another on earth are not broken by death but remain forever. The liturgy appropriates this sentiment and even transposes it in an atmosphere of light and hope unknown to the non-Christian religions. The heavenly Jerusalem, common fatherland of all believers, is the Christian reply to this human aspiration.

Communion with the saints in heaven

The thought of our communion with the saints in heaven and especially with the Virgin Mary, still more than the thought of our communion with the departed, holds an important place in the liturgies, at least in those of the present day. For the thought of this communion underlies not only the commemoration of the saints which is found in the anaphoras since the fifth century, but also the creation of the cult and the feasts of the saints, which have flourished luxuriantly in all the rites, beginning with the fourth-fifth century.

We know that the veneration of the saints in the Church developed out of the veneration of the martyrs, and that originally the cult of a martyr was closely bound up with his tomb and with the anniversary of his martyrdom.[11] This annual and local veneration consisted essentially in the celebration of the Eucharist. St. Cyprian, speaking of three martyrs of Carthage, tells his people, "You know that we offer the sacrifice in their memory (*pro eis*) every year when we commemorate the day of their passion."[12] And it was while he was celebrating the vigil that would terminate with the Mass for the anniversary of St. Polycarp in 250, at Smyrna, that the priest Pionius was arrested.[13] When the veneration of the Blessed Virgin and of the confessors began in the fourth-fifth century, their anniversaries were celebrated in the same way.

The sense of these rites is that we remain in communion with the saints, and that this communion is realized preeminently in the liturgical action, particularly in the celebration of the sacrifice. The Mass is the meeting place *par excellence* of the Church on earth and the Church in heaven.

By reason of this conviction, the commemoration of the departed in all the anaphoras, beginning with the fifth century, is prolonged into a commemoration of the saints, regarded as the most illustrious of the Christians, the ones whose communion with us is particularly important and worthy of note.[14]

---

[11] Cf. Righetti, II, 268 ff. The most ancient notice of a liturgical veneration of the martyrs is found in the *Martyrium Polycarpi*, 18.

[12] *Ep.* 39, 3; ed. Bayard, I, 99 (PL 4, 323). For the translation of "pro eis" see note 15 below.

[13] *Acta Sanctorum*, Feb. 1.

[14] Cf. Jungmann, *The Mass of the Roman Rite*, II, 159–160, 170–179. Examples of the commemoration of the saints in the Eastern

And to make a memorial of the saints means to offer them the homage of our veneration, and at the same time to ask them to intercede on our behalf that God, by reason of their merits and their prayers, may grant us His protection : a twofold movement, which occurs especially in the Mass. "Then we make a memorial also of the departed," says St. Cyril of Jerusalem, "first of all, of the patriarchs, the prophets, the Apostles, the martyrs, that by reason of their prayer and their intercession God may accept our entreaty." [15]

Thus the liturgy considers the saints as our intercessors; and this is obvious, for example, from the collects or the litany of the Roman rite. To this idea is added the idea that the feasts of the saints are occasions for us to praise God for the marvels He has wrought in them. Finally, we venerate and honor the saints themselves for the perfection to which they have attained with the help of God's grace, and we propose them to ourselves as examples, with the hope of joining them one day in heaven.[16] Such are the different aspects of our communion with the saints of paradise, that communion which the liturgy expresses in so many ways.

It expresses it very explicitly in the feast of All Saints, found today in all the rites and originating in a commemoration of all martyrs, of which there is evidence in certain Eastern churches as early as the fifth century. In the Roman liturgy the feast of November 1, which goes back at least to the sixth century under various forms and on different dates, expresses very felicitously the profound unity of the earthly Church and its worship with the heavenly Church and its worship. The *Vidi turbam magnam* ("I saw a great throng"), which is a sort of central theme of the feast; the enumeration in hymns, antiphons and responsories of the different categories of saints whom we invoke, honor and strive to imitate; the description of the great liturgy which the saints and the angels celebrate unceasingly in heaven — all this, at the end of the liturgical year, constitutes a wonderful synthesis of the relations between the Church militant and the Church triumphant.

In certain of the Latin liturgies we find likewise the idea that our earthly worship is a sketch and a participation of the worship which not only the

---

anaphoras will be found in F. E. Brightman's *Eastern Liturgies* (Oxford, 1896), p. 56 (Syrian anaphora of St. James), p. 388 (present Byzantine anaphora), etc.

[15] *Catech. myst.*, V, 9 (PG 33, 1116). Originally, it was said that the sacrifice was offered or that the prayers were said at Mass *for* (ὑπέρ, *pro*) the martyrs or the saints, just as it was said that the Mass was offered *for* the dead. The ὑπέρ or *pro* was taken in the broad sense of "on the subject of, in relation to." Jungmann in *Die Stellung Christi im liturgischen Gebet*, p. 234, notes that in the Coptic Jacobite liturgy, at the time for the gospel the deacon invited the people to pray by saying to them in Greek, "Pray for (ὑπέρ) the holy

gospel," to which the people answered, "Kyrie eleison" (cf. Brightman, *Eastern Liturgies*, p. 155). Later, the attempt was made to be more precise, and some authors had difficulty explaining this ὑπέρ. Beginning with the fifth century, although traces of the ancient formula are still found, there is no longer any hesitation about the meaning to be given it: "At the altar we do not commemorate them (the martyrs) in the same sense as the others who have departed in peace, as if we prayed for them, but rather in order that they may pray for us and we may follow in their footsteps" (St. Augustine, *In Io. Tract.* 84, 1 [PL 35, 1847]).

[16] In the Roman canon this last idea appears especially in the *Nobis quoque peccatoribus*.

angels but also the saints render to God in heaven. Several Mozarabic or Gallican prefaces actually mention the saints along with the angels in the formula of introduction to the *Sanctus*. For example, here is the ending of a Mozarabic *Inlatio* for the feast of St. Bartholomew: "May that unceasing chant which the angels thrice sing out in heaven and all the saints proclaim, be heard daily on earth in our offices; together with the choirs of angels, the throngs of saints and the voices of all who praise You, may we too praise You, the Holy One of all the holy ones, saying . . ." .[17] A *Contestatio* of one of the Masses of the *Missale gallicanum vetus* ends similarly: "He it is (the Word) whom all the angels together with the multitude of the saints praise in endless song, saying . . ." .[18]

2. The Liturgy and the Angels

In order to understand the place occupied by the angelic world in the liturgy, we must refer to the biblical teaching on the relations among angels, men and inferior creatures.

Angels and men in revelation

Now the Old and the New Testament teach clearly that in God's plan these three orders do not constitute three worlds independent of one another, but a single cosmos ordained to a single end. Each order tends to that end in its own way, but in close connection with the other two; so that any event touching one or another of these orders has consequences for the other two also.

The fact that the angelic world belongs to the cosmos appears already, on the second level of attention, in chapters 2 and 3 of Genesis: when God banished man from paradise after the fall, "at the east of the garden of Eden He placed the cherubim, and the flaming sword, which turned every way, to guard the way to the tree of life" (Gen. 3:24).

In biblical tradition the cherubim are angelic beings who live with God and defend His dwelling-place. Here they are carrying out the orders given by God consequent upon Adam's sin; they have become enemies of man in so far as man has made himself the enemy of God. For the author of the narrative, it goes without saying that these angels were at God's side when He was creating man, and that they were man's friends as long as he was God's friend.[19] By rebelling against God, man separated himself also from the angels and put himself on the side of the evil being who was hiding under the appearance of a serpent. Man and angel belong to the same cosmos and

[17] *Liber moz. sacr.*, n. 843; cf. nn. 77, 150, etc.

[18] Mass 2; text edited in an appendix in Mohlberg's *Missale gallicanum vetus* (Rome, 1958), p. 78.

[19] It is probable that in Gen. 3:22 ("Indeed! the man has become like one of us, knowing good and evil!") God is supposed to be addressing the angels. A similar setting is found again repeatedly in the Old Testament: 3 Kings 22:19–22; Job 1:6–2:7; Is. 6:8.

are involved in the same history : they cannot be disinterested in each other.

This theme, so evident from the very first chapters of Genesis, will be continually repeated, presupposed, developed, in the Old Testament. The angels will appear there essentially as God's servants, constituting His heavenly court and carrying His messages or executing His orders on earth.

Surrounding Yahweh we find the cherubim of Ezechiel (1 and 10), who are assistants at the throne, or God's throne itself.[20] The seraphim of Isaias (6:1-3) also surround the throne of God, and sing the *Sanctus* as in a liturgical service. A good many psalms recall the praise which the angels address to God, and give us to understand that this praise is one of their principal functions.[21]

The angels are also at the service of Yahweh in His relations with the world and especially with men. They accompany Him when He shows Himself to men,[22] and they are always at His disposal to fulfil His orders. Such are the watchmen and the hundreds of thousands of whom Daniel speaks ; [23] the seven who stand in God's presence (Tob. 12:15); the angels of the nations : Michael for Israel (Dan. 10:13-21 ; 12:1) and other angels for other nations (Is. 24:21 ; Dan. 10:13-21). Malachy alludes to the angel of the testament, probably the angel to whom has been entrusted the special role of intermediary between God and Israel for the conclusion and the execution of the pact of Sinai.[24] Other angels help men in the name of God (Gen. 24:7; Ex. 14:19; 23:20-23; Judges 5:20), protect men and intercede for them (Tobias; Job 5:1 ; 33:23-24; Ps. 33:8; Zach. 1:12), present their prayers to God (Tob. 3:24-25; 12:12-15), console them (3 Kings 19:5; 4 Kings 1:15; Dan. 3:49; 6:22). Angels are also sent by God to punish men; among them are the exterminating angels (Ex. 12:23; 2 Kings 24:16; 4 Kings 19:35; 1 Par. 21:15-16; Ps. 77:49; Ezech. 9-10).

In the later Jewish theology, both that of the apocrypha and that of the rabbis, the angelology was greatly developed, with insistence on the idea of their belonging to the cosmos and of the role they play in it.[25] This period introduces the guardian angels who intervene in various circumstances of life, and the angels who accompany souls to the presence of God after death. At the same time, great importance is given to the angels charged with directing the stars and the elements; ingenious schemes are worked out for dividing the angels into hierarchical classes; the veneration of the angels and recourse to their intercession is developed more and more.

The New Testament also states that there is unity between the angelic

---

[20] Cf. Ps. 17:11; Dan. 3:55. Cherubim surmounted the ark of the covenant in the tabernacle (Ex. 37:7-9) and surrounded it in Solomon's temple (3 Kings 6:23 ff.; 2 Par. 3:10 ff.).

[21] Cf. Ps. 28; 102; 148.

[22] Gen. 18-19; Deut. 33:2-3; Ps. 67:18; Zach. 14:5.

[23] Dan. 4:10-14; 7:10; cf. Ezech. 9:1-10.

[24] Mal. 3:1. Cf. the apocryphal *Book of Jubilees* 6:19-22; 14:20; and, in the New Testament, Acts 7:38 and 53; Gal. 3:19; Heb. 2:2.

[25] Cf. Joseph Bonsirven, *Le judaïsme palestinien au temps du Jésus-Christ*, I (Paris: Beauchesne, 1935), 222-239.

world and the human world, but its teaching takes on a special coloring from the fact of the Incarnation: having come down from heaven to earth, the Word incarnate here establishes the kingdom of God and restores — and this in a much more exalted and spiritual way — the unity of the cosmos which was ruptured by sin (cf. Col. 1:15–20).

Two aspects of the New Testament angelology deserve to be underlined: first, the presence and the action of the angels throughout the life of Christ: the ministers of God are also the discreet, self-effacing servants of Jesus; second, the intervention of the angels in the life of the Church: not only do they rejoice in the conversion of sinners, but they come to the aid of the Apostles or of the faithful (Acts 5:19; 8:26; 10:3–8; 12:15; 1 Cor. 4:9).

Finally, the Apocalypse illustrates in many scenes this participation of angels and men in a single history and a single liturgy. For the author of the Apocalypse, the Church on earth and the heavenly Jerusalem constitute two stages of one and the same construction, one and the same city, with continual relations between them. The inhabitants of heaven, angels as well as saints, pray for their brethren on earth and present the prayers of their earthly brethren to God; the angels reveal to men on earth the designs of God, and come to their aid in the struggle against Satan. The Church on earth gradually sends its members to heaven. When the number of the elect is filled up, there will be only the heavenly Jerusalem, with its cosmic and eternal liturgy.

The angels and the Mass

Undoubtedly the author of the Apocalypse in his description of the heavenly liturgy is inspired more than once by the Christian rites of which he had experience. But the liturgy itself, in recalling the relations between men and angels, is simply putting into practice the teaching of the Bible.[26]

As far as the Mass is concerned, it is especially in the theme of the angel of the sacrifice that the patristic and liturgical tradition expresses the idea of the unity between the world of the angels and that of men. As there was mention in the Apocalypse (8:3–5) of an angel who offered the prayers of the saints on a golden altar standing before the throne of God, it was an easy step to suppose that this mediation was exercised principally with respect to that supreme prayer which is the Mass. This idea appears very often in the liturgies.[27]

[26] On the place of the angels in the liturgy, the following may be read: Erik Peterson, *Das Buch von den Engeln* (Leipzig: Jakob Hegner, 1935); H. Düllmann, "Engel und Mensch bei der Messfeier," *Divus Thomas* (Freiburg), 27 (1949), pp. 281 ff.; Jean Daniélou, *Advent* (New York: Sheed & Ward, 1950), pp. 81–100; *id.*, *The Angels and Their Mission* (Westminster, Md.: Newman, 1957); *id.*, *The Bible and the Liturgy* (Notre Dame, 1956), pp. 130

f., 198–200 and 211–215. We have made extensive use of these studies in our presentation.

[27] Cf. Bernard Botte, "L'ange du sacrifice," *Cours et conférences des Semaines liturgiques*, VII (Louvain, 1929), 209–221; *id.*, "L'ange du sacrifice et l'épiclèse de la messe romaine au moyen âge," *Rech. de théol. anc. et médiév.*, I (1929), 285 ff.; G. Fitzengard, *De sacrificio coelesti secundum S. Ambrosium* (Mundelein, 1944).

In the Roman liturgy it is expressed in the *Supplices te rogamus*: In suppliant attitude we pray You, O God all-powerful, command that these gifts be carried by the hands of Your holy angel to Your altar on high, in the sight of Your divine majesty . . . ." Various interpretations of this text have been proposed. Some have thought that the angel mentioned here was Christ, or the Holy Spirit.[28] Actually the concern is with an angel, or rather with the angelic ministry in general. This interpretation is the most obvious, and is supported by the canon of St. Ambrose: ". . . we ask You and pray You to accept this oblation on Your heavenly altar *by the hands of Your holy angels*." [29] The same idea is found again, in much the same terms, in the Egyptian liturgy of St. Mark: "The gifts of sacrifice, of offering, of thanksgiving, that have been offered You, receive, O God, on Your holy, heavenly, spiritual altar in the heights of heaven, through the ministry of Your archangels." [30]

In a more general way, the liturgies affirm that the angels are present at the sacrifice of the Mass. Beginning with the sixth century, this idea is brought out by the Byzantine tradition in the hymn of the *Cheroubikon* which is sung at the time when the oblations are carried solemnly to the altar: "We who mystically represent the cherubim and sing the trisagion hymn to the life-giving Trinity, lay aside all earthly cares, for we are to receive the King of the universe *who comes escorted by unseen armies of angels*. Alleluia." [31]

Not only do the angels assist at the sacrifice, but they celebrate it with the human ministers. At the little entrance the priest recites this prayer: "Master, Lord our God, who have established in heaven orders and armies of angels and of archangels for the liturgy of Your glory, bring it about that together with our entrance the entrance also of the holy angels be made, who *celebrate the liturgy together with us* and together with us sing glory to Your goodness." [32]

And in the liturgy of the presanctified there is sung at the time of the great entrance, "Now *the heavenly powers adore invisibly with us*. For here is the King of glory advancing. Here is the mystic sacrifice already accomplished, coming with its escort. Let us approach with faith and holy desire, that we may become sharers of life eternal." [33]

In the Greek version of the Syrian liturgy of St. James the *Cheroubikon* is as follows: "Let all human flesh be silent; let it stand with fear and trembling and have no earthly thought. For the King of kings, Christ our God, comes to be immolated and to give Himself as food to the faithful. *He is preceded by the choirs of angels with all the powers and dominations; the cherubim with many eyes and the seraphim with six wings, who cover their faces and cry out the hymn. Alleluia*." [34]

[28] Cf. Righetti, III, 336.
[29] *De sacr.*, IV, 6, 27 (PL 16, 445).
[30] Brightman, *Eastern Liturgies*, p. 129.
[31] Ἱερατικόν, p. 182.

[32] *Ibid.*, p. 171.
[33] *Ibid.*, p. 247.
[34] Brightman, *Eastern Liturgies*, pp. 41–42.

In an Egyptian liturgy which dates probably from the sixth century, the deacon announces at the time of the kiss of peace, "Have your hearts in heaven. If anyone has had any dispute with his neighbor, let him be reconciled. . . . For the Father of men, His only Son and the Holy Spirit are present, watching our actions and examining our thoughts; *and the angels are moving among us and mingling with us."* [35]

This idea of the presence of the angels at the Eucharistic sacrifice has nothing arbitrary about it. It is based on these two data of revelation : the angels constitute God's court, and hence are present wherever God is present; moreover, they are our fellow citizens, our guardians and our intermediaries with God. By this twofold right they are present at the Mass, at that mystery in which heaven and earth are united.

It is to these arguments that the Fathers have recourse to explain the presence of the angels at Mass. St. Ambrose, for example, says that "there can be no doubt that an angel is present when Christ is present, when Christ is immolated." [36] St. John Chrysostom, in turn, writes that when the priest approaches the altar to offer the unbloody sacrifice on it, "angels surround the priest; the whole sanctuary and the space around the altar is filled with heavenly armies in honor of Him who is on the altar." [37] And St. Gregory the Great explains in the *Dialogues,* "Who among the faithful could doubt that at the very moment of the immolation, the heavens open at the priest's voice ? In this mystery of Jesus Christ the choirs of angels are present; the lowest beings are associated with the highest, the earthly join the heavenly, and the visible and the invisible become a single reality." [38]

These two themes of the angel of the sacrifice and the angels present at the Mass help us to understand the meaning of the insertion of the *Sanctus* into the anaphora. The triple *Sanctus* already figured in the liturgy of the synagogue, where it was called the *Kedushah,* that is, sanctification, obviously the sanctification of the name of God.[39] There would be nothing surprising in the fact that this acclamation should have entered very early into the prayer of the Christians, who each day asked God that His name be "sanctified" on earth as it is in heaven by the angels.

[35] Anton Baumstark in *Oriens Christianus,* 1901, pp. 1 ff.

[36] *In Lc.,* 1, 12 (CSEL p. 28, 12 ff.). Cf. *De sacr.,* I, 2, 6 (PL 16, 419), where the "angels" who surround the body of Christ are rather the ministers of the altar.

[37] *De sacerdotio,* VI, 4 (PG 48, 681).

[38] *Dialogues,* IV, 58 (PL 77, 428).

[39] Thus in the prayer called *Shemoneh Esreh:* "You are holy, and holy is Your name, and holy ones praise You every day. Blessed are You, O Lord, holy God. *Reader:* We will sanctify Your name in the world even as they sanctify it in the highest heavens, as it is written by the hand of Your prophet: And they cried one to the other and said, *Congregation:* Holy, holy, holy, is the Lord of hosts; the whole earth is full of Your glory. *Reader:* To those over against them they say, Blessed — *Congregation:* Blessed be the glory of the Lord from His holy place. *Reader:* And in Your holy words it is written, *Congregation:* The Lord shall reign for ever, your God, O Zion, unto all generations. Alleluia. *Reader:* Unto all generations we will declare Your greatness, and to eternity we will hallow Your holiness; and Your praise, O our God, shall never depart from our mouth, for a great and holy God and King are You" (cf. W. O. E. Oesterley, *The Jewish Background of the Christian Liturgy* [Oxford, 1925], p. 143).

The first allusion to the use of the *Sanctus* in the Christian liturgy is found most probably in St. Clement of Rome.[40] From the fourth-fifth century, starting with the euchology of Serapion, the insertion of the *Sanctus* into the anaphora is widespread in the East, and from there it passes to Spain, Gaul and Italy. It must have been accepted at Rome in the first half of the fifth century.[41] After that, it is found in all the liturgies. It was normally sung by the whole assembly.[42]

Why do we sing this angelic acclamation ? Since the anaphora of the Mass is essentially a prayer of blessing, praise and thanksgiving, the insertion of the *Sanctus* into this prayer signifies that it is by blessing, praising and thanking God in the Mass that we unite ourselves as closely as possible to the liturgy of heaven. By singing the *Sanctus* we express and we live the union of the angelic world and the human world.

Actually all the Christian liturgies have made it clear, by the modifications they have made in the text of Isaias, that their *Sanctus* was no longer merely that of the seraphim in Solomon's temple, but rather that of the angelic bands in the heavenly Jerusalem (cf. Apoc. 4:8).[43] To this song of praise, this acclamation of heaven, the Christian people associate their song and their liturgy, thus demonstrating their union with the Jerusalem on high.

The angels and baptism

The angels play a part likewise in the other sacraments. The liturgical and patristic tradition speaks of the angel of baptism, who takes care of the catechumens, intervenes in the blessing of the baptismal water, assists at the baptism and then watches over his charge throughout his life.

The present Roman Ritual also, in the first part of the baptism of adults, which is nothing more than the ancient rite for making a catechumen, clearly alludes to the angel of baptism: "God of Abraham, God of Isaac, God of Jacob, God who appeared to Your servant Moses on Mount Sinai and led the children of Israel out of the land of Egypt, assigning to them the angel

---

[40] I *Cor.*, 34, 5–7: "Let us consider how the whole multitude of His angels stand by Him and minister to His will. For the Scripture says, 'Ten thousand times ten thousand stood by Him and thousands of thousands ministered to Him, and they cried, "Holy, holy, holy is the Lord of the armies, the whole creation is full of His glory." ' Let us too, gathered together in concord and unanimity, cry out to Him constantly as with one voice, that we may share in His great and glorious promises." As Jungmann notes in *The Mass of the Roman Rite*, II, 132, it is remarkable that Clement does not merely quote the hymn according to the vision of Isaias (6:3), but introduces it by the passage from Daniel (7:10), just as most of the Eastern liturgies do, later on. The last sen-

tence from Clement, moreover, seems to allude to a liturgical assembly.

[41] Cf. Righetti, III, 322–323.

[42] Cf. Jungmann, *The Mass of the Roman Rite*, II, 128 ff.

[43] Cf. *ibid.*, pp. 134–135: "More important is the addition in the song of the word 'heaven': *coeli et terra*; this is true of all the Christian liturgies, and only of them. . . . No longer is it the temple of Jerusalem that resounds with the triple *Sanctus*, nor is it only the seraphim who cry out one to another; heaven has become the scene, and all the choirs of heavenly spirits, the *militia coelestis exercitus*, are united in the singing. *Socia exultatione* they sing their song of praise, and their cry is *sine fine*."

of Your mercy to protect them day and night; we pray You, O Lord, see fit to send Your holy angel from heaven to protect likewise this Your servant N. and lead him to the grace of baptism. Through Christ our Lord." [44]

The intervention of the angels in the consecration of the baptismal water is probably derived from John 5:4: "The angel of the Lord descended from time to time into the pool and stirred the water." With regard to this intervention, Erik Peterson in his *Buch von den Engeln* cites several texts from Tertullian and from various liturgies.[45] Tertullian says, for example, that "the waters are somehow given medicinal quality through the intervention of the angel" [46] and that we "are purified in the water by the ministry of the angel and thus prepared to receive the Holy Spirit" [47] or even that "the angel of baptism, as mediator, prepares the way for the coming of the Holy Spirit by washing away sins." [48]

The same idea is found again in a formula for the blessing of baptismal water from the Gelasian sacramentary: ". . . send upon these waters, prepared for washing and giving life to men, the angel of holiness, that, once the sins of the past life have been washed away and the guilt has been effaced, he may make a pure dwelling-place for the Holy Spirit in those who are regenerated." [49]

On the presence of the angels at the moment of baptism, Origen says, "When the sacrament of the faith was given you, the heavenly virtues, the ministries of the angels, the assembly of the firstborn were present." [50] Didymus of Alexandria also states, "Visibly, the font generates our visible body by the ministry of the priests. Invisibly, the Spirit of God, invisible to every intellect, immerses in Himself and regenerates at the same time our body and our soul, *with the assistance of the angels*." [51]

The interest of the angels in baptism often finds expression among the Fathers in the theme of their admiration before the neophyte coming out of the font.

St. Cyril of Jerusalem says to the newly baptized, "The angels dance around you in chorus, saying, 'Who is this who comes up in white garments and leaning on her beloved?'" [52]

And St. Ambrose develops the same idea in explaining to the neophytes who are about to approach the altar, "You have begun to approach. The angels have observed you and have seen you approaching; they have observed that human condition which formerly was soiled by the black stain of sin, and have seen it suddenly resplendent. This has made them ask, 'Who is this that

---

[44] Ordo baptismi adultorum, n. 17.
[45] Pp. 66–67.
[46] De baptismo, 4 (PL 1, 1204).
[47] Ibid., 6 (PL 1, 1206).
[48] Loc. cit.
[49] I, 74; ed. Wilson, p. 116.
[50] In Ios. hom. IX, 4 (PG 12, 874).

[51] De Trin., II, 12 (PG 39, 672 B). Other patristic texts are cited by Erik Peterson, Das Buch von den Engeln, pp. 68–69. Cf. also P. Lundberg, La typologie baptismale dans l'ancienne église (Paris, 1942), pp. 44–45.
[52] Catechesis 3: De baptismo, 16 (PG 33, 448).

goes up from the desert whitened ?' The angels are in admiration, therefore. Do you want to know why ? Listen to the Apostle Peter say that there has been given us that which the angels desire to see. Listen again : 'What eye has not seen, nor ear heard, this is what God has prepared for those who love Him.' " [53]

This doctrine of the angel of baptism should not seem arbitrary to us. For, if baptism causes us to be born to the supernatural life and reconciles us with God, it reconciles us at the same time with the angels and makes us their fellow citizens, members of the Church destined to join them as dwellers in the heavenly Jerusalem. It is perfectly normal, therefore, that they interest themselves in, and assist at, so important an act of our life and of theirs. If there is joy among the angels over one sinner doing penance, there is undoubtedly joy among them also over one person being born to the divine life.

The angels and the other sacraments

The same verse of Luke (15:10) forms the basis of the liturgical and patristic theme of the angel of penance, so called both because he exhorts to penance and because he uncovers hidden sins or plays a certain part in their forgiveness.[54]

For the intervention of the angels in the sacrament of matrimony, we may cite a text of Tertullian, who speaks of "the happiness of the matrimony which the Church brings about, the offering confirms, the blessing seals, the angels announce and the Father ratifies." [55]

The angels assist also at the consecration of a bishop : the *Apostolic Constitutions* contain the reminder that, when the people are invited to bear witness to the qualities of the candidate, they must do so "as if they were in the tribunal of God and Christ, in the presence of the Holy Spirit and of all the holy spirits charged with ministering" (cf. Heb. 1:14).[56]

The angels and the liturgy of the departed

There is no need for explaining in full detail the very important role which belongs to the angels in the liturgy of the sick and of the departed.[57] In the present Roman Ritual the action of the angels is mentioned in the prayers *Proficiscere, anima christiana* and *Commendo te* of the commendation of a

---

[53] *De sacr.*, IV, 2, 5 (PL 16, 437).
[54] Cf. Erik Peterson, *Das Buch von den Engeln*, pp. 72–73. On Ash Wednesday, in the first prayer for the blessing of the ashes which were formerly placed on the public penitents, the priest asks God, " . . . deign to send Your holy angel from heaven to bless and sanctify these ashes . . . ."

In the *Divine Comedy*, at the entrance into purgatory, an angel marks seven P's on Dante's forehead as symbols of the seven capital sins (*Purg.*, IX, 103–114), which will be canceled

one at a time, as he leaves each of the circles of purgatory, by other angels (*Purg.*, XII, 98 and 115–136).
[55] *Ad uxorem*, II, 9 (PL 1, 1302).
[56] VIII, 4, 5; ed. Funk, I, 472.
[57] An extensive inquiry into the role of the angels at the moment of death and in the voyage of souls, according to the Alexandrian and Cappadocian Fathers, has been made by A. Recheis, *Engel, Tod und Seelenreise* (Rome, 1958).

soul, as well as in the antiphons *Subvenite, sancti Dei* and *In paradisum* of the funeral service.[58]

All these prayers show the angels coming with the saints to meet the soul of the departed, and leading it and welcoming it into heaven. The Roman ritual of funerals in a prayer of blessing of the tomb, goes so far as to mention an angel charged with guarding it: "O God, by whose mercy the souls of the faithful find rest, see fit to bless this tomb and assign Your holy angel to guard it . . . ."

In the next chapter, on the subject of the struggle against Satan in the liturgy of the dead, we shall have a word to say on the theory according to which the angels and the devils are supposed to intervene in the particular judgment.

The angels and the Divine Office

The presence of the angels in the liturgy of praise is a classic theme.

As early a writer as Origen said of prayer recited in common: "If the angel of the Lord is with those who fear Him, . . . it is to be supposed, when they are officially gathered for the glory of Christ, that the angel of each one will be with each one of those who fear God, that is, with the one whom he is assigned to guard and direct; so that when the faithful are gathered, there are two assemblies, that of men and that of the angels."[59]

And St. Benedict in his Rule describes the monk's attitude at the Divine Office: "We believe that the divine presence is everywhere . . . . But we should believe this especially without any doubt when we are assisting at the Work of God. To that end let us be mindful always of the Prophet's words, 'Serve the Lord in fear' and again 'Sing praises wisely' and 'In the sight of the angels I will sing praise to You.' Let us therefore consider how we ought to conduct ourselves in the sight of the Godhead and of His angels, and let us take part in the psalmody in such a way that our mind may be in harmony with our voice."[60]

This conviction has remained vital in the monastic tradition. We need only recall this anecdote reported by Alcuin: "It is told that . . . Bede said, 'I know that the angels are present at the canonical hours. . . . What would happen if they did not find me with the other brethren? Would they not say, "Where is Bede?"'"[61]

Finally, the angels are mentioned very often in the blessings and consecrations of the ritual. By way of example, let us cite these two prayers for

---

[58] The *Proficiscere* appears in the Gelasian sacramentaries of the eighth century. The mention of the Blessed Virgin and of St. Joseph is a later addition. Several prayers for the departed in the ancient Gelasian, III, 91 (ed. Wilson, pp. 295–299), ask that they be guided and welcomed by the angels. The same idea is found in the offertory of the Mass for the Dead: " . . . but may St. Michael, the standard-bearer, bring them into the holy light."

[59] *De orat.*, 31 (PG 11, 553).

[60] Ch. 19.

[61] *Ep.* 219; ed. Froben, I, 282, Or *Ep.* 16 (PL 100, 168). Other texts are cited by Erik Peterson, *Das Buch von den Engeln*, pp. 76 ff.

the protection of houses: "Listen to us, Lord, holy Father, all-powerful, eternal God, and deign to send Your holy angel from heaven to guard, sustain, protect, visit and defend all who dwell in this house." [62] The following prayer is said at the end of Compline: "Visit this house, we pray You, Lord, and keep far from it every ambush of the enemy; may Your holy angels dwell here, to guard us in peace, and may Your blessing be always upon us."

The angels and the liturgical year

The Christmas cycle, in which the angels appear very often, reminds us each year of the role they play in the history of salvation and especially of the part they played with regard to the Incarnation.

The *Gloria in excelsis Deo*, which the gospel has them singing at the birth of Jesus, quickly entered the Christian liturgy. It developed into a great doxology which takes the form of a paraphrase and an amplification of the angelic hymn. Employed first at the beginning of Lauds, it was later sung at the Mass. Every time we recite it, it reminds us of the reestablishment of peace between the human world and the angelic world, thanks to the coming of Christ on earth.

This idea forms the inspiration of a "collect for peace" for Christmas day in the *Missale gothicum*: "All-powerful, eternal God, who have made this day sacred by Your Incarnation and by the Blessed Virgin Mary's giving birth; who, as the corner stone, by Your Incarnation have restored unity in place of the long-standing discord between angels and men caused by the transgression of the tree; grant to Your servants in the joy of this solemnity that, as they rejoice to see You share their earthly condition, they may be brought to union with the heavenly citizens, over whom You have raised the body You assumed." [63]

Finally, to have a somewhat more complete view of the role of the angels in the liturgy, we must recall that they soon became the object of a direct veneration.

This veneration, which is centered especially around the person of St. Michael, appears in the East in the fourth century, and in the fifth century it is already flourishing in the West. It was originally tied in with the numerous sanctuaries dedicated to the archangel throughout the Christian world. The Leonine sacramentary already has five Mass formularies on September 30 for the anniversary of the dedication of the basilica which had been consecrated to St. Michael on the Via Salaria. [64] The Gelasian and the Gregorian sacramentaries include a similar feast on September 29, in connection with the dedication of the sanctuary on Monte Gargano, famous since the end of the fifth century. In this feast St. Michael is considered as the head of the heavenly armies. Thus all the angels are venerated together with him.

---

[62] This prayer, now sung at the end of the *Asperges* which precedes the Sunday high Mass, is found as early as the Gelasian sacramentary, III, 76; ed. Wilson, p. 286.

[63] Ed. Bannister, n. 16.

[64] Nn. 844–859; ed. Mohlberg, II, 106–108.

The feast of the guardian angels on October 2 was celebrated in Spain and in France from the fifteenth century, but it was not extended to the universal Church until 1670.[65]

To conclude this study of the place of the saints and the angels in the liturgy, we shall quote a pasage from St. Augustine. Perhaps better than anyone else, the bishop of Hippo felt and expressed the profound unity between the world of the angels and that of men in the general framework of the city of God, a unity which is reflected in our earthly liturgy because that liturgy is the anticipation, under the veil of the mystery, of the cosmic liturgy of the heavenly Jerusalem :

"All together we are the members and the body of Christ ; not only we who are present in this place, but all Christians throughout the earth ; and not only we who are alive at this time, but, actually, every just person who has passed through this life and will pass through this life, from Abel the just until the end of the world, as long as men beget and are begotten ; every just person who exists now, not in this place but in this life, and every just person who is yet to be born — all together form the one body of Christ, and each one is a member of Christ. If all, then, are His body and each one is a member, He is surely the Head of this body. He is the Head of the body which is the Church, says the Scripture, the Firstborn, who holds the primacy in all things. And since it is also said of Him that He is always the Head of every principality and power, this Church which is now a pilgrim is united to that heavenly Church where the angels are our fellow citizens. . . . Thus it is made a single Church, the city of the great King." [66]

We form but one Church, therefore, with the angels and with the saints of all time. This unity will be perfect in the heavenly Jerusalem, but even now it is real, and it finds its highest manifestation in the liturgical action, that action which assembles "all the believers from the beginning to the end of the world, in addition to the legions and armies of the angels, so that there is but one city under one king, one province under one emperor, happy in eternal peace and salvation, praising God forever, blessed forever." [67]

---

[65] Cf. Righetti, II, 329–334.
[66] Sermo 341, IX, 11 (PL 39, 1499–1500).

[67] St. Augustine, Enar. in Ps. 36, sermo III, 4 (PL 36, 385).

13 THE TWO CITIES: THE STRUGGLE AGAINST SATAN IN THE LITURGY

If there is one truth of faith to which Christians today attach hardly any importance, it is certainly the existence of Satan and the reality of his activity against the designs of God.[1] In minimizing this doctrine, Christians are forgetting that an essential aspect of the Christian life is its character as a continual struggle not only against evil in itself and against our evil tendencies, but also, in a more concrete and more personal way, against Satan and his troops.

When they read the gospel accounts of cures worked by Jesus on behalf of sick people possessed by a devil or an evil spirit, many believers are tempted to see nothing in such possession but a popular interpretation of appearances without objective value.[2]

---

[1] Cf., e.g., Henri-Irénée Marrou, "The Fallen Angel," *Satan* (New York: Sheed & Ward, 1952), pp. 67–68: "Apart from professional theologians, professors whose habit it is to plod through the encyclopedia of dogma with steady and methodical steps, and apart from those privileged souls who are so far advanced in the way of perfection and the life of the spirit that they know every aspect of it, one might say by experiment, I am certain that among the Christians of our day there are very

few who *believe* really and effectively in the devil; for whom this article of faith is an active element of their religious life. Even among those who say they are and think they are and want to be faithful to the Church's teaching, we should discover many who have no difficulty in acknowledging that they do not accept the existence of 'Satan.' "

[2] On the healing of the possessed by Christ, cf. F. M. Catherinet, "Demoniacs in the Gospel," *Satan*, pp. 163–177.

Similarly, in reading the history of the desert Fathers, they attribute to *naïveté* their tendency to see Satan everywhere and to be constantly at war with him; or else they see in this tendency a Christian transformation of the tendency of the popular Greek and Roman mentality to find demons everywhere.

To be sure, there are no grounds for a sweeping condemnation of the modern mentality, which began to take shape during the sixteenth century as a reaction against the psychotic preoccupation with Satanism and sorcery which had prevailed from the fourteenth to the beginning of the sixteenth century.[3] Still, this modern disposition does tend to minimize and almost to deny an important point of revelation.

For revelation teaches us that a factor of struggle and of drama enters into the relations between man and God. Some angels rebelled against God, and introduced physical and moral evil into the cosmos. From that time on, the history of the world and of man involves a continual struggle between God and Satan, between the followers of God and the followers of Satan. They are two kingdoms, two cities, always at war. This struggle extends to the whole universe; and wayfaring man, *homo viator,* whose destiny is not yet fixed, is the stake.

Anyone who neglected this dimension of the Christian life would render himself incapable of understanding the liturgy in one of its essential aspects. Inversely, there is no better means of penetrating this datum of faith to the depths than to examine it and live it in the liturgy.

1. The Struggle Against Satan in the New Testament

We shall not attempt here to follow throughout the Bible the development of the revelation concerning the devils. We shall merely try to show how the New Testament sees in Christ's life and in that of the Christian an unceasing struggle against Satan.[4]

Satan urged man to rebel against God; he was the instigator of original sin, and he continues unflaggingly to incite man to sin. Together with sin, he introduced death into the world, the death of the body and that of the soul, and every physical and moral evil (Rom. 5:12; Heb. 2:14). His harmful influence is exercised especially in the ailments which the authors of the New Testament, taking a purely religious point of view, consider always as consequences of sin and hence as manifestations of Satan's power (Matt. 10:1; 12:22-28; Luke 13:16; John 5:14; 2 Cor. 12:7).

By getting man involved in his rebellion, Satan has made him his slave (John 8:34 and 44; Rom. 6:16-20). This domination of Satan makes itself felt in a special way in paganism and idolatry, which are not mere deviations

---

[3] Cf. Emile Brouette, "The Sixteenth Century and Satanism," *Satan*, pp. 310-348.

[4] Cf. Louis Bouyer, "The Two Economies of Divine Government: Satan and Christ," in *God and His Creation* (Chicago: Fides, 1955), pp. 465-497; Stanislas Lyonnet, "Le démon dans l'écriture," *Dict. de spir.*, III, 142-152.

of the intellect but really worship offered to devils (1 Cor. 10:19–21; 2 Cor. 4:3–4).

Being master of man, Satan is likewise master of the lower creatures, which because of man's sin are subject to vanity and to corruption (Rom. 8:20–21). He is "the prince of this world" (John 12:31; 14:30), that is to say, of all the forces of evil at work in the world. He is "the god of this world," "of this *saeculum*" (1 Cor. 2:6–8; 2 Cor. 4:4), that is to say, of the forces of evil in as much as they can operate during the space of time granted them. This kingdom is also that of the flesh and of darkness.

Christ and Satan

In such a perspective, Christ's activity appears as a victorious struggle against Satan, and the establishment of the kingdom of God implies the destruction of the kingdom of Satan: "For this did the Son of God make Himself manifest, that He might destroy the works of the devil" (1 John 3:8; cf. Matt. 12:28). Christ comes to free man from the devil's power under all its forms: sin, death, sickness. Immediately after His baptism, "Jesus was led by the Spirit into the desert to be tempted by the devil" (Matt. 4:1). This hand-to-hand combat in which He engages with the devil just before undertaking His work of salvation shows well enough what will be the meaning and the end of that work.

It is with the Passion that this duel reaches the crucial point. St. John has brought to light, more effectively than the other evangelists, this dimension of the mystery of the cross. For him, the time of the Passion is the "hour" of Jesus, that hour which the Father has set and which the Son has accepted with full freedom (John 12:27–33; cf. 7:30; 13:1). The two adversaries plunge into the battle (John 14:30), of which the issue is known in advance (John 12:31; 16:11).

St. Paul for his part insists on the triumph of Christ, whose exaltation is shown by His descent into hell, His resurrection from the dead and His ascension (Eph. 4:9; Phil. 2:8–11). In going up again from hell to earth and from the earth to heaven, the Lord has shown that His dominion extends to the whole universe.

This action of Christ's is continued by the Apostles. When they are sent out on a mission for the first time, Jesus gives them "power and authority over all the devils, as well as the power to cure diseases; and He sent them forth to preach the kingdom of God, and to heal the sick" (Luke 9:1–2; cf. 10:17–19). The apostolic mission has a twofold aspect: to establish the kingdom of God, and to destroy the kingdom of Satan; the one is not found without the other. There is nothing surprising, therefore, about these two themes meeting in Christ's last commissions to His Apostles (Mark 16:15–18) or about the fact that St. Paul, in defining his mission before King Agrippa, says that he is sent to the pagans "to open their eyes that they may turn from darkness to light and from the dominion of Satan to God" (Acts 26:18; cf. 16:16–18; 19:11–17).

The Christian and Satan

The life of the Christian, like that of Christ, will be a continual struggle against the diabolical powers. The deepest reason for this is that living as a Christian means imitating and continuing Christ, and this imitation is at the same time mystical and moral: it causes us to participate in Christ's way of being and, as a consequence, in His way of seeing and of feeling, acting and reacting, in the presence of God and of creatures.

This conformation to Christ is achieved radically in baptism, but it also requires a moral effort which must be exerted throughout one's life. Like his model, like his leader, the Christian will have to cross swords with Satan.

In this struggle "against the Principalities and the Powers, against those that rule the world of darkness, against the evil spirits abroad in the air," the believer must have recourse to the defensive and offensive arms indicated by St. Paul (Eph. 6:11–18). He must show himself watchful and sober (2 Cor. 2:11; Eph. 4:27; 1 Pet. 5:8). The Scripture recommends prayer and fasting especially (Matt. 17:21; Mark 9:29), and the Lord in the *Our Father* has him ask, "Do not expose us to temptation, but deliver us from the evil one" (Matt. 6:13).[5] But it is the invocation of the name of Jesus that the New Testament presents as the weapon most potent against the devil (Matt. 7:22; Mark 9:38; 16:17; Luke 10:17; Acts 16:18; 19:13; Phil. 2:10). Finally, the Christian must expect to undergo a particularly violent assault at the moment of death. Here again he must imitate his Lord, who won His final victory only by His cross.

The Christian's struggle is included, moreover, within a battle which is that of the whole Church. It is worthy of note that the texts of the New Testament which show the Church founded on Peter are situated in the perspective of the struggle against Satan: it is to guarantee the Church against the attacks of Satan that Christ founds it on Peter (Luke 22:31–32; Matt. 16:17–19).

And the entire Apocalypse takes the form of an explanation of history considered as a struggle to the death between the city of God, which groups the angels and the saints around God and the Lamb, and the city of the devil, which gathers around Satan the devils, the pagan powers that are persecuting the Church, and the worshipers of the beast. This struggle is carried on till Satan's final assault and the definitive triumph of the kingdom of God.[6]

Thus the New Testament is extensively concerned with the struggle of the children of light against the prince of darkness; and it considers that struggle

---

[5] In itself, ἀπὸ τοῦ πονηροῦ can mean "from evil" or "from the evil one." If the second rendering is adopted, this is because the New Testament on this point is very concrete and personal: the Christian needs to be delivered not only from evil in general, but above all from Satan, who is the source of all evil and of every temptation.

[6] Cf. M. E. Boismard, *L'Apocalypse* (*Bible de Jerusalem*) (Paris, 1950), pp. 12–15.

essentially as a continuation of, and a participation in, the battle waged by the Son of God made Man. This whole teaching is summed up by the author of the letter to the Hebrews in a sentence which will often be the subject of commentary in patristic literature: "Therefore, because His children have blood and flesh in common, so He in like manner has shared in these, that by His death He might destroy the one who had the empire of death, that is, the devil, and might deliver those who throughout their lives were kept in servitude by the fear of death" (Heb. 2:14-15).

2. Aspects of Patristic Demonology

When the Fathers speak of the devils, most often they simply repeat the data of the New Testament. They do attempt, however, to make distinctions and draw conclusions from those data, and this in three directions: to determine the nature of devils and in what exactly their rebellion consisted; to become better acquainted with the psychology of temptation and the rules for discernment of spirits; to determine the power of the devils over man and over the elements. The first two of these questions are rather the concern of dogmatic theology and of spirituality; they awake almost no echo in the liturgy. The third, however, interests us directly, and is worth dwelling on.[7]

Action of the devils on the human body, on paganism, on the elements

The New Testament taught that Satan is present behind every evil, physical or moral; that his influence over the human body and sensible things is real, and can go as far as inhabitation and possession properly so called; finally, that his action makes itself more vividly felt over everything that is related to the worship of idols.

The patristic tradition accepts these data of faith, but seeks further to explain them, to depict their expression in the concrete. Here we are on the level, no longer of the faith, but of the explanation of the faith.

Of the many opinions expressed at that time, some were taken from the Jewish apocryphal books like the *Testament of the Twelve Patriarchs* or the *Book of Henoch,* while others were a Christian transposition of certain characteristics of the Greek demonology.

Thus, for example, we are told that the devils make their way into the human body and there take up their dwelling, or even that devils specializing in one or another vice — the seven or eight capital sins, for instance — find a home in some particular part of the human body and there arouse the passions.[8]

---

[7] On the devil in patristic literature, the best study at present is that which has appeared in the article "Démon" in the *Dict. de spir.*, III, 152-219, with the collaboration of Jean Daniélou, "Dans la littérature ecclésiastique jusqu'à Origène," Antoine and Claire Guillaumont, "Dans la plus ancienne littérature monastique," François Vandenbroucke, "En Occident."

[8] This idea appears in the *Testament des*

Another opinion widespread at that time is that the devils are masters wherever paganism prevails: they identify themselves with the pagan gods, they hide in the statues of the idols to receive the honors offered the gods, to breathe the odor of the sacrifices and of the incense, which delights their senses, to preside over the pagan worship, utter oracles, foster magic and astrology.[9]

The whole pagan life, not only the functions of worship but also the whole civil, military, commercial activity, the theater, the honors — all this is considered as connected with the pagan worship and therefore infested by the diabolical action. It is a huge machine which Satan uses to hold men in bondage. To this whole complexus Tertullian gives the name of *pompa diaboli,* the devil's "pomp."[10]

Another affirmation, based on biblical data and still more on Jewish and Greek speculations, is that the devils, especially in pagan surroundings, are constantly acting on the elements, the plants and the animals, for the purpose of doing evil to man and preventing him from attaining his salvation.

Tertullian says, for example, that "their business is to corrupt mankind. . . . Therefore they inflict upon men's bodies diseases and other bitter misfortunes, and upon the soul sudden and extraordinary outbursts of violence. They have their own subtle, spiritual properties for assailing each part of human nature. Much power is allowed their spiritual faculties, with the result that, without being apprehended by sight or any of the other senses, they are more evident in the outcome of their activity than in the activity itself. So it is, for example, in the case of fruit or crops, when something imperceptible in the air casts a blight upon the flower, kills the bud, and injures the development; as if the air, tainted in some unseen manner, were spreading abroad its pestilential breath."[11]

On these three points — inhabitation of the human body by devils, usurpation of the whole pagan life, action on the elements — the conceptions borrowed from Judaism or from the Greek way of thinking did not give birth to a new doctrine, but simply probed or prolonged the teaching of the New Testament. The liturgical rites which will develop in response to these preoccupa-

---

douze patriarches, Ruben, III, 3–7 (French translation in Joseph Bonsirven, *La Bible apocryphe* [Paris, 1953], p. 118). It is found again in the *Corpus hermeticum,* e.g., XVI, 14–15 (ed. Nock-Festugière, II, 236), and in the heterodox literature, such as the pseudo-Clementine writings, e.g., *Homilia* IX, 10 (PG 2, 248–249), or the gnostic Valentine, according to Clement of Alexandria, *Strom.,* II, 20, 114 (PG 8, 1057). More than one Christian author echoes the idea; for instance, Tatian, *Oratio adversus Graecos,* 18 (PG 6, 848); Clement of Alexandria, *Pedag.,* II, 1, 15 (PG 8, 404); Origen, *In Ios. Hom.* XV, 6 (PG 12, 904); Minucius Felix, *Octav.,* 27, 1–4 (PL 3,

323–325).

[9] In the Greek conception, the "demons" intermediate between the gods and men were generally considered as beneficent spirits. The Christians regard them, on the contrary, as maleficent beings, satellites of Satan, demons in the present sense of the word. Cf., e.g., Justin, *Apol.* II, 5, 2–6 (PG 6, 452–453); Athenagoras, *Legatio,* 23–26 (PG 6, 941–952).

[10] Cf. J. H. Waszink, "Pompa diaboli," *Vigiliae christianae,* I (1947), 13–41.

[11] *Apol.,* 22, 4–5 (PL 1, 405–406); translation by Sister Emily Joseph Daly, C.S.J., in *The Fathers of the Church,* X (New York: Fathers of the Church, Inc., 1950), 69.

tions will have to be regarded, therefore, as being inspired basically by biblical and Christian data, even if they include some traces of speculations foreign to that primary source.

Struggle against the devils in the Christian life and after death

Moreover, in making explicit what was found in the New Testament only in germ, the patristic tradition has brought out the anti-demoniac significance of a series of manifestations of the Christian life. Such is the case, for example, for baptism, which St. Paul (Rom. 6:1–11) presented from the first as a participation in Christ's victory and a liberation from sin. Such is the case also for martyrdom,[12] in which the Apocalypse (12:11) lets us see a victory over Satan.

The ancient tradition regards baptism, martyrdom, the ascetical life of virgins and of monks, as realities closely linked; for martyrdom is the full flowering and the ratification of baptism, while virginity and the monastic life are substitutes for martyrdom.[13] Renunciation, death to self, is always a struggle against Satan. Origen is so imbued with this idea that he describes the whole of asceticism as a combat against the devils.[14] And the monastic life, especially in the eremitical form, as an eminent instance of the struggle against Satan, is an essential theme of the *Life of St. Antony* by St. Athanasius, a theme which the whole of monastic hagiography continues to illustrate.[15] Evagrius Ponticus especially becomes the theoretician of this aspect of the monastic life.[16]

We must mention also an opinion which Origen borrowed from the Greek world and which has found an echo in the liturgy still perceptible in our day. Origen believes that after death the soul, in ascending toward God through the celestial spheres which surround the earth, is subjected to repeated examinations. At the entrance to each sphere are posted devils, described sometimes as lions ready to devour the soul or at least to bar its passage, sometimes as examiners or collectors (*telonai*), to whom the soul must not only give an answer but also pay a tribute, more or less considerable according to the number of sins with which it is still burdened.[17]

---

[12] Evidence from Hermas, St. Ignatius of Antioch, Tertullian and various Acts of martyrs will be found collected by Jean Daniélou, "Démon dans la littérature ecclésiastique jusqu'à Origène," *Dict. de spir.*, III, 179–182. The "Passion of SS. Perpetua and Felicitas" has been studied from this point of view by F. J. Dölger, "Der Kampf mit dem Aegypter in der Perpetua-Vision. Das Martyrium als Kampf mit dem Teufel," *Antike und Christentum*, III (1932), 177–188.

[13] Cf. Edward A. Malone, *The Monk and the Martyr: The Monk as the Successor of the Martyr* (Washington: Catholic University of America Press, 1950).

[14] Cf. S. Bettencourt, *Doctrina Origenis ascetica, seu quid docuerit de ratione animae humanae cum daemonibus* (Studia anselmiana, 16; Vatican City: Libreria Editrice Vaticana, 1945).

[15] We may cite, for example, the biographies of St. Paul the Hermit, of St. Hilarion, of Malchus, written by St. Jerome, or the descriptions of the life of the monks contained in the *Historia monachorum*, in the *Lausiac History*, in the *Sayings of the Fathers*, in the *Conferences* of Cassian.

[16] Cf. article "Démon dans la plus ancienne littérature monastique," *Dict. de spir.*, III, 204–205.

[17] *In Lucam hom.* 23 (PG 13, 1861–1862). It will be noted that Origen is aware of attack-

This imaginative way of representing the particular judgment enjoyed a great vogue in the ancient East and also in certain regions of the West until the thirteenth century.[18] The soul's journey across the celestial spheres in company with the good angels — and especially with St. Michael, the great psychopomp — who assist it in the trials to which the devils subject it, is a theme which recurs often in the writings of the Fathers, in the apocryphal books and in the liturgical texts. With images borrowed from Greek cosmology and demonology, the Christian authors illustrate the affirmation of the Scripture that the whole Christian life is a struggle against Satan.

3. Theological Judgment on the Affirmations of Christian Antiquity about the Struggle against Satan

What must be thought of all these assertions of the New Testament and of the Fathers about the struggle against the devils? Is the believer bound to accept them *en bloc,* or can he discriminate between that which is truth of faith and that which is free opinion or even fanciful hypothesis?

In the first place, it is beyond doubt that a certain number of these scriptural or patristic data are not presented as dogmatic statements by any means. No one is obliged to believe that St. Michael plays a special role as psychopomp, or that there are devils who specialize in certain vices, or that the air is the favorite dwelling-place for the spirits of evil. Similarly, the whole imagery with which a writer like Origen surrounds the voyage of the souls after death not only is not imposed upon the believer, but should be discarded as an error.

Let us note further that there can be no question of admitting without scrutiny the reality of all the diabolical visions recounted in the ancient hagiographical and monastic literature. Of course the theologian has no objection on principle against these apparitions; but the historian, if he knows anything at all about the ancient mentality on this point, knows that he must accept these accounts only with cautious prudence.

After these cases have been eliminated, there remain in the New Testament and in the patristic writings a great number of statements which it seems hard for us to take literally. Aside from some exceptional cases where diabolical possession seems likely or even certain, we are inclined to consider as purely

---

ing a difficult subject: "Periculosum quidem, sed tamen strictim breviterque tangendum."

[18] Cf. J. Rivière, "Rôle du démon au jugement particulier chez les Pères," *Rev. des sciences relig.,* IV (1924), 43–64; A. Recheis, *Engel, Tod und Seelenreise.* Obviously in giving such a description of the particular judgment the Fathers are speaking as poets, not as theologians; somewhat as a preacher today might appeal to the imagination in describing the torments of hell or the joys of paradise. Although St. Cyril of Alexandria indulges in

extremely detailed descriptions (*Hom.* XIV, *De exitu animae* [PG 77, 1073–1076]), he begins with this reminder: "This Judge has no need of accusers and of witnesses, of proofs and of refutations. It is He who places before the eyes of the guilty all that we have done, said and willed" (*ibid.,* 1072). These descriptions did not raise any dogmatic difficulties, therefore, even if some of the listeners or of the orators themselves did not distinguish very clearly between imaginative presentation and doctrinal statement.

natural the phenomena which Christian antiquity attributes to Satan's influence: action of the elements, sickness, psychic disturbances, temptations, etc. We are tempted to reverse St. Paul's statement and say that it is against flesh and blood that we must struggle, and not against the Principalities, the Powers and the rulers of this world of darkness (cf. Eph. 6:12).

The question, at bottom, is: What is meant by *natural?* This question may be answered from two different points of view, and hence may receive two answers, which complete rather than oppose each other. The Scripture and the Fathers take one viewpoint, while we, instinctively, take the other.

In Greek and in Latin, the idea of nature is linked to that of birth. The nature of a being is everything that constitutes it at its birth; everything that belongs to it by the fact of its birth is natural to it. Everything that supervenes later, everything that modifies, for better or for worse, the original state of this being, is considered as foreign to its nature, as not natural. Hence the notion of nature is not a philosophical notion, based on the distinction between the essential and the accidental, but a notion that might be called historical, a notion which starts out from a state of fact, from a concrete situation.

This conception is that of the Scripture and of the Fathers when, with or without the word, they speak of the nature of man, when they seek to distinguish what is natural to him from that which comes to him from causes foreign to his nature. What is natural to man in this perspective is what belonged to him in his primitive, original state, when he came forth from the hands of God. Whatever may have been produced later on and modified his condition no longer forms part of his nature.

This notion was received in an almost universal way in the Christian world until the thirteenth century, that is, until the time when people began to consider things no longer from a concrete and historical viewpoint but from an abstract and entitative viewpoint. This change of perspective was accentuated, beginning with the sixteenth century, by the fact of the polemic against Protestantism and Baianism.

In this new perspective, nature becomes almost synonymous with essence. The nature of a thing is its essence as principle of its specific operations. What is natural to a thing now is that which constitutes its essence, that which is derived necessarily from its essence or that which is required by its essence as a necessary means for attaining an equally necessary end.

This philosophical notion abstracts from the historical condition, the concrete situation of beings. That is declared natural to man which answers to his metaphysical structure, without any concern for knowing whether it belonged to his original state. Thus sickness, death and passions are natural to man, and the philosopher does not have to appeal to a cause foreign to human nature in order to account for them.

It is easy now to understand the apparent opposition between the ancient mentality and the modern mentality. Is man's struggle against evil a struggle against natural forces or a struggle against Satan? It all depends on one's idea of nature. If a person conceives of nature from a philosophical point of view, he will say that sickness, death, passions are in conformity with the nature of man and of things. But if he takes the historical point of view, he will say that this struggle of man against evil is not natural, because it did not form part of his original condition.

There is much more in this than a question of words. The problem is to know whether man is actually engaged in a purely natural undertaking or whether he finds himself faced with an adversary, faced with Satan.

Now it is a fact that evil, both physical and moral, entered the world not simply by man's sin, but by man's sin instigated by Satan. This intervention of the devil to bring about man's fall was not just an episode of the struggle between good and evil, but a consequence and a manifestation of Satan's enmity towards God. The state of privation which resulted for man, privation of grace and of the preternatural gifts, is a state of sin, that is, of aversion to God and servitude to Satan; and all the consequences of this original sin, all the evils which weigh down man and the world, are so many marks of the devil's power.

Today we take too little notice of these preternatural gifts which God had granted to Adam and which all men should have enjoyed. They went beyond the requirements of our metaphysical nature, but they belonged in fact to the primitive condition of human nature. Their loss threw man into a state other than his original state, other than that which God had willed for him.

In this perspective, the purpose of Christ's coming on earth was not to perfect, to crown as it were, a world and a nature which of themselves would be neutral with regard to God, as is supposed by a naturalism too widespread in our day. This coming is truly a "redemption," a "repurchase," a "liberation" of man and of the cosmos. And Christ comes to liberate us not only from a state of hostility towards God, but also and especially from a person hostile to God. As St. Paul writes, "God has snatched us from the power of darkness and transferred us into the kingdom of His beloved Son" (Col. 1:13).

The salvation brought by Christ restores grace to us, but not yet the preternatural gifts. It makes us enter even now into the kingdom of God, but it does not yet free us from the influence of Satan, it does not excuse us from the fight. This influence, which makes itself felt through all the evils that touch us, is exercised in certain cases by means which are above nature, in the philosophical sense, but most often by natural means. A better knowledge of the nature of man and of things, a more exact science of natural forces and processes, shows us that Satan has recourse to means surpassing nature less frequently than the ancients thought. But our improved knowledge and science should not make us forget that evil entered the world because of Satan and hence the Bible, and the liturgy depending on the Bible, are right when they present the struggle against evil as a struggle against Satan.

4. The Struggle against Satan in the Liturgy of the Initiation

The Scripture and the Fathers bring out the importance of the battle against Satan in sacred history and in the mystery of Christ. Since the liturgy is simply the prolongation and the expression in worship of that history and of that mystery, it is to be expected that the struggle against the powers of evil should occupy a large place here also. Actually there are a great many liturgical customs and texts bearing on this point. Even without studying them all, we shall easily be able to see that the sacraments, the sacramentals and the liturgical year always picture Satan as the constant adversary of the kingdom of God.

Baptism

This struggle against the devils is expressed first of all in the rites of the Christian initiation, and especially in those of baptism. Three principal themes inspired by the Scripture will be developed by the baptismal liturgy: in as much as it is a death to sin, baptism frees man from the bondage of Satan and brings him to the liberty of the children of God; in as much as it is birth to the life of Christ, baptism is the first act of a fight which will be waged throughout the Christian's life, under the opposing influences of the Prince of light and the prince of darkness; finally, for the converts from paganism, baptism is a renunciation of that whole worship of idols and that whole pagan environment in which Satan reigns as master.

It seems that as early a writer as Justin makes allusion to the exorcismal value of baptism.[1] At any rate, the anti-Satanic significance of baptism appears explicitly at the time of Tertullian in the rite of the renunciation of Satan.[2] In the fourth and fifth centuries it is brought to light fully by the ceremonies that accompany baptism and by the explanations of the Fathers.

Besides its expression in the exorcisms and in the renunciation of Satan, this struggle against the devils finds expression in the blessing of the baptismal water and, if the patristic commentaries are to be believed, in almost all the other rites of baptism. A cursory examination of the rites in use from the fourth to the seventh century [3] will help us understand the exact import of the anti-Satanic elements which the present Roman Ritual has kept in its "order of baptism."

---

[1] *Dial.*, 30 and 85 (PG 6, 540 and 676). In these two passages Justin says that the devils are put to flight by calling on the name of Jesus, and he follows this name with a profession of faith which might well be that of baptism.

[2] *De spectac.*, 4 (PL 1, 635–636); *De corona*, 13 (PL 2, 97); *De anima*, 35 (PL 2, 710).

[3] Cf. Jean Daniélou, *The Bible and the Liturgy*, pp. 19–69.

The rites over the "audientes"

When a candidate presents himself for admission to the first stage of the catechumenate, that of the *audientes* or *auditores,* the sacred minister's first gesture is to breathe on his face. This insufflation is a mark of contempt for Satan, as indicated by the formula of exorcism which accompanies it: "Depart from him, unclean spirit, and give place to the Holy Spirit, the Consoler."[4] It should help the Christian to take cognizance of the power wielded by Satan over all men. This is a point to which St. Augustine often recurs in his battle against Pelagian naturalism, in making the observation that this rite of exorcism is employed even for infants, though they have not committed any personal sin.[5]

After the insufflation, the sacred minister lays his hands on the candidate, to signify sanctification under its positive aspect.

Then the candidate's forehead is marked with the sign of the cross. This is the *consignatio* or *sphragis*.[6] The sign of the cross is first of all the sign of belonging to Christ, of consecration to Christ; but it is also a sign leading to recognition and protection, the mark and the standard of the soldiers of Christ. It was easy to find an anti-Satanic value in it; so much the easier as the cross had been the instrument and the symbol of Christ's Passion and of His victory over Satan. It is not without reason that this victory is recalled more than once in the New Testament in a context where there is question of the death on the cross.[7]

Hence the Fathers and the liturgies have underlined the anti-demoniac significance of the *consignatio crucis.* Thus St. Cyril of Jerusalem writes that in an upright conscience the Lord "stamps His salutary and wonderful *sphragis*, which the demons fear, which the angels recognize, so that the former flee to hide themselves while the latter surround the soul as a member of the family."[8]

To understand the full meaning of this *consignatio*, we must recall that the Christians had frequent recourse to the sign of the cross as a protection against the devils.

We read, for example, in the *Apostolic Tradition* of Hippolytus, "When tempted always reverently seal your forehead with the sign of the cross. For this sign of the Passion is displayed and made manifest against the devil if you make it in faith, not in order that you may be seen by men, but with

[4] This rite is always included in the Roman Ritual (*Ordo baptismi adultorum*, n. 8; *ordo baptismi parvulorum*, n. 3).

[5] Cf., e.g., St. Augustine, *De gratia Christi et de peccato originali*, II, 40, 45 (PL 44, 407–408); *De nupt. et concup.*, I, 20, 22 (PL 44, 426–427); *Contra Iul.*, VI, 5, 11 (PL 44, 828–829).

[6] In the West, it was done at this time in the ceremony; in the East, at different points of the ceremony in different countries.

[7] Cf. John 12:31–33: " 'Now judgment is passed on the world; now will the prince of this world be cast out. And I, when I am lifted up from the earth, will draw everything to Myself.' And this He said to indicate what death He would die." Cf. 1 Cor. 2:2–6; Phil. 2:8–11.

[8] *Catech.* 1, 3 (PG 33, 373).

Christian spirit (*per scientiam*) putting it forward as a shield. If indeed the adversary sees the power of the Spirit outwardly displayed from within . . . he takes to flight trembling." [9]

Lactantius says likewise, "Anyone who has seen how the devils adjured in Christ's name flee from the bodies they have been possessing, knows what terror the sign of the cross inspires in the devils." [10]

St. Cyril of Jerusalem insists often on the anti-Satanic power of this sign, and advises the Christian to trace it on his forehead on every occasion: "Let us not be ashamed of the cross of Christ, therefore. Even if others hide it, make its sign yourself openly on your forehead, that the demons, seeing the sign of the King, may flee trembling. Make this sign when you eat and drink, when you sit down, when you go to bed, when you rise, when you speak, when you are on the way — in a word, on every occasion." [11]

And St. Augustine writes that unless the sign of the cross "is made on the forehead of the believers, on the water itself by which they are regenerated, on the oil of the chrism with which they are anointed, on the sacrifice by which they are nourished, nothing of all this is done as it should be." [12]

That seal of the living God which, according to the Apocalypse (7:2-3), is to mark the foreheads of the faithful of the last times to protect them from the influence of the devils, has been interpreted by tradition, therefore, as being the sign of Christ, the sign of the cross.

At Rome and in Africa, beginning with the third-fourth century, after the candidates had been signed with the cross, they were given a taste of salt which had previously been exorcised and blessed. [13] This rite signified that they were to be nourished on the divine wisdom, but it also had the sense of a protection against Satan, as is shown by the prayer of exorcism said over the salt: ". . . We pray You, therefore, Lord our God, that in the name of the Trinity this salt be made a health-giving *sacramentum* to put the enemy to flight." [14]

The rites over the "competentes"

It can be seen from what we have said so far that the admission to the catechumenate was considered as a liberation from Satan and an adherence

---

[9] *Trad. apost.*, 37; ed. Dix, pp. 68–69. In the last sentence I leave out some words of difficult interpretation. In them, apparently, Hippolytus means that in tracing the sign of the cross on his forehead, the Christian manifests outwardly the force of the Holy Spirit, whose temple he has become by his baptism; the spirit of evil must flee before this sign of the presence and the force of the Holy Spirit.

[10] *Inst.*, IV, 27 (PL 6, 531–532).

[11] *Catech.* 4, 14 (PG 33, 472). This text is cited by Jean Daniélou, *The Bible and the Liturgy*, pp. 62–63, who gives other examples of the efficacy of the sign of the cross, one

drawn from St. Athanasius, *Life of St. Antony*, 13 (PG 26, 864), the other from St. Gregory of Nyssa, *De vita S. Gregori thaumaturgi* (PG 46, 952 A-C). Cf. also St. Cyril of Jerusalem, *Catech.* 4, 13 (PG 33, 472), and *Catech.* 13, 3, 22, 40 and 41 (PG 33, 773, 800, 820–821).

[12] *In Io. tract.* 118, 5 (PL 35, 1950).

[13] This rite is still used in the Roman Ritual (*ordo baptismi adultorum*, nn. 13–15; *ordo baptismi parvulorum*, nn. 6–7).

[14] *The Gelasian Sacramentary*, I, 31; ed. Wilson, p. 47. The text of the Roman Ritual is substantially the same.

to Christ. Such also was the sense of the rites of preparation for baptism which were carried out all during Lent over the *competentes* or *electi*, that is, the catechumens who would be baptized at Easter. In order to be inscribed among the *competentes*, the candidate had to undergo an examination in a setting which expressed symbolically the struggle against Satan.

Thus it is that in Syria, as we learn from the *Catecheses* of Theodore of Mopsuestia, during this examination the candidate remains standing on a haircloth, barefoot, clad only in a tunic, with hands extended in an attitude of prayer and with eyes lowered.[15] He wants to show thereby the servitude in which the devil held him captive, and to arouse the compassion of the judge.[16] The haircloth on which the candidate stands is first of all a symbol of penance, but it also recalls the garments of skin with which God clothed Adam and Eve after the fall. Hence, for Theodore, this pre-baptismal test recalls the temptation of Adam in paradise, and also that of Christ in the desert.[17]

The ceremony is completed with the inscription in the registers of the Church, which is like the positive aspect of this new victory over Satan.

During Lent the *competentes* are required to take instructions and submit to scrutinies. The instructions have the essential aim of explaining the Apostles' Creed and the Our Father, which the candidates must learn by heart. The scrutinies are rites of purification, consisting especially in exorcisms and prayers.

While the instructions are primarily catechetical in import, they include also an aspect of struggle against the devil. According to the Gelasian sacramentary, after the creed has been recited before the candidates, the bishop makes a brief commentary on it, saying among other things, "You, therefore, should retain in your hearts this very brief formula which contains everything, so that this profession of faith may serve you as protection at all times. For the power of these arms is always invincible, and serves the good soldiers of Christ against all the surprises of the enemy. Let the devil, who never stops tempting man, find you always armed with this creed; that, having conquered the adversary, whom you renounce, you may preserve incorrupt and immaculate to the very end the grace of the Lord, with the help of Him whom you acknowledge."[18]

But it is in the liturgy of the scrutinies that the anti-Satanic character of baptism stands out most clearly. These scrutinies took place on the third, fourth and fifth Sundays of Lent, as well as on the morning of Holy Saturday. Originally, at least, they were not an examination of the candidates' knowledge or character, but a rite by which their body and soul were "scrutinized" to make sure that the devil was not hiding in them, and to eliminate all

---

[15] *Catechesis* XII, prologue; ed. Tonneau, p. 323.
[16] *Catechesis* XII, 24; ed. Tonneau, p. 361.
[17] *Catechesis* XII, 22; ed. Tonneau, p. 359.

On all this, cf. Jean Daniélou, *The Bible and the Liturgy*, pp. 20–22.
[18] I, 35; ed. Wilson, p. 56.

diabolical influence by recourse to exorcisms and prayers, with the addition of the anointing and the explicit renunciation of Satan on Holy Saturday morning.[19] That is why the clerical exorcists were the principal ministers of the scrutinies.

Bishop Quodvultdeus of Carthage, a contemporary of St. Augustine, enumerates the *sacramenta* involved in the scrutinies: exorcisms, prayers, religious chants, insufflations, haircloth, inclinations of the head, the humiliation of bare feet.[20]

According to *Ordo romanus* XI, which dates from the seventh century or perhaps from the end of the sixth century, the scrutiny properly so called opens with the deacon's invitation, "Pray, *electi*. Kneel." The silent prayer of the catechumens is undoubtedly ended with a collect said aloud by the priest, to which all answer "Amen." Then the deacon invites the godfathers and godmothers to trace the sign of the cross on the forehead of their godchildren. Next, an acolyte pronounces a first exorcism over them. The same ceremonies are repeated a second and a third time. Finally the priest says a prayer, "Aeternam ac iustissimam pietatem tuam . . ." and has the candidates signed once more by their godparents.[21]

Substantially the same rites have always been used in the Roman liturgy for the baptism of adults, while they have been sharply curtailed for the baptism of infants.[22]

The formularies used for the exorcisms all have much the same character. Satan is addressed in a contemptuous way: unclean spirit, adversary, enemy of the faith and of the human race, seducer, source of all evil and all sin, traitor, ancient serpent, etc.; he is reminded of his sins, the punishments God has inflicted on him, the victories Christ has won over him. He is commanded brusquely to flee, to leave the place, to give honor to God and to Christ. The names of the divine Persons and the name of the Savior Jesus Christ are invoked against him. The sign of the cross is made, and, since more recent times, holy water is used.

Thus a formula of exorcism mentioned by *Ordo romanus* XI, of which we find the text in the Gelasian sacramentary, says, "Therefore, accursed devil, recognize your condemnation and give honor to the living and true God; give honor to Jesus Christ, His Son, and to the Holy Spirit; withdraw from these servants of God, because our God and Lord Jesus Christ has seen fit to call them to His holy grace and blessing and to the gift of baptism. By this sign of the holy cross which we place on their foreheads and which do you, accursed devil, never dare to violate." [23]

---

[19] Cf. Righetti, IV, 43 ff. *The Gelasian Sacramentary*, I, 29 (ed. Wilson, p. 45), defines the scrutiny as "heavenly mystery by which the devil with his pomp is destroyed and the gate of the heavenly kingdom is opened."

[20] *Sermo ad compet.*, 1 (PL 40, 660–661).

[21] *Ordo romanus* XI, 11–27; ed. M. Andrieu, *Les Ordines Romani du Haut Moyen Age*, II (Louvain, 1948), pp. 420–424.

[22] *Ordo baptismi adultorum*, nn. 16–28; *ordo baptismi parvulorum*, nn. 7–9.

[23] *The Gelasian Sacramentary*, I, 33; ed. Wil-

Among the scrutinies, the most solemn and most important is that which takes place on Holy Saturday morning. Besides an exorcism of the usual kind and the *redditio symboli*, it includes three rites which all have a directly anti-Satanic character: the *aperitio aurium* (opening of the ears), the anointing and the renunciation of Satan.

The *aperitio aurium* is connected with the exorcism which precedes it, and it is substantially the development of the simple sign of the cross with which the exorcisms often end. The meaning of this rite is clearly expressed by the formula which accompanies it, preserved in the present ritual: "Ephpheta, which means 'Be opened,' so that you may perceive the fragrance of God's sweetness. But you, O devil, depart; for the judgment of God has come." [24]

The anointing with oil on the breast and between the shoulders — in the East it was done on the whole body — is a preparation for the struggle against the devil: the catechumen who is going to confront Satan needs to be filled with the strength of Christ, not only for the hand-to-hand combat of baptism, but also for the fight to be pursued throughout his life. [25]

"We came to the font," says St. Ambrose; "you entered, you were anointed. . . . You were anointed as an athlete of Christ, as if you were a wrestler." [26]

And the Eastern tradition is unanimous in this interpretation. [27] Thus in the sacramentary of Serapion the anointing is accompanied with this prayer: "We do this anointing over those who approach for the divine regeneration, praying that our Lord Jesus Christ set healing and strengthening forces to work on their behalf, and thereby find out and heal every trace of sin and iniquity or of diabolical influence in their soul, their body and their mind; that, by His grace, He grant them forgiveness, that, freed from sin, they may live in justice and, re-created by this anointing, purified by the bath and renewed in the Spirit, they may have the strength henceforth to overcome all the hostile powers and the illusions of this life." [28]

At Rome the renunciation of Satan followed the rite of anointing and originally took place in the baptistry itself. It is one of the most ancient anti-Satanic elements of the baptismal ritual. [29] It sums up the whole doctrine of

---

son, p. 48. This formula of exorcism follows upon a prayer, "Deus Abraham . . . ," asking God to send His angel to protect the catechumens.

[24] *The Gelasian Sacramentary*, I, 42; ed. Wilson, p. 79; *Ordo baptismi adultorum*, n. 34; *ordo baptismi parvulorum*, n. 13.

[25] *The Gelasian Sacramentary*, I, 42; ed. Wilson, p. 79; *ordo baptismi adultorum*, n. 36; *ordo baptismi parvulorum*, n. 15. The liturgies and the Fathers consider this anointing as preparatory to the whole Christian life.

[26] *De sacr.*, I, 2, 4 (PL 16, 419).

[27] Cf., e.g., St. Cyril of Jerusalem, *Catech.* 20, 3 (PG 33, 1080): "Just as the insufflations of the faithful and the invocation of the

name of God, like flames of roaring fire, burn the devils and put them to flight, so the oil exorcised by the invocation of God and by prayer receives such power that it not only burns and destroys the vestiges of sin but also puts to flight all the invisible powers of evil." See other texts in Jean Daniélou's *The Bible and the Liturgy*, pp. 40–42.

[28] *Sacram. Serap.*, 22, 15; ed. Funk, II, 185.

[29] As early a writer as Tertullian bears witness to it: *De corona*, 3, 2 (PL 2, 79). It is found in *The Gelasian Sacramentary*, I, 42 (ed. Wilson, pp. 78–79) and is preserved in the Roman Ritual, *ordo baptismi adultorum*, n. 35; *ordo baptismi parvulorum*, n. 14.

baptism as liberation from Satan and adherence to Christ. The formula is notably the same in the various liturgies.

The object of the renunciation is expressed in three members: Satan, his pomps, his angels or his works. The "pomps of Satan" designate the manifestations of pagan worship, especially the processions and the games which the Christians were still tempted to attend.[30] As for the "angels of Satan," it does seem that these should be identified with the devils;[31] some of the Fathers, however, understood the expression as applying to men who served as instruments in Satan's hands to do evil and tempt the believers;[32] in this sense it would approximate the variant "and his works," preserved by the Roman tradition,[33] which designates sins of every kind.

In the Eastern liturgies the meaning of the renunciation is further underlined by the attitude of the catechumen. To renounce Satan, he turns toward the west and extends his hands. The ancient Greek tradition placed the gates of Hades to the west, and in this same direction the patristic tradition placed the kingdom of darkness.

As St. Cyril of Jerusalem explains, "The devil, being darkness, has his empire in darkness. That is why you renounce this prince of darkness and of obscurity while turned symbolically toward the west."[34]

At the same time the catechumen extends his hand or his hands, a gesture which accompanies the conclusion of pacts, but also their denunciation, and he breathes three times in the direction of Satan as a sign of contempt. After this he turns toward the east, hands raised and eyes heavenward as a sign of prayer, and professes his adherence to Christ.[35]

The blessing of the baptismal water

Among the rites which surrounded the baptism itself on Easter night, the one having most directly an anti-Satanic sense was the blessing of the baptismal water. Tertullian already speaks of it as a current practice.[36]

Very probably this sanctification of the water included two aspects right from the beginning: to cast out all diabolical influence by an exorcism, and to bring down the divine protection and power, with a special reference to the Holy Spirit.[37] The prayer of consecration of the water which is found in

[30] Cf. J. H. Waszink, "Pompa diaboli," *Vigiliae christianae*, I (1947), 13–41.

[31] The expression would be inspired by Matt. 25:41; cf. 2 Cor. 12:7; 2 Pet. 2:4; Jude 6; Apoc. 9:11; 12:7–9.

[32] Cf. e.g., Theodore of Mopsuestia, *Catechesis* XIII, 7–9; ed. Tonneau, pp. 377–383.

[33] Found already in Hippolytus, *Trad. apost.*, ch. 21; ed. Dix, p. 34.

[34] *Catechesis* 19, 4 (PG 33, 1069). Cf. Jean Daniélou, *The Bible and the Liturgy*, pp. 26–34.

[35] These rites are preserved in the Byzantine

liturgy of baptism; cf. E. Mercenier, *La prière des Eglises de rite byzantin*, I, pp. 339–341.

[36] *De baptismo*, 4, 4 (PL 1, 1204). Cf. Righetti, IV, 58, and the bibliography cited there.

[37] Cf. St. Ambrose, *De sacr.*, I, 5, 18 (PL 16, 422–423): "As soon as the priest enters he performs the exorcism over the creature which is water, and afterwards utters the invocation and offers the prayer that the font be sanctified and that there be in it the presence of the eternal Trinity." Cf. *ibid.*, I, 5, 15 (PL 16, 422).

the Gelasian sacramentary[38] and which is still used in the Roman liturgy, is obviously constructed on this scheme.

Such a rite simply exemplifies the teaching of revelation: after the fall, Satan has great power over man and over the world; and before making use of creatures, especially for a sacred purpose, it is necessary to sanctify them by withdrawing them from the diabolical influence. It may be that there is also some survival in this rite of the Greek opinion which regarded certain elements, such as water and air, as the favorite abodes of demons.[39]

Even the decoration of the baptistries sometimes points up the anti-demoniac character of the rite: in some of them a hart panting after water is represented, with a serpent in its mouth, to indicate that the catechumen arrives at the water of salvation only after having conquered the devil.[40]

The post-baptismal anointing

The rites which follow baptism — anointing with chrism by a priest, white garments, lighted candle — stress the new life to which the neophyte has just been born. The anointing, however, has also an anti-Satanic sense. This sense, to be sure, is not brought out in the formula of the anointing itself; but it is clearly affirmed in the prayer which precedes the preface of consecration of the chrism on Holy Thursday:

". . . Lord, we pray You that by the anointing with this chrism You grant purification of soul and body to those who are coming to the bath of divine regeneration; so that, if any remnant of adverse spirits still adhere in them, it may go away on contact with this consecrated oil. Let no place be granted the evil spirits; let no opportunity be granted the deserting powers; let no possibility of hiding be given the perverse tempters; but, for Your servants who are coming to the faith and are to be cleansed by the operation of the Holy Spirit, may the preparation of this anointing be helpful toward the salvation they will receive in the sacrament of baptism by means of the birth of heavenly regeneration."[41]

The terms of this prayer permit us to state that, according to the mind of the ancient Church, all the anointings made with the chrism have a very marked anti-demoniac sense.

Confirmation

This observation holds particularly for confirmation, an anointing which

[38] I, 44; ed. Wilson, pp. 85–86.

[39] Cf., e.g., Tertullian, *De baptismo*, 5, 2–5 (PL 1, 1204–1205).

[40] Cf. Jean Daniélou, *The Bible and the Liturgy*, pp. 36–37.

[41] *The Gelasian Sacramentary*, I, 40; ed. Wilson, p. 70. This prayer is now used for the blessing of the oil of the catechumens. In the Roman Pontifical, the anti-Satanic sense of the anointings made with the chrism and with the oil of the catechumens is underlined again by the exorcisms made over the oil before it is blessed and also by the last stanza of the hymn *O Redemptor*: "Do You see fit to consecrate, O King of the everlasting country, this juice of olive, as a sign of life against the claims of the devils."

the neophyte receives from the bishop immediately after his baptism. Moreover, since confirmation is the seal and, as it were, the fulfilment of baptism, it is normal that, among other ends, confirmation have the end of strengthening the new Christian for that fight against Satan which he will have to wage throughout his life, though under conditions which are no longer those that prevailed before his baptism.

This idea is expressed, for example, in the prayer for the blessing of the chrism in the euchology of Serapion: "God of hosts, protector of everyone who turns to You and places himself in Your powerful hand and under Your only-begotten Son, we call upon You, that, through the divine and invisible power of our Lord and Savior Jesus Christ, You give this chrism a divine and heavenly power. May the baptized who will be anointed with it, with the salutary sign of the cross of the only-begotten Son, by which Satan and all the hostile powers have been routed and discouraged, be regenerated and renewed by the bath of regeneration. May they become sharers more and more in the gift of the Spirit. Fortified by this seal, may they remain stable and immovable, unhurt and inviolable, protected from threats and surprises, living in the faith and the knowledge of the truth to the very end, and awaiting the hope of life and of the eternal promises of our Lord and Savior Jesus Christ."[42]

And St. Cyril of Jerusalem explains thus the anointing at confirmation, which in Jerusalem was done on the breast: "Then you have been anointed on the breast, that, clothed with the breastplate of justice, you may be able to withstand the surprises of the devil. For, just as Christ after His baptism and the descent upon Him of the Holy Spirit, went out to do battle against the adversary, so also you, after the sacred baptism and the mystical anointing, clothed with the complete armor of the Holy Spirit, stand against the hostile powers and make war on them, saying, 'I can do all things in Him who strengthens me, in Christ.'"[43]

The Eucharist

The initiation of the new Christian, freed from the bondage of Satan and enrolled in the *ecclesia*, finds its completion only in the participation in the Eucharistic sacrifice. And, to be sure, it is above all the positive aspect — the new life in Christ — which is brought forward in the Eucharistic liturgy. Still, following St. Paul, who noted the total opposition between the table of the Lord and the table of demons (1 Cor. 10:20–21), tradition has often pointed out the meaning of participation in the Eucharist as struggle against Satan.

A secret prayer of the Leonine sacramentary, repeated later by other sacramentaries, makes this petition: "All-powerful, eternal God, who command

[42] *Sacram. Serap.*, 25, 16; ed. Funk, II, 186–187.

[43] *Catech.* 21, 4 (PG 33, 1092). Cf. *Catech.*

3, 13 (PG 33, 444), and 17, 35–37 (PG 33, 1009–1012).

those who participate in Your table to abstain from the diabolical banquet, grant to Your people, we pray You, that, rejecting a taste for profane and deadly food, they may approach with pure minds the banquet of eternal salvation." [44]

During the night of Easter, while going from the baptistry to the church, where they would participate in the sacrifice for the first time, the neophytes solemnly chanted Psalm 22, which they had learned during Lent. When they came to the words "You have prepared before me a table in the face of those who attack me," it was easy for them to understand these words as referring to the Eucharist as protection and weapon against Satan.

This is the interpretation proposed to them by St. Cyril of Jerusalem, who, after having insisted on the reality of Christ's body and blood in the Eucharist, continues, "The blessed David explains all its force to you when he says, 'You have prepared before me a table in the face of those who attack me.' Here is what he means: 'Before Your coming, the demons had prepared for men a table contaminated and polluted and full of diabolical influence. But after Your coming, Lord, You have prepared a table before me.' When man says to God, 'You have prepared a table before me,' what else does he mean but the mystical and spiritual table which God prepares for us in the face of the devils, that is, against them? And rightly: the former table was communion with the demons, but this one is communion with God." [45]

The theme of the Eucharist as protection and weapon against Satan recurs often in the Fathers.

Let us cite St. John Chrysostom: "God has given me also another weapon of protection. Of what kind? He has prepared a table for me, He has shown me a food with which He will fill me, that after I have been refreshed here I may overcome the enemy with more strength. When the enemy sees you go out from the Lord's banquet, he flees you as if you were a lion breathing fire from your mouth. Faster than the wind he leaves you and does not dare approach. When that cruel enemy sees your tongue red with blood, believe me, he does not resist. When he sees your mouth glowing red, he turns back, terrified." [46]

And St. Cyril of Alexandria says, "Consider again how useful it is to touch His holy flesh. It puts to flight many ailments and a throng of demons, it subverts the power of the devil and in a moment heals a great multitude. . . . May He (Jesus) touch us also, therefore, or better, may we touch Him in the mystical *eulogia*, that He may free us from infirmity of soul, from the devils' attacks and tyranny." [47]

[44] *Sacram. leon.*, n. 76; ed. Mohlberg, II, 11; *The Gelasian Sacramentary*, I, 9; ed. Wilson, p. 9; Ambrosian Missal, *oratio super populum* for the feast of the Circumcision.

[45] *Catech.* 22, 7 (PG 33, 1101). Cf. Jean Daniélou, *The Bible and the Liturgy*, pp. 177–183.

[46] *Homily to the Baptized* (rejected by Migne, but now considered authentic), in Jesús Solano's *Textos eucaristicos primitivos*, I, n. 952.

[47] *In Lucam*, 4 (PG 72, 552); Jesús Solano, *Textos eucaristicos primitivos*, II, n. 606. Cf. *De adorat. in sp. et verit.*, 3 (PG 68, 285); J. Solano, *ibid.*, n. 533.

How common among the faithful was this belief in the efficacy of the Eucharist against the spirits of evil, is demonstrated by this story of St. Augustine's: "Hesperius, a former tribune, lives in our region. He has a farm at Fussala, called Zubedi. Having observed that his house was being subjected to the harmful influence of evil spirits, who afflicted his animals and his servants, in my absence he asked our priests that one of them should come to the place to pray and cast out the devils. One of them went. There he offered the sacrifice of Christ's body, praying with all his heart that the vexation cease. By God's mercy, it ceased immediately." [48]

Still more characteristic, perhaps, was the ancient custom of giving the Eucharist even to the possessed, on condition that they behave suitably and show themselves submissive to the Church; for it was held that this was the best remedy against possession and that it would be dangerous to deprive these sick people of it.

Thus canon 41 of the Council of Orange in 441 prescribes, "If possessed persons already baptized are taking measures for their own purification, delivering themselves to the care of the clergy and obeying their orders, by all means let them communicate, that they may be protected by the power of the sacrament from the attacks of the devil who infests them, or that their purgation may continue if they are already on the way to being cleansed." [49]

In the *Conferences* of Cassian, Abbot Serenus criticizes the custom in certain churches of excluding the possessed permanently from communion: "We do not recall that holy communion was ever forbidden them by our elders. Rather, they thought that, if possible, holy communion should be administered to them even daily. For you must not think that holy communion thus becomes the food of devils, according to that gospel saying, 'Do not give holy things to dogs,' which you have wrongly interpreted in this sense. Rather, it becomes protection for soul and body. When the possessed person receives holy communion, it burns the spirit who dwells in his members or who seeks to hide himself there, and puts him to rout as if it were a fire. Recently we have seen Abbot Andronicus and many others cured by this means. On the other hand, the enemy will keep harassing the possessed person more and more if he sees him deprived of this heavenly medicine. The longer he finds him kept away from this spiritual remedy, the more intensely and frequently will he tempt him." [50]

This awareness of the value of the Eucharist as protection against the devil rendered still more obvious, in the ancient Church, the seriousness and the danger of excommunication: one who had been cut off from ecclesiastical communion could no longer take part in the Eucharist, and he found himself exposed defenseless to Satan's attacks.

That is the reason, says St. Leo, that this penalty should be inflicted only

---

[48] *De civ. Dei*, XXII, 8, 6 (PL 41, 764).
[49] Hefele-Leclercq, *Histoire des Conciles*, II,

I (Paris: Letouzey et Ané, 1908), 442–443.
[50] *Conference* 7, 30 (PL 49, 709–710).

in the most serious cases and after mature consideration: "Communion must not be easily denied to any Christian. And this decision must not be made by a bishop in anger. . . . We have known some to be excluded from the grace of communion for deeds and words of little moment. Thus a soul for which Christ's blood was poured out, being punished with such cruel torture, has been abandoned wounded and, as it were, unarmed and stripped of all defense, an easy prey to the devil's attacks." [51]

The liturgies also echo this idea.

Thus, the anaphora of book VIII of the *Apostolic Constitutions* makes explicit mention of it in the epiclesis, which asks for the coming of the Holy Spirit on the offerings, "that He may make this bread the body of Your Christ and this chalice the blood of Your Christ, so that all those who partake of them will be strengthened in the true religion, will obtain remission of their sins, will be defended from the devil and from his frauds." [52]

The same idea is found again in this postcommunion of the Leonine sacramentary: "We pray You, Lord, that, having received Your mysteries with reverence, we may be armed against the weakness of our condition and against the devil's ambush." [53] Then there is this secret from the Gelasian sacramentary: "May Your sacraments, Lord, guard us and protect us always against diabolical attacks." [54] The same idea is expressed again in this *Post pridie* of the Mozarabic liturgy: "Sanctify the mystery, O Lord, give joy to the minister, illuminate the temple, decorate the altar, give order to the people, cure the sick, grant healing, listen to the prayers, that all, freed from the devil's deceits, may fear not him who lies in ambush for them but Him who cures them." [55]

This whole exposition should make us understand how essential in the ancient discipline of the Christian initiation was the idea of the Redemption and the Christian life as a struggle against Satan and as liberation from Satan's rule. Original sin, the situation of hostility toward God resulting from it, man's need to be freed from Satan's power — all this was affirmed so clearly and so concretely in the baptismal liturgy that Christian antiquity was preserved from all tendency to naturalism. If this liturgy recovered

---

[51] *Ep.* 10, ch. 8 (PL 54, 635). The context shows that the concern is indeed with Eucharistic communion (cf. note b of the editor in PL), which, from the fifth century on, could be designated by the term *communio* alone (cf. A. Blaise, *Dictionnaire latin-français des auteurs chrétiens*, under the word *communio*, 5). Thus the idea of St. Paul that one who is excommunicated is abandoned to Satan (1 Cor. 5:5; 1 Tim. 1:20) has its concrete application in the lot of one who is deprived of Eucharistic communion. This is normal, since communion in the sacrifice is the efficacious sign of ecclesiastical communion.

It might be asked whether the ancient custom of placing the consecrated host in the mouth or on the breast of the deceased did not also have an antidemoniac significance. Cf. Righetti, II, 390 f.

[52] *Const. apost.*, VIII, 12, 39; ed. Funk, I, 510; ed. Quasten, *Monumenta eucharistica et liturgica vetustissima*, IV, p. 46.

[53] *Sacram. leon.*, n. 1304; ed. Mohlberg, II, 167.

[54] III, 11; ed. Wilson, p. 230. This is the secret of the fifteenth Sunday after Pentecost in the Roman Missal.

[55] *Liber moz. sacr.*; ed. Férotin, n. 1395.

something of its old strength, would not the danger of naturalism which threatens Christians in our day be lessened perceptibly?

5. The Struggle against Satan in the Liturgy of the Sacraments Other than Those of the Initiation

The theme of the struggle against Satan appears not only in the sacraments of the initiation, but also in the others.

The liturgy of penance

It is quite natural that penance was considered as a second baptism. This idea is valid for the sacrament of penance as such, whatever be the disciplinary and liturgical form in which it is clothed. It was easier to grasp, however, and more effective when this sacrament had a public character and was given only once in a lifetime. For then it was not only by its effects but also by its non-repetition that it appeared as a second baptism, and the parallelism with the first baptism was thereby more sharply outlined.[56]

At any rate, it was easy to pass from the idea of penance as the new or second baptism to the idea of penance as the new or second liberation from that bondage to Satan into which the Christian has fallen again by the sins committed after baptism. Here is how Tertullian, for example, presents the matter to us:

"Reluctantly I speak of a second, rather a last, hope, for fear that in mentioning penance as a remedy still available, I seem to allow room for sinning again. . . . Let no one decide to be more perverse because God is more clement, returning to sin every time he is pardoned. . . . We have escaped once; let us not expose ourselves further to danger, with the hope of getting out unhurt. . . . But the implacable enemy never stops using his evil arts; rather, he becomes most furious when he sees a person fully liberated; he blazes up most, just when he is being extinguished. It is inevitable that he grieve and groan to see so many works of death destroyed in a person by the pardon of sins; to see wiped out so many entries which were going to stand in the record for that person's condemnation. He is maddened at the thought of that same sinner, now become a servant of Christ, one day judging himself and his angels. That is why he spies on the person, attacks him, besieges him, to see whether by some means he can either blind the eyes through fleshly concupiscence, or entrap the mind with worldly allurements, or shake the

---

[56] Cf., e.g., a fragment of the anonymous *Contra Novatianos*, published among the works of St. Athanasius (PG 26, 1316): "Just as the man baptized by a priest is enlightened by the grace of the Holy Spirit, so likewise he who makes his confession in penance obtains forgiveness through the priest by the grace of Christ." The same idea is found in St. Leo, *Ep.* 108, 2 (PL 54, 1011): "God's manifold mercy comes to the aid of fallen mankind in such a way that the hope of eternal life is restored not only through the grace of baptism but also through the medicine of penance." The *Shepherd of Hermas* calls baptism the first penance and canonical penance the second penance, to which recourse can be had only once (*Mand.* IV, 3).

faith through the fear of the secular power, or make the person decline from the right road by means of perverse doctrines. He will keep tempting the person, trying to trip him up. Hence God, foreseeing these murderous arts of his, has still left another way open, although the door of baptismal innocence is closed and barred. He has placed in the vestibule the door of the second repentance, which opens to whoever knocks on it; but only for one time, because this is already the second time; and after this no more: the next knock will go unanswered." [57]

After such assertions, it is normal that the development of the liturgy of penance should have led to the expression in the rites themselves of this idea that the sinner's fall is due to the devil's instigation, his envy, his cunning, [58] and that the sinner's return to divine grace and to communion with the Church is a liberation from Satan's power.

It was by excommunication that the sinner was placed officially among the penitents. This juridical and public act which separated the Christian from the community and denied him participation in the sacraments was considered as an abandonment into the hands of Satan "for the death of the flesh, that the spirit may be saved." [59]

The Middle Ages gave the scene a dramatic character. [60] And the present Pontifical, which is still quite medieval, brings out this aspect of excommunication: ". . . we separate him from the reception of the precious body and blood of the Lord and from the society of all the Christians and exclude him from the pale of Holy Mother Church in heaven and on earth. We declare him excommunicated and anathematized. We judge him damned to everlasting fire with the devil and his angels and all the reprobate, until he shall disentangle himself from the snares of the devil, return to correction and to penance and satisfy the Church of God which he has injured. We abandon him to Satan for the death of the flesh that his spirit may be saved in the day of judgment." [61]

The same idea appears in the prayers for public penitents said during the Mass. Thus, according to book VIII of the *Apostolic Constitutions*, the dismissal of the penitents is preceded by a litany which begins in this way: "Penitents, pray. All of us make ardent supplication for our brethren who are in penance, that the merciful God show them the way of repentance, receive their self-accusation and confession, 'speedily crush Satan under their feet' (Rom. 16:20), free them from 'the devil's snares' (2 Tim. 2:26) and from the violence of the demons, and keep them from every unlawful word, every shameful action and every evil thought." [62]

---

[57] *De poenit.*, 7, 2–10 (PL 1, 1240–1241).

[58] Cf., e.g., the prayers for the reconciliation of penitents in *The Gelasian Sacramentary*, I, 38–39; ed. Wilson, pp. 63–68. There it is recalled that man has been led into sin "invidia diaboli . . . diabolica fraude . . . diabolica incursione."

[59] 1 Cor. 5:5. Cf. St. Leo, *Ep.*, 10, ch. 8 (PL 54, 635), cited at note 51 above.

[60] Righetti, IV, 192 f.

[61] *Ordo excomm. et absolv.*, last part of the anathema *Quia diabolo suadente*.

[62] *Const. apost.*, VIII, 9, 2; ed. Funk, I, 484.

In such a perspective the reconciliation of the penitents was naturally regarded as their liberation from the power of Satan. St. Jerome tells us all the essentials in a few words: "The bishop offers his oblation for the layman, lays his hands on him, invokes upon him the return of the Holy Spirit, and thus, making the people pray, reconciles to the altar the one who had been abandoned to Satan for the death of the flesh that the spirit might be saved. He does not restore a member to health until all the members have wept together. The father readily forgives the son if the mother in her commiseration prays him to do so." [63]

The formulas of reconciliation in the Gelasian sacramentary ask: "that the enemy not exult in the harm done to Your family . . . that the enemy no longer have power over his soul . . . . Renew in him, most kind Father, whatever has been corrupted by earthly frailty or violated by diabolical fraud." [64] The same ideas are found again, magnificently developed, in several collects of the Mozarabic liturgy.[65]

The liturgy of the sick

The liturgy of the sick has always comprised and still comprises: penance, the anointings with oil, the viaticum and the "commendation of the soul." In all of this the anti-Satanic aspect is conspicuous. And this will be no cause for surprise if we remember the connection in the New Testament between sin, sickness, death and Satan, as also between liberation from sin, liberation from sickness, liberation from death and liberation from Satan. We may recall, for example, what is said in Mark 6:12-13 about the mission of the twelve: "And going out, they preached that men should do penance; and they cast out many devils, and anointed many of the sick with oil and cured them."

The idea of the struggle against Satan is expressed already in the formula for blessing the oil which will serve to anoint the sick. The most ancient text known is that of the *Apostolic Tradition* of Hippolytus.[66] But the custom is probably even more ancient: St. Irenaeus speaks of gnostics who had the custom of anointing with oil mixed with water the faithful who were about to die, "that the dead may not be taken and kept by the superior principalities and powers, and that their inner man, invisibly, may rise higher." [67]

---

[63] *Adv. lucif.*, 5 (PL 23, 159).

[64] *The Gelasian Sacramentary*, I, 38–39; ed. Wilson, pp. 65–66.

[65] *Liber ordinum*, prayers *Placabilem autem* and *Adiuvate me*; ed. Férotin, cols. 98 and 100.

[66] *Trad. apost.*, 5; ed. Dix, p. 10.

[67] *Adv. haer.*, I, 21, 5 (PG 7, 666–667). The text is cited by C. Ruch in the article *Extrême onction* in the *Dict. de théol. cath.*, V, cols. 1931 f. He observes that, on the testimony of

Irenaeus himself, "the gnostics in their worship used, indiscriminately, gross and superstitious practices, ceremonies derived from the pagan mystery cults, and more or less disfigured Christian rites. . . . One may justifiably ask, therefore, whether the Marcosian ceremony is not a transposition of a Catholic rite intended to save the soul from sin and from the devil, to do away with the obstacles which would prevent it from reaching paradise."

In the East the first formulas of blessing already affirm the anti-Satanic import of the anointing: "In the name of Your only-begotten Son Jesus Christ we bless these creatures; we pronounce over this water and this oil the name of Him who suffered, was crucified, arose and is seated at the right hand of the Unbegotten. Grant curative powers to these creatures, that whoever drinks of them or is anointed with them may be freed from every fever, from every demon, from every sickness; may they be a remedy of healing and of wholeness for those who receive them in the name of Your only-begotten Son . . . ." [68] Or again: "Sanctify, through Christ, this water and this oil . . . give them healing power, to banish ills, put the devils to flight, foil every ambush." [69]

The Roman sacramentaries provide only one collect for the blessing of the oil of the sick, in which the idea of struggle against Satan remains implicit. [70] But in the ninth century a very explicit exorcism takes its place before this collect. [71]

In the present ritual of extreme unction there are constant reminders of the anti-Satanic character of the sacrament. On entering, the priest sprinkles the sick-room with holy water and asks, "Let no demons have access here; let the angels of peace be present." He invokes Christ's blessing on those who live there, asking that He turn away all hostile powers from them, rescue them from all dread and bewilderment, and that God send His angel "to watch over, cherish, protect, be with, and defend all who live in this house." [72] Before proceeding to the anointings, the priest says a prayer which is none other than the formula employed in the eleventh century for the anointing of the head: "In the name of the Father, and of the Son, and of the Holy Spirit. May any power that the devil has over you be utterly destroyed, as I place my hands on you . . . ." [73]

The theological meaning of extreme unction is well expressed in the Mozarabic liturgy by an antiphon which simply brings together three passages from the gospel: "The Lord said to His disciples, 'Receive the Holy Spirit'; 'In My name cast out the devils'; and 'Lay your hands upon the sick and they shall be healed.'" [74] To sanctify the soul, to expel devils, to heal the body — such indeed are the three ends of the sacrament of the sick according to the liturgy and tradition.

After the anointings the viaticum is in order. What we have said above about the value of the Eucharist as protection against Satan allows us to understand how fitting is the formula which accompanies this rite: "Receive, my

[68] *Sacram. Serap.*, 17; ed. Funk, II, 178–180.

[69] *Const. apost.*, VIII, 29, 3; ed. Funk, I, 532.

[70] *The Gelasian Sacramentary*, I, 40, collect *Emitte, quaesumus*; ed. Wilson, p. 70. This collect has been kept by the Roman Pontifical.

[71] At first this was the exorcism *Exorcizo te, creatura olei*, now used for the blessing of the chrism; now it is the *Exorcizo te, immundissime spiritus*.

[72] *Ordo ministr. sacram. extremae unctionis*, n. 5.

[73] *Ibid.*, n. 7.

[74] *Liber ordinum*; ed. Férotin, col. 72.

brother, this food for your journey, the body of our Lord Jesus Christ, that He may guard you from the malicious enemy and lead you into everlasting life. Amen." [75]

The *commendatio animae* is the last liturgical act by which the Church assists the living. The prayer *Commendo* especially develops the idea of the struggle against Satan. This prayer, which is taken from a letter of St. Peter Damian, is partly an expression of hopes or desires and partly exorcistic in character. After having expressed the hope that the angels and the saints will come to meet the soul, it continues, "May the most foul tempter with his mob fall back before you. May he tremble at your coming with your escort of angels and flee into the dread chaos of eternal night. . . . May shame and confusion strike the cohorts of hell; and may the slaves of the tempter not dare to bar your way."

These last words seem to echo the ancient belief that souls in their ascent toward heaven are subjected to a series of trials and examinations by the devils. Very likely this imaginative way of representing the soul's voyage underlies also the fourteen petitions, "Deliver, O Lord, the soul of Your servant . . . ."

The liturgy of the ordination of exorcists

In the liturgy of ordination, the idea of the fight against the devil is manifest above all in the existence of the order of exorcist and in the rites for that order.

It is known that the power to exorcize was regarded at first in the Church as a personal charism, with which any Christian might be endowed. The exercise of this charism, however, must have been subjected very soon to the control of the hierarchy, so as to constitute an official function, at least in the West; for, around 251, exorcists are mentioned along with lectors and ostiaries in a letter of Pope St. Cornelius to Fabian of Antioch; [76] but this does not mean necessarily that the office of exorcist was regarded henceforth as an order properly so called. [77]

At the end of the fourth century, in the East, the *Apostolic Constitutions* specify, "The exorcist is not ordained by the laying-on of hands. This reward given to combatants depends on the free benevolence and grace of God through Christ in the outpouring of the Holy Spirit. The identity of one who receives the charism of healing is indicated by a divine manifestation, which makes known to all the grace that is in him." [78]

The manner and form of the ordination of exorcists are known from the seventh canon of the so-called Fourth Council of Carthage, a text which dates from the end of the fourth to the end of the sixth century: "When the

[75] *De communione infirmorum*, n. 19.

[76] Fragment preserved by Eusebius, *Hist. eccl.*, VI, 43, 11; ed. Bardy (Sources chrétiennes), II, 156. Cf. St. Cyprian, *Ep.* 23; ed. Bayard, I, 62.

[77] Cf. articles "Exorcisme" by H. R. Philippeau and "Exorcistat" by A. Bride in *Catholicisme*, IV, cols. 941–947.

[78] *Const. apost.*, VIII, 26, 2; ed. Funk, I, 528.

exorcist is ordained, the bishop gives him the book in which the exorcisms are written, saying, 'Receive it and commit it to memory, and have power to lay your hands on the possessed person, whether he be baptized or catechumen.'"[79] With slight modifications, this formula is still included in the Roman Pontifical.

The other texts comprised in this ordination — an admonition and two prayers — insist on the idea that the exorcists receive the *potestas*, the *potestas et imperium*, to cast out devils; they are *imperatores spirituales* and at the same time *medici probabiles*, endowed with the gift or the charism of healing (*gratia curationum*).

Although the exorcists soon had to relinquish the greater part of their functions to the higher clergy, the existence of their order shows how seriously the Church regards her struggle against Satan. Today the order of exorcist is nothing more than a step toward the priesthood, and the exorcism of the possessed is most often reserved to specially delegated priests. Still, the fact that every priest continues to receive these powers, and to use them, moreover, in the virtual exorcisms over things or over catechumens, shows clearly that, in the mind of the Church, the fight against the devils remains an ever-present reality.[80]

The liturgy of marriage

In the ritual of marriage also, the idea of the struggle against Satan has left some traces. One of the motives for the Church's insistence on blessing a Christian marriage is to protect the new home from those attacks of the devil to which St. Paul alludes (1 Cor. 7:2–5).

What must be done, says St. John Chrysostom, is "to call in the priests and by prayers and blessings to reinforce the unity of sentiment which should prevail in marriage, that the husband's love and the wife's chastity may increase; that everything may tend to introduce virtue into the house; that all the devil's machinations may be removed; and that the partners themselves, united with the help of God, may lead a happy life."[81]

The liturgy has followed through this idea, and the theme of the protection of the newly married against the devil is found in the most ancient formularies of the marriage ritual that have come down to us. The Leonine sacramentary contains a solemn blessing of the bride in which God is asked to give her all the virtues, all the strength necessary, that "the excommunicated father of lies may usurp no power over her."[82] The Gelasian sacramentary gives, besides this blessing, the text of a prayer to be said over the couple after com-

---

[79] Hefele-Leclercq, *Histoire des Conciles*, II, 1, p. 112.

[80] Mention is still made of the Church's struggle against the powers of darkness in the admonition which precedes the ordination to the diaconate.

[81] *In Gen. hom.* 48, 6 (PG 54, 443).

[82] N. 1110; ed. Mohlberg, II, 140, 11, 24–25: "Nihil ex hac subsicibus ille auctor praevaricationis usurpet." This clause is found again, somewhat altered, in the nuptial blessing of the Roman Ritual.

munion, in which God is asked especially to "fend off all the attacks of the enemy, that even in marriage they may imitate the holiness of the Fathers." [83]

In the sixth-seventh century, if not earlier, there appears the blessing of the bridal chamber, still mentioned in our ritual. A great many formulas used for this blessing implore the Lord to ward off from the nuptial chamber all attacks of evil spirits and all wrongdoing.[84] No doubt the Middle Ages were too ready to believe that the devils often rendered marriages sterile by recourse to supernatural means. Still it is accurate to say that every evil is somehow the expression of a Satanic influence; hence the Church makes no mistake in asking God to protect the new home from any action of Satan.

Our ritual has also a blessing for an expectant mother, in which God is asked to watch over His handmaid and to defend her against all persecution and spite of the enemy.[85] Such a prayer was inspired in the Church not by a childish fear of the devil, but by a supernatural conception of the history of salvation, that history of which God is the master, but a master who leaves some real power in the hands of the adversary.

6. The Struggle against Satan in Some Sacramentals

In the two preceding sections we have studied, along with the sacraments, the principal rites which accompany them and bring out all their riches. Hence our present inquiry will bear only on those sacramentals which have no direct connection with the sacraments.

One need only peruse the Ritual and the Pontifical now in use to be impressed by the great number of rites in which the theme of the struggle against Satan and his kingdom appears in a more or less vivid fashion. An enumeration has shown this theme recurs in about fifty of the sacramentals, in connection with the most varied circumstances in the life of the Christian and of the Church, from the blessing of a house or that of a lime-kiln to the consecration of a virgin, the dedication of a church or the liturgy of the departed.[86] We shall confine ourselves here to a few remarks on the blessing and the use of holy water, the prayers against bad weather, the consecration of virgins, the monastic profession and the liturgy of the departed.

Holy water

The use of water blessed for a purpose outside of baptism seems to have found little favor in the Church of the first centuries, as being too much like the lustrations to which Judaism, paganism and certain heterodox sects had recourse.[87] But in the East, apparently from the fourth century, there is a trace of a blessing of water and of its ritual use outside of baptism.

The sacramentary of Serapion contains a prayer meant originally for the

[83] III, 52; ed. Wilson, p. 267.
[84] These formulas will be found in A. Franz, *Die kirchlichen Benediktionen im Mittelalter* (Freiburg im B.: Herder, 1909), II, 180–185.
[85] *Rituale Romanum*, VIII, 5.

[86] Cf. Egon von Petersdorff, "De daemonibus in liturgia memoratis," *Angelicum*, 19 (1942), 326–328.
[87] Tertullian, *De baptismo*, 5 (PL 1, 1204–1205).

blessing of the oil of the sick, later adapted to serve also for blessing bread or water: "We call upon You, who have all power and strength, Savior of all men, Father of our Lord and Savior Jesus Christ, and we pray You to send from heaven the healing power of Your only-begotten Son upon this oil, that for those who will be anointed with it — or who will receive these creatures — it may serve to keep away all disease and infirmity, as an antidote against every devil, to put every impure spirit to flight, to expel every evil spirit, to extirpate every fever or chill or debility, to receive grace and the remission of sins, that it may be for them a remedy of life and of salvation, restoring health and wholeness to the soul, the body and the mind, and giving perfect salvation. O Lord, may every diabolical action, every demon, every assault of the adversary, every wound, every torment, every sorrow, every pain or thrust or jolt or evil shade, fear Your holy name which we are now invoking, and the name of Your only-begotten Son, and keep away from the interior and the exterior of Your servants, that glory may be given to the name of Him who for us was crucified, who rose from the dead, who bore our sorrows and our wounds, and who will come to judge the living and the dead." [88]

It is hardly necessary to point out the anti-Satanic value this text gives to the use of the blessed oil or water. It will be noted likewise that the themes developed in this prayer are very close to those that will be found later in the formulas for the blessing of water.

In the West, the blessing and the use of holy water appear in the course of the sixth century. The ancient Gelasian sacramentary already contains the complete rite: blessing of the water, exorcisms over the water and the salt, prayers for the sprinkling; [89] and most of these formulas are found again in the *Ordo ad faciendam aquam benedictam* of the Roman Ritual. There God is asked to purify from all diabolical influence the persons, things and places on which the holy water will be sprinkled:

"Pour into this element the power of Your blessing, that Your creature, serving Your mysteries, may have supernatural power for expelling demons and curing diseases. Whatever this water sprinkles in the homes of the faithful, let it be preserved from every impurity, delivered from all harm. Let no harmful spirit dwell there, no breath of corruption; may all the traps of the hidden enemy be removed, and may everything opposed to the safety and repose of those who live there be put to flight by the sprinkling of this water; and thus may the well-being implored with the invocation of Your holy name be safe against every attack."

Very soon, holy water was employed in most of the liturgical blessings; and today it is still, with the sign of the cross, the most frequently used sacra-

---

[88] *Sacram. Serap.*, 29; ed. Funk, II, 190–192. It appears that this prayer was composed for the blessing of oil, but later employed also for bread and water. To the original title "prayer for the oil of the sick" have been added the words "or for bread or water"; and in the body of the prayer itself has been inserted the mention of "these creatures," which fits the context poorly.

[89] III, 75–76; ed. Wilson, pp. 285–288.

mental. This constant recourse to holy water shows us how important a place the struggle against Satan holds in the life of the Church, and should hold likewise in the life of every Christian.

Prayers against bad weather

The sprinkling of holy water finds a place in the "procession for averting tempest" which the Roman Ritual provides.[90] While the bells are sounding, the litany is recited, followed by Psalm 147, some versicles and five collects; one of them, which is found also in the missal among the collects against bad weather, is conceived thus: "We pray You, Lord, that the spirits of iniquity be driven away from Your family, and the scourge of stormy skies depart."

This rite is a modest vestige of a practice very popular in the Middle Ages, the blessing or conjuration of storms.[91] It was inspired by the notion, an accurate one, that bad weather, in so far as it does harm to man, is due somehow to the devil's action; but, since the distinction was not well drawn between natural and supernatural means used by the devil, this practice easily degenerated into superstition.

The consecration of virgins

We have recalled above how the Church of the first centuries, making explicit the data of the New Testament, regarded the life of virgins and of monks as eminent forms of the struggle which the Christian carries on against Satan. In the liturgy this theme is quite apparent in the rites of the consecration of virgins and of monastic profession.

The most ancient formula for the consecration of virgins is found in the Leonine sacramentary; it is the preface of consecration still used in our days.[92] In it God is asked to accept the offering of the virgin and grant her the graces necessary for the fulfilment of her vow.

In this framework of prayer is sketched a theology of Christian virginity, which begins by recalling the fall of man, deceived by the devil, then shows how God, to lift him up again, inspires in chosen souls the desire of a greater perfection and a total consecration, which gives them the strength to overcome even the deepest tendencies of nature.

These souls have a particular need of divine grace, for the ancient enemy rages against them in a very special way. May God therefore grant them His protection, "that the ancient enemy, who surrounds the nobler resolutions with more subtle traps in his desire to spoil the palm of perfect continence, may not insinuate himself through some negligence of the mind and rob those who have made a vow of virginity of that which should be found even

---

[90] X, 8: *De processionibus ad repellendam tempestatem.*

[91] Cf. Righetti, IV, 399 ff.; A. Franz, *Die kirchlichen Benediktionen im Mittelalter,* II,

49–123.

[92] *Sacram. leon.,* n. 1104; ed. Mohlberg, II, 138–139.

in the conduct of married women." The whole life of the consecrated virgins, then, will be a struggle against Satan.

The same theme recurs in the prayer *Deus plasmator corporum* of the present Pontifical: "They desire to live in Your grace. May the champion of evil and enemy of good, fail in his efforts to gain title of ownership over these vessels consecrated to Your name." And the prayer *Exaudi* for the blessing of the garments asks that these "be a strong armor of defense against all the arrows of the enemy."

The monastic profession

Since the monastic profession has been considered as a second baptism, a good deal of thought has been given to establishing a certain parallelism between the rites of profession and those of baptism.[93] Just as the convert turns away from paganism to embrace a new life, so the monk leaves the world to enter a state of perfection. Like baptism, therefore, the monastic profession is a renunciation of Satan and his pomps and an adherence to Christ, and the monk's whole life is a struggle against the devil.

These themes are already expressed, with a thoroughly Roman sobriety, in the prayer "for those who are renouncing the world" of the Gelasian sacramentary, a prayer which seems to be the ancient Roman formula for the consecration of a monk: "Be pleased, Lord, we pray You, to open the doors of Your grace to Your servants who are renouncing the pomps of the world and who, despising the devil, are taking refuge under the banner of Christ. Receive with a favorable countenance those who come to You, that the enemy may not be able to triumph over them. Grant them the aid of Your unwearying arm; surround their minds with the armor of the faith, that, happily protected on all sides as by a wall, they may feel the joy of having escaped the world."[94]

The same ideas are found again in the Mozarabic liturgy: "Receive, I pray You, Lord, this Your servant N. who is fleeing to You from the tempest of this world and the entrapments of the devil, that in being received by You he may feel the joy of being saved from the present world and rewarded by You in the world to come."[95]

It will be noticed that in these texts the struggle against the devil is presented as a flight: to make profession of the monastic life is to flee the world and the devil, to withdraw from their dangerous company.

In the primitive monastic tradition the concern was not with fleeing, but with attacking: to make profession was to engage oneself in a still more violent struggle against the devil, to go out and provoke him. The concept is preserved in the Greek Euchology, which has also kept in an explicit way the idea of the monastic profession as second baptism.

[93] Cf. Ph. Oppenheim, "Mönchsweihe und Taufritus," *Miscellanea Mohlberg*, I, 259 ff.

[94] III, 82; ed. Wilson, p. 290.
[95] *Liber ordinum*; ed. Férotin, col. 86.

To the monk who is going to receive the great habit and make profession, the priest declares, "Brother, today you receive the second baptism, in the superabundance of the gifts of the merciful God; and you are purified of your sins and become a son of light." [96]

By reason of his state, the new monk will be obliged to fight harder against Satan: "And think no longer that in the life you have led hitherto you have struggled valiantly against the invisible powers of the enemy; but think that, from now on, you will have greater travails in the struggle against him. But he will not be able to conquer you if he finds you protected by a strong faith and charity towards Him who leads you, and by promptness to every obedience and humiliation." [97]

Finally the priest prays to God for the newly professed monk: "Arm him with Your power and clothe him with the panoply of Your Holy Spirit; for his fight is not against flesh and blood, but against principalities, against powers, against the rulers of the darkness of this world, against the spirits of evil. Gird his loins with the power of truth, and clothe him with the breastplate of Your justice and Your exultation, and equip his feet with readiness to spread the gospel of peace. Make him wise enough to take up the shield of faith with which he may ward off all the fiery darts of the Evil One, and to receive the helmet of salvation and the sword of the Spirit, which is Your word." [98]

Moreover, the various articles of the habit with which the new monk is clothed are regarded as the pieces of armor just mentioned. [99] Finally — a significant detail — the epistle read at the Mass of profession is precisely the passage of St. Paul's letter to the Ephesians (6:10–17) in which the Christian is invited to put on this armor and take these weapons in hand for the fight against Satan.

The liturgy of the departed

This theme of the anti-Satanic combat holds a prominent place also in the liturgy of the departed. We have already described how the ancients represented the voyage of the soul after death: the demons subject it to a series of examinations, while the angels come to its aid. It is in this perspective that the liturgy views the last battles of the Christian against the powers of evil. Here are some examples taken from the Gelasian sacramentary:

"Receive, O Lord, the soul of Your servant N., returning to You from the land of Egypt. Send Your holy angels to meet him, and show him the way of justice. Open the gates of justice to him, and drive the princes of darkness away." [100]

"Be pleased, O Lord, to give him a place of light, refreshment and peace. May he be permitted to pass the gates of hell and the ways of darkness, and

---

[96] Εὐχολόγιον (Rome: Polyglot Press, 1873), p. 242.

[97] Ibid., p. 243.

[98] Ibid., pp. 244–245.

[99] Ibid., p. 248.

[100] III, 91; ed. Wilson, p. 296.

dwell in the habitations of the saints, and in the holy light which You promised long ago to Abraham and to his descendants." [101]

"May Michael, the angel of Your covenant, assist him. Free his soul, Lord,
from the princes of darkness and from the places of punishment." [102]

In the historical and present-day liturgies, many other allusions, more or
less obvious, may be found to this perilous journey of the soul. The prayer
Deus cui proprium est of the funeral ritual asks God to watch over the soul
of the departed: "Do not deliver him into the enemy's hands, or put him out
of mind for ever, but command that his soul be taken up by the holy angels
and brought home to paradise."

Surely the most remarkable text is the offertory of the *Requiem* Mass, which
is developed completely in the framework of this imagery: "Lord Jesus
Christ, King of glory, free the souls of all the faithful departed from the pains
of hell and from the deep pit. Save them from the lion's jaws, that they may
not be the prey of Tartarus and may not fall into the darkness; but may St.
Michael, the standard-bearer, bring them into the holy light which You promised long ago to Abraham and to His posterity." [103]

This prayer and other similar prayers kept in our liturgy for the dead must
be understood in the light of the present theology of the Last Things. Today
they cannot be anything but prayers asking God to free the soul from the
pains of purgatory, whatever sense their author may originally have given
them, and whatever imagery he may have employed.

At any rate, it does remain true that as long as the soul is detained in
purgatory, we can speak of its struggle against Satan; for the fact that it does
not yet enjoy the beatific vision is a trace, or rather a consequence, of the
devil's power over souls since the fall of Adam. This power, with all its consequences, will be fully and definitively destroyed only at the general resurrection, as St. Paul proclaims: "The last enemy to be destroyed will be death"
(1 Cor. 15:26).

7. The Struggle against Satan in the Temporal and the Sanctoral

To complete our study of the struggle against Satan in the liturgy, we still
have to examine the liturgical cycles. This we shall do with the help of the
missal especially, and of the breviary occasionally.

The Christmas season

The time from Advent to the Epiphany has for its central theme the mystery of Christ as manifested coming of the Lord, prepared for, announced and

---

[101] *Ibid.*, p. 297.
[102] *Ibid.*, p. 298.
[103] On this offertory cf. Bonifacio M. Serpilli, *L'offertorio della Messa dei defunti* (Rome: Tip. Agostiniana, 1946); Marino Soressi,

"L'offertorio della messa dei defunti e l'esca-
tologia orientale," *Eph. lit.*, 61 (1947), 245–
252. It seems to have been composed for a
country in which the Eastern influence was felt,
probably Ireland.

prefigured in the Old Testament, realized historically in Palestine, realized *in mysterio* in the Church, and finally preparing for and prefiguring the manifested coming in the last times.

But, as is obvious in all the liturgies, Christ comes to save men, to ransom them; and this redemption necessarily involves a fight against Satan, from whose bondage man is to be freed. It may be expected that this aspect of the mystery will be brought to light in the Christmas cycle. Actually, in the present Roman Office, it hardly appears except in the hymn *Creator alme siderum* [104] and in the lessons of the second nocturn of Christmas, taken from a sermon of St. Leo, which bring out clearly the anti-Satanic meaning of the Incarnation:

"The Son of God, in the fulness of time fixed by the inscrutable divine counsel, assumed human nature to reconcile it with its Creator, that the author of death, the devil, might be conquered by that same nature which he himself had once conquered. In this conflict, which He joined for our sake, the Lord fought by rules of strict and perfect equity: the all-powerful God entered the lists with the cruel enemy not in His majesty but in our lowliness, opposing to him the same form and nature that we have, subject to mortality like ours, but free from all sin. . . . Be conscious, O Christian, of your dignity . . . remember that you have been snatched from the power of darkness and transported to the light and the kingdom of God." [105]

The same theme appears frequently in the ancient sacramentaries. Thus the Leonine gives these two prayers for the feast of the Nativity:

"Grant, we pray You, Lord our God, that He who was born today to destroy the devil and pardon sins, may purify us from the infiltration of sin and defend us against the attacks of the enemy." [106]

"O God, who have not allowed the human nature You created to perish by the malice of the devil, apply the remedies of Your mercy, that man may not be overcome by the enemy's deceit but rather obtain redemption from Your goodness." [107]

In the Gelasian sacramentary the idea is expressed that we need the divine protection against Satan to enable us to celebrate Advent and Christmas worthily:

"By virtue of these gifts, O Lord, we pray You, keep ever far from us the machinations of the devil, that we may celebrate with pure minds the Nativity of our Redeemer." [108]

---

[104] In the second and fourth stanzas. The original text of the second stanza, still kept in the monastic breviary, is not so explicit as the text established by the revision made under Urban VIII:

"Qui daemonis ne fraudibus	"Who, lest the fraud of hell's black king
Periret orbis, impetu	Should all men to destruction bring,
Amoris actus, languidi	Didst, by an act of generous love,
Mundi medela factus es."	The fainting world's physician prove."

[105] Second nocturn of Christmas, lessons 4–6.
[106] N. 1251; ed. Mohlberg, II, 160.
[107] N. 1272; ed. Mohlberg, II, 163.

[108] I, 3 (secret for the vigil of Christmas); ed. Wilson, p. 3.

"Hasten, Lord our God, do not delay, and free us by Your power from the devil's fury." [109]

The *Missale gothicum* asks God that the feast of Christmas free us from Satan,[110] and points out that Christ, by submitting to the law of circumcision, has made the devil's yoke fall from our neck.[111]

The Ambrosian Missal, in a preface for the feast of the Blessed Virgin on the sixth Sunday of Advent, establishes a parallel between Eve and Mary, and shows that Mary's action has destroyed the work that the devil had accomplished in Eve and through Eve.

Finally, in the Mozarabic Missal, the *Inlatio* of the fourth Sunday of Advent, recalling the manifested coming of Christ in its various phases, sees it as wholly directed toward the liberation of man from the slavery of Satan.[112]

Lent

It is in the Easter cycle, however, and especially in the season of Lent, that the theme of the struggle against Satan assumes the greatest importance. We have already indicated its place in the liturgy of the initiation and in the penitential liturgy, which were celebrated precisely during this period in ancient times.

But it is not only for catechumens and public penitents that Lent is preeminently the time for the fight against the devil; it is so for all the faithful who yearly celebrate and live the mystery of Christ the Redeemer. For the whole Church, Lent is the time of the annual retreat, centered on this mystery of Christ the Redeemer. Prepared for, announced, prefigured by the Old Testament, salvation was accomplished radically by Christ at the time of His earthly life, especially in His Passion and His glorification; now it is applied *in mysterio* to the catechumens and the penitents, as well as to all Christians; when the parousia comes, it will be perfected.

For all the faithful, the great means for realizing this mystery are, first of all, participation in the sacraments in their full liturgical dimension — sacraments of the initiation for the catechumens, penance and the Eucharist for the excommunicated, the Eucharist for the rest — and then also prayer, fasting, good works, almsgiving, reading and meditation of the Bible, and in general the more courageous practice of the Christian virtues.

Lent ought to be an intensification of the whole Christian life, centered on participation in the "paschal mysteries." It should be an effort on the part of all the faithful to approach temporarily the kind of life which the ascetics are seeking to lead uninterruptedly. It would be well to read again the exhortation of St. Leo in the second nocturn of the first Sunday of Lent.

[109] II, 84 (prayer for Advent); ed. Wilson, p. 219. Other prayers for Advent or Christmas ask that Christ by His coming free us from the slavery of sin, which is an aspect of the servitude of Satan. Cf. in the Roman Missal the collect of the third Mass of Christmas.

[110] *Missale gothicum*; ed. Bannister, p. 4.
[111] *Ibid.*, p. 18.
[112] *Liber moz. sacr.*; ed. Férotin, n. 32.

In such a perspective, it is normal that the liturgies of times past as well as those of the present day should present Lent as the ideal season of the struggle against Satan. And this theme, in fact, recurs often. Thus, the collect with which the imposition of ashes on Ash Wednesday is completed, sees the whole of Lent in this light: "Grant, O Lord, that we may begin with holy fasting the defensive operations of the Christian warfare, that in our fight against the spirits of evil we may be protected by the fortifications of self denial."

The whole Mass of the first Sunday of Lent, in the Roman rite and also in the Ambrosian, illustrates this same idea. The gospel (Matt. 4:1–11) tells of the temptation of Jesus in the desert, and the epistle (2 Cor. 6:1–10) lists the Christian virtues in a text which recalls the description of the Christian's armor in Eph. 6:11–18. The idea in choosing these readings for the first Sunday of Lent is evidently to show a parallel between the forty days on which the faithful are preparing to enter and the forty days passed by Christ in the desert, these two periods being considered as times of battle at close quarters against the devil. This parallel is reinforced by the use of Psalm 90 for the choir parts of the proper: the sacred text which Christ had invoked against Satan is now invoked by the Church as she wages the same battle.

The importance of this battle in the ascetical practices of Lent is underlined also by the Mozarabic liturgy. Among the examples which should inspire the Christian at this time, the supreme one is that of our Lord Jesus Christ, "who after a full forty days in the solitude of the desert brought to nothing all the temptations of the devil." [113] "By His fasting He won a glorious victory over the devil, and by His example showed His own soldiers how to fight." [114] Hence during Lent "with all care, beloved brethren, we should observe the practice of the fast and the struggle against the devil as against enemies of another breed, in daily attacks, day and night; for the devil subverts with bad thoughts a person whom he has not been able to trick into evil deeds, and solicits with false images in sleep the one whom he has not been able to tempt while awake." [115]

And, as this struggle holds so important a place in the Lenten liturgy, we must undoubtedly think of Satan as the prime antagonist envisioned in the numerous texts of this season in which the Church asks God's protection against enemies.[116]

From Passion Sunday to the Ascension

In the second part of the Easter cycle, that is, from Passion Sunday to the Ascension, the liturgy, modeling itself on the New Testament, insists on this idea that Christ's Passion, His death, His descent into hell, His Resur-

---

[113] *Liber moz. sacr.*; ed. Férotin, n. 318.

[114] *Ibid.*, n. 477.

[115] *Ibid.*, n. 473. On the theme of fasting as a weapon against Satan, cf. *ibid.*, nn. 345, 346, 514.

[116] Thus, in the Roman Missal: the prayer *super populum* of Tuesday and the postcommunion of Wednesday of the first week, the collect of the second Sunday, etc.

rection and His Ascension are so many acts of His struggle against Satan and
of His triumph over Satan.

Thus it is that during Passion Week the Roman liturgy describes the
ever mounting opposition between Jesus and His enemies, who are instruments of Satan. This conflict will end only with the victory of Christ, who
in the gospel of the Saturday (John 12:10–36) exclaims, "The moment in
which the world will be judged has come; now the prince of this world will
be cast out. And I, when I am lifted up from earth, will draw all to Myself."

On Palm Sunday this theme is brilliantly illustrated by the procession with
palms, which is a proclamation of Christ's victory and the Christian's victory
over the devil. This is clearly expressed in the prayer of blessing preserved
in the new *Ordo* of Holy Week: "Bless these branches of palm, we pray You,
Lord, and grant that the bodily actions Your people are performing in Your
honor today may be perfected with the deepest spiritual devotion in victory
over the enemy and a pervading love for the work of Your mercy." This
symbolism of the procession with palms was explained more in detail in the
prayer *Deus, qui miro dispositionis ordine*, which was not kept in the present
Ordo.

Especially after the discovery of the cross in the fourth century, the liturgies develop also the scriptural and traditional idea that Christ's death on
the cross is a victory over the devil. In the Roman liturgy this concept is expressed particularly in the adoration of the cross on Good Friday: we adore
and glorify the cross as standard of Christ, standard of the triumph won over
the powers of hell. This triumphal significance of the cross has been sung by
Venantius Fortunatus in the first stanzas of the hymn *Pange lingua*:

"Sing, O tongue, the winning of the glorious struggle, and proclaim the
noble triumph on the trophy of the cross: how the Redeemer of the world
conquered by immolating Himself.

"Moved with compassion for the deceit foisted on our first father when he
incurred death by eating the fatal fruit, the Creator then chose a tree to repair
the damage done by that earlier tree.

"Order required that such be the way of our salvation: that artifice should
overcome the artifice of the two-faced traitor, and that the instrument of
man's healing be that which the enemy had used to hurt him."

The same idea is found again in the preface of the cross, which is said in
the Roman rite throughout Passiontide: ". . . You who founded the salvation
of mankind in the tree of the cross, that from the very source of death, life
might spring up again, and that he who conquered by a tree might himself
be conquered on a tree, through Christ our Lord."

And the same theme is repeated in the two feasts of the Finding and the
Exaltation of the Holy Cross, which are like an echo of the adoration of the
cross on Good Friday. The antiphons of these feasts in the Roman liturgy
are very characteristic: "Here is the cross of the Lord! Away with you,

hostile powers! Victory goes to the lion of Juda, the offspring of David."
"By the sign of the cross deliver us from our enemies, O our God!" "By the
tree we were enslaved, and by the holy cross emancipated." Analogous texts
would be found in the Mozarabic,[117] Gallican [118] and Byzantine [119] liturgies.

Christ's descent into hell, His Resurrection and His Ascension are presented
likewise by liturgical tradition as a triumph over Satan. A text of the Mass
of the third Sunday after Easter in the Mozarabic liturgy recalls that Christ
"descended into hell, conquered death, made the devil powerless, abolished
the laws of Tartarus . . . ." [120] And a preface of Easter night in the Gelasian
sacramentary praises Him because "having breached the walls of hell, He
has brought us today the glorious standard of His Resurrection, and on His
return has taken man, cast down by the jealousy of the enemy, and led him
into the midst of the astonished stars." [121]

The sanctoral

The martyrs, and, above all, the female martyrs

In the feasts of the sanctoral, the idea of the struggle against Satan is developed in connection with martyrdom, especially the martyrdom of women.
Because it is a total gift of oneself to God, martyrdom is the highest manner
of imitating Christ, and hence the summit of Christian perfection. At the
same time it is the most conspicuous victory of the Christian over Satan, or
rather the victory which Christ Himself, living in His members, wins over
Satan. This defeat, in the opinion of tradition, is particularly humiliating for
the devil when it is inflicted by a woman; for woman is weaker than man,
and moreover it was the woman who was the instrument of the serpent's
triumph in paradise.

This theme appears very often in the Leonine sacramentary, especially in
the prefaces of the martyrs. As we know, these proper prefaces became fewer
and fewer in the Roman sacramentaries, and our present missal does not
contain any of them, so that the idea of martyrdom as victory over Satan has
completely disappeared from our liturgy. Let us cite at least two examples
taken from the Leonine sacramentary.

A preface for the feast of St. Cecilia makes this eulogy: "It is truly fitting
. . . You who, that the triumph over the enemy of the human race might
be greater, not only destroyed the tyranny of the devil through Christ our

[117] Cf. Liber moz. sacr.; ed. Férotin, nn. 739–
747, in particular n. 743.

[118] Cf. Missale gothicum; ed. Bannister, nn.
317 ff.; The Bobbio Missal; ed. Lowe, nn. 288
ff., in particular the contestatio at n. 292.

[119] Cf. the feast of September 14 and that of
the third Sunday of Lent, Τριῴδιον (Rome:
Polyglot Press, 1879), e.g., p. 349, third stich;
p. 351, stichs 2–4; p. 353, cathisma; p. 356,
ode 5, third stich, etc.

[120] Liber moz. sacr.; ed. Férotin, n. 704; cf.
nn. 615, 616, 679, 707, 752, 753.

[121] I, 45; ed. Wilson, p. 88; cf. I, 63, 64, 65
(prefaces). In the present Roman liturgy this
idea appears in the hymns of Easter Aurora
caelum purpurat and Ad regias Agni dapes, in
the lessons of the second nocturn of Easter
Monday and Tuesday (in the Monastic Breviary), in the hymns of the Ascension Salutis humanae sator and Aeterne rex altissime.

Lord; and not only through the blessed martyrs of the male sex do You take a well-deserved revenge on the deceiver for the fall of the first man; but also through the weaker sex You justly take revenge against the enemy of our mother Eve; that he who laid low both sexes, taking advantage of their foolish trust of him in their paradisiac happiness, now, by Your grace, may be ground under foot by the one and the other." [122]

And a preface in honor of St. Stephen says, "It is truly fitting . . . because not only, through Jesus Christ our Lord, have You granted us, Your adopted sons, that cruel hell's deadly sting should be destroyed, together with him who had received the power to inflict it, the devil, and that death, contracted as punishment for sin, when it was undergone to satisfy justice, should lead to a reward; but such has been the generosity of Your superabundant grace that human nature receives all this not only in the person of our Redeemer but also in that of the faithful who have acknowledged Him. St. Stephen it was, levite of the New Testament and first martyr after the Lord's Passion, who first took this role and won this victory." [123]

It is very regrettable that this idea of martyrdom as victory over Satan has disappeared from our liturgy. It corresponded to a biblical concept (Apoc. 12:7–12) which had been widely echoed by tradition, and it surely holds an important place in the theology of martyrdom. In the present missal I can find only two collects relying on the intercession of the saints in asking God for His protection against the devil.[124]

The angels and the Virgin Mary

Another biblical theme, which has passed into all the liturgies, historical and present-day, is that of the intervention of the angels in the struggle against Satan. Its development is found especially in the feast of St. Michael, in that of the guardian angels, and in the prayers to St. Michael recited by order of Leo XIII after low Mass and before the exorcism "against Satan and the apostate angels." [125]

As to the role of the Virgin Mary in the fight against Satan, there is no mention of it in the liturgies until a very late date, and it is only in the most recent compositions that it has assumed real importance. This does not signify by any means that Mary's role in this domain is secondary, but only that Christians did not become vividly aware of it until an age in which the liturgies had almost completely taken shape.

The earliest explicit mention in the liturgy of the opposition between Satan and Mary, and at the same time the most ancient prayer invoking Mary's

[122] *Sacram. leon.*, n. 1180; ed. Mohlberg, II, 149.

[123] *Ibid.*, n. 678; ed. Mohlberg, II, 86. This theme recurs in the prefaces of the Leonine with an insistence that is truly striking; cf. nn. 29, 159, 161, 164, 784, 826, 837, 839, 1183, 1185. It is developed also by the *Liber moz. sacr.*; ed. Férotin, nn. 72, 81, 96 etc.

[124] Postcommunion of the Mass of St. John Capistran, March 28, and collect of the Mass of St. Ubald, May 16.

[125] Roman Ritual, XII, 3.

intercession against the devil, seems to be in a Mass of the *Missale gothicum*, composed at the end of the seventh or the beginning of the eighth century. In the *Contestatio* of the Mass of the Assumption, Mary is called "splendid bridal chamber from which the worthy Bridegroom comes forth; light of the nations; hope of the faithful; plunderer (*praedo*) of the demons." [126] This title of *praedo* undoubtedly means that Mary snatches the devils' prey away from them. And the prayer after the *Pater* in the same Mass asks, "Deliver us from every evil, from every sin, O God, author and Creator of all good things; and, through the intercession of the blessed Mary, Your Mother, defend us with daily protection against the daily plots of the enemy; Savior of the world. . . ." [127]

We can hardly say that there are any similar texts in the liturgies of the Middle Ages. A recent inquiry has found one in the thirteenth century, then some in the *Sacerdotale romanum* of the sixteenth century, and several, finally, in the Offices composed in the nineteenth and twentieth centuries.[128]

The anti-Satanic theme does appear rather often in the recent feasts of the Blessed Virgin. We recall, with a reference to Genesis, that Mary has conquered the serpent and has crushed his head. And we ask her to defend us against the devil's schemes: "Tower impregnable to the dragon, star propitious to the shipwrecked, protect us from deceits and guide us by your light." [129]

The ferial Office

To complete this overall view of the struggle against Satan in the liturgy, let us make an observation at this time which will be repeated and illustrated in a following chapter: there are many psalms which mention enemies and their assaults; sung by Christians, these psalms can and should be understood as directed against Satan and his satellites. And this is not a postulate invented by an artificial allegorism, but, as will be established later, a demand founded on theological principles. This simple observation shows us the place occupied in the ferial Office by the fight against Satan.

One hour of the Office especially insists on this idea: the hour of Compline. The short lesson warns us that the devil prowls around us like a hungry lion, the hymn asks God's protection against the images and dreams which would be inspired by the devil, finally the collect implores God to keep him away from us and to put us under the protection of the angels.

[126] *Missale gothicum*; ed. Bannister, n. 98.

[127] *Ibid.*, n. 102.

[128] Egon von Petersdorff, "De daemonibus in liturgia memoratis," *Angelicum*, 19 (1942), 332.

[129] Hymn *Praeclara custos virginum* of the feast of the Immaculate Conception. The same theme recurs in the lessons from Genesis read at the first nocturn and in the antiphon at the *Benedictus* of this feast, in the hymns and in the ninth lesson of February 11, in the hymn for Lauds of October 11, etc. Mention of the Blessed Virgin is made also in the exorcism "against Satan and the apostate angels" which Leo XIII inserted in the Roman Ritual, XII, 3; this is the first time a liturgical exorcism mentions Mary.

The traditional psalms of Compline are Psalms 4, 90 and 133, which the Roman Office has kept only for Sunday Compline, but which the monastic Office repeats every day.

It is obvious that Psalm 90 was chosen for its anti-Satanic sense. Even if the Hebrew text makes no explicit mention of the devil, the Septuagint did not depart from the deeper meaning of the psalm by bringing the devil into the picture, since the whole Eastern and biblical tradition sees a close connection between the sickness and danger of all kinds mentioned here, and the spirits of evil. In reciting every Sunday or even every day this psalm which reminds him of the temptation of Christ, the all-powerful protection of God and the solicitude of the angels, how could the Christian forget that the struggle against Satan forms part of his daily life?

In conclusion, it must be repeated that the fight against Satan, in which all ages and all beings are engaged, is an essential element of revelation and therefore of the liturgy, and that anyone who ignores it cannot fully understand either revelation or the liturgy.

This history of God's interventions in the world and of the response made to those interventions has taken a dramatic turn: there are two cities at war. And the drama of every being is included in this universal drama. The liturgy, faithful echo of revelation, keeps reminding us of this. It shows us the Church "always in battle array, waging constant war against her enemies, of whom the Apostle says, 'Our fight is not against flesh and blood, but against principalities and powers, against the rulers of this world of darkness, against the evil spirits of the air.'" [130]

Only in this light can we understand why the liturgies keep exhorting the faithful to the struggle against Satan. Besides the formulas of a more specific character which we have been examining, they use generic formulas to ask God's protection on the faithful and on the Church against the devil and his angels.

"Be strong in war, and fight against the ancient serpent, and you will receive the eternal kingdom," advises the Roman liturgy in the antiphon at the *Magnificat* of the second Vespers of Apostles.

The Mozarabic liturgy, coming to the end of the paschal feasts and viewing Lent, and in fact the whole Christian life, as a struggle against Satan, prays most appropriately:

"Do not permit us, Lord, to forget the good things You have given us, raising us up to salvation when we were lost. Place between us and the irredeemable devil a perfect hatred, not that he may be enabled by Your leave to harm us, but that he may not be able to cause any further lapses in those whom You have enlightened with the knowledge of Your truth." [131] The continuing

---

[130] Roman Pontifical, ordination of deacons.
[131] *Liber moz. sacr.*; ed. Férotin, n. 713. Other prayers asking protection against the devil are found in the Leonine sacramentary, nn. 78, 140, 182, 184, 266, 391, 418, 516, 518, 520, 533, 631, 1272.

need for this divine protection is well explained in the same Mozarabic liturgy:

"Grace has adopted man, but the devil is not yet confined to hell. Sin has lost its violence, but not its nature. We are able to fight, but we are in no position to stand safely at ease. The enemy has been despoiled but not annihilated, and of course he will rage against those who used to be under his dominion but whom he has now lost." [132]

[132] *Liber moz. sacr.*, ed. Férotin, n. 657.